John A. Pfitsch, M.A. and Barbara Teetor Waite, Ph.D.

From Underdog to Winner

In Pursuit of 100% Performance

Frendship Publications

ISBN-13: 978-0998498805
ISBN-10: 0998498807

Cover photo: Rosenbloom Field, Grinnell College, taken by Erin Hurley

Printed in the United States of America

First Printing, First Edition 2017
Frendship Publications

Gratitude

Coach is no longer with us, at least in the physical sense. He can't accept my apology for not giving this project top priority much sooner. But, wherever he is in the metaphysical sense, I hope he knows how honored and grateful I feel to be the one to whom he entrusted his manuscript, personal story, and lifetime of ideas.

Many thanks to members of the Grinnell College "family," who supported this project through thick and thin, some of whom worked, played, sweated, cried, and cheered alongside John Pfitsch. This list includes but is not limited to: Emily Pfitsch and members of the Pfitsch Family, Kit Wall, Dee Fairchild, Patty Johnson, Jim Powers, and Jayn Chaney.

A few people seemed to drop everything to help keep the creative juices flowing on this project. They are George Drake, Professor Emeritus and President Emeritus of Grinnell College, Ted Schultz, Sports Information Director at Grinnell College, and many helpful members of the library system at Grinnell College: Richard Fyffe, Catherine Rod, Allison Haack, and Sam Dunnington. Thank you to Sarah Clopton and Cyndi Harvey from The University of Kansas for confirming important facts. All of these contributions might have been "short and sweet," but they made "forever" differences in the outcome of this project.

A special thanks to the earliest readers of this book: Emily Pfitsch, Kit Wall, Dee Fairchild, and Patty Johnson. Their guidance helped me "see" Coach more vividly and "hear" his voice more clearly. And to Suzanne Kelsey, thank you for the wonderful support only a dear friend, who is also a writer, can provide.

A hearty thank you to Bob Rotella, a mentor and hero to me and many others, for putting his stamp of approval on this book. He was the first to teach me about acceptance and trust, for which I will always be grateful.

Barbara Teetor Waite, Ph. D.
October, 2016

Dedication

For all those practitioners who wonder, "what the heck am I doing?" and all those academicians who wonder, "what the heck am I doing?" we're in this together and together we're better.

Table of Contents

Foreword

Whether we're striving to win a world championship or neighborhood tournament, whether we're the underdog or favorite, the desire to succeed energizes and prepares us to perform our best. The authors of *From Underdog to Winner* spent years of their lives studying the keys to optimal performance, particularly the power of the human mind and the impact of positive relationships on our capacity to overcome obstacles and adversity.

As this book points out, sport psychology research isn't always conducted by academicians. It may be more or less "scientific," but I believe there's great value in the everyday experiences of athletes and coaches. They are in the best position to observe and study the phenomena occurring on the field and court. If we are open to communicating with one another and sharing our information and experiences, we can produce remarkable results.

Although I never met John Pfitsch, I have a feeling I would have enjoyed hearing his stories. He was a thinker and doer, someone I would have admired for many reasons. His "out-of-the-box," progressive approach to training athletes makes me wish I'd been one of his players. His student-athletes and fellow practitioners undoubtedly valued their relationships with him. I'm sure his impact is still felt in their lives.

My colleague, Barb Waite, offers a creative and analytical look at Coach Pfitsch's raw and innovative theories. She brings them to light and examines their merit. Her informal discussion with Coach Pfitsch will undoubtedly appeal to a wide and contemporary audience. Her critical insight into the meaning and depth of his theories, particularly regarding his relationships with those whom he coached and worked, highlights the importance of an academician's role in the process of creating and disseminating the wisdom of the practitioner. Cheers to the process, one in which I hope we can all take part!

Bob Rotella, Ph. D.
Performance Consultant and Author, *How Champions Think*

The Kick-off

In the final minutes before the game, spectators, mostly family and friends, found their places on cold, metal bleachers. If I'd taken a moment, I would have noticed the larger than normal crowd packing the stadium. I would have seen the natural turf scuffed up in places due to previous games and pre game prep. I would have admired the durability of a scoreboard from a previous era, felt pride as I gazed upon the sun-bleached banner hanging from beneath the wooden press box and shared the enthusiasm of boosters grilling hot dogs and burgers just outside the gate. If I'd listened, I would have heard their voices, sensed their gaiety. I would have noticed the chill in the air and the moisture lingering from the morning fog. But my job was singular and clear and only part of the greater plan. I was the kicker, just one of the kickers. A coin was tossed; selections made; events set in motion. The outcome, a chain and collection of outcomes, changed my life; yet in the moment, I stayed focused on the task at hand. My task. My life. The emotional energy outside the task could have become exhilarating, too exhilarating. I struggled to take in what had meaning and purpose to my purpose. Details were missed, even those important to the complete story. At the moment and in so many moments, my personal story was the only important one. Looking back, the day I'm about to describe feels like the kick-off to one of my life's more memorable series of events, one which can only be seen in its completeness with a long and contemplative look back, and a bit of imagination to fill empty spaces.

Eyes forward, I steadied the steering wheel with my left hand and groped for the campus map on the passenger seat beside me. The paper crinkled as I grasped it. I glanced at my watch and immediately regretted taking time to drive through downtown Grinnell.

Grinnell, Iowa, a town of fewer than 10,000 people, sat conveniently close to Interstate 80. My directions read "Exit 182, 146 North to 10th Ave. turn right." One simple turn and I'd be there. Taking a detour through the heart of Grinnell was too tempting. Midwestern cliches jumped to mind as I passed Bill's Jewelry, the colorful marquee of the Strand Theatre, and McNally's Market. I turned east on 6th and south on Broad, (the other main street,) to see more small businesses, a bike shop with vintage and new bikes hanging in the massive front windows and a coffee shop called Saints Rest. A small city park conjured up images of families picnicking on blankets while children played tag and danced to music from local talent performing under the circular gazebo in the center.

As I hurriedly drove back north, peaceful small town ambience faded into institutional brick and stone, symbols to me of eager expectation and intellectual challenge. Classic arches and loggia with gothic and castle-like facades made an Ivy League impression. If architecture was any indication, Grinnell College was a place of high educational ideals.

Once on 10th Avenue, I scanned both sides of the street for clues, the words "Physical Education" or "Athletics" on a sign, a building, anywhere. A line of tennis courts appeared to my left. The nets were down. The courts looked well-maintained. Someone cared about the sport I loved. Snow dusted the green grass between the street and sidewalk. It was a beautiful Fall day in Grinnell. A glance at my watch let me know I couldn't take time to enjoy it beyond a quick notice. I centered the map on the steering wheel as I rolled forward.

Kerthump. Kerthump. The car lunged up and over railroad tracks. Damn. I must have passed it. Seeing no cars in either direction, I turned around in the middle of the street. Gotta love small towns. Kerthump, kerthump. Aha! Physical Education Complex on my left. I turned into a drive taking me behind the

2

building. Thank God for Visitor Parking. There was nothing called "fashionably late" when it came to professional meetings. The soles of my beat-up snow boots soaked up warmth as I climbed the wide steps leading to heavy, institutional glass doors. I turned and noticed a slightly ethereal cloud of evaporation. No snow or ice remained on the warm concrete. These are smart people, these Pioneers.

The Pioneers of Grinnell College were known for their smartness, selectivity and huge endowment. Established by Congregationalists and abolitionists in the 1800s, the college developed into a hotbox of critical thinking and a litmus test for social justice. From this outsider's view, the campus combined old buildings, nice tennis courts, and new ideas. I was there to study the latter.

The Physical Education Complex was a humongous brick box, actually a few brick boxes attached to one another. Apart from heated steps, there was nothing very fancy about it. Functional, yes. No surprise there. I laughed to myself. Athletic department buildings of the 1970s weren't typically decked out with crown molding, chandeliers and marble. Familiarity with the motif and the general lack of pretense put me at ease. Built post World War II and pre pretense, the immense brick buildings housed not only the athletic department, but the physical education department, classrooms, locker rooms, and a gym or two, hence the large blocky look. The shiny vinyl floors and brick walls accented wherever possible with school colors, in this case, scarlet and black, calmed me further as I followed instructions scribbled on the margins of the campus map still in my hand. I walked down a hallway where I was pleased to see Tom McCullen standing outside an open office door. He smiled and shook my hand. We exchanged pleasantries. I followed him into a square room with steel gray desks, unmatched chairs, and harsh fluorescent lights.

The most prominent clue this was John Pfitsch's office, a seasoned veteran of the coaching trenches, was the collection of trophies, plaques, and certificates plastering walls and shelves.

Conference Champion, Coach of the Year, Academic All American. Accolades closed in around me. Tom said, "Wait here. He'll be back in a minute."

I turned slowly in every direction. Despite the accolades, the office felt void of pretense, too. No cherry cabinetry. No glass bookcases. Displays perched upon common everyday shelving. Photos, many framed in plain black wood and hanging on the wall, some propped against trophies, sucked up my attention like a vacuum scooping up dust balls. I saw men, all men, some younger, some older. I stopped looking, eyes glazed over. Easy for me to lose interest when they all looked alike, when they all were men. Familiar emotion bubbled up and distracted me. I wondered how many other women of my generation felt the same when observing memorabilia of men in sport. Was it difficult to appreciate other's achievement after being denied equal or even remotely similar opportunities? I touched a lanyard of scarlet and black hanging from a trophy and traced it with my fingers down to a silver whistle. I wanted to place it between my lips and blow! Silly, I told myself, and moved on. Colorfully inscribed coffee mugs on the shelf suggested laborious hours and good humor; a champagne bottle suggested celebration. I was in a workroom and a shrine to male sport achievement.

I knew enough about Coach John Pfitsch to expect a busy, energetic man. Tom, Coach Pfitsch's men's soccer team assistant, had given me interesting bits and pieces as he sat in my sport psychology seminar at University of Iowa. He described with enthusiasm the innovative methods Coach Pfitsch used with the soccer team and invited me to meet the man behind the ideas. I was hopeful, not overly optimistic, to reap professional benefits from this encounter. After all, he was a coach, a Division III coach. I was a professor at a major university with a Ph. D. in sport psychology. I didn't want to be rude, but what could he teach me about sport psychology? What had I not already learned from the bible of sport psychology: its body of research literature? What could one coach, one person, a person without a line of research

4

from which to draw, offer in addition to that? At the very least I expected to enjoy meeting Coach Pfitsch, the character, the seasoned coach with colorful stories to tell. I prepared to spend an hour, no more, listening to stories of his glory days.

The "old man" entered the room with preschool-like excitement. He was dressed in a white t-shirt and black polyester warm up pants, unmistakable coach attire, not exactly chic, even for a coach. He glanced at me, undoubtedly the only novel item in the room, and with a voice that broke ice like a wrecking ball, said: "Who the hell are you? What did— Tom said— What the hell kind of name is Waite?"

I guess I expected a little more "warm and fuzzy." Meet Coach Billy Goat Gruff.

I know now Coach John Pfitsch was relatively small in stature and in his late 70s. But on this day these details were quickly eclipsed by enormous energy, making it impossible to estimate age, even size, with any true accuracy. I noticed his hair was short, straight, graying, and neatly trimmed over each ear. He carried himself with the stiff confidence of a World War II veteran, an officer. He pulled on his matching black warmup jacket sporting the red Maltese-like cross I recognized as a Grinnell College emblem. As he spoke, he pointed to one of the chairs closest to him. I sat. He threw one leg over the corner of his desk and plopped down. He looked down on me. I sat up straighter.

"Waite as in Ralph or Waite as in Steve?" (Steve Waite had played basketball for University of Iowa as I'd been told a number of times since moving to Iowa.)

"Or did you say 'Waits?' as in Tom?"

I truly was not prepared for the man they called "Coach." I stammered, not so much from nervousness or intimidation, but a very strong desire to keep up. "Waite is my married name. It's English, I believe. I'm not— I'm here to learn about the mental training you do with your athletes."

"Scholar-athletes," he said with a grin and a twinkle in his eye. "Emphasis on scholar." He dragged the words across the pea gravel in his throat.

I smiled. I liked the twinkle as much as the emphasis. "Tom is in a sport psychology seminar of mine at U. of I." I thought I better lay it all out from the start. He needed to know he was speaking to an expert. After years of dealing with it, I had a short fuse when it came to condescension in the male-dominated world of sport. I didn't have the patience to bring him up to speed.

His eyes narrowed and he raised his voice slightly. "Then why the hell do you care what I have to say?"

I smiled out of confusion and an attempt at manners. His eyes, his words, his tone momentarily held me in crosshairs. I surmised from his pause, he wasn't kidding about the question. He wanted a response.

"Tom said you have innovative ideas, ideas I might find interesting, theories about mental training."

"Are you a shrink?"

I laughed. This man listens. "No. Not a shrink. In fact, I have to be careful how I use the term psychologist. I'm definitely not a clinical psychologist."

"A shrink."

"Right. Most people seem to think psychiatrists and psychologists are all shrinks and a sport psychologist, therefore, is a shrink. I'm not a shrink."

He looked at me with skepticism. I'd seen the look before. I quickly added a variation of the explanation I'd used for years: "My training and research is about performance, sport performance: how to take athletes from point A to point B, to maximize potential. To be more precise, I study performance and the variables associated with it."

"How to win."

"Not necessarily."

"How to win at all costs."

I laughed. "No. Well, no. The ultimate goal being to reach full potential."

"100% performance." He looked pleased and folded his arms across his chest.

I hesitated, sensing the test continued. "Yes. I guess you could put it that way."

"So if I was to win every game I ever played, like Dan Gable, that would be success to you?"

"Well, he didn't win every match he wrestled." My knowledge of the famed Dan Gable might impress him. Why was I trying to impress him!

He smiled ever so slightly.

Not wanting to offend a potential fan of an Iowa icon, I quickly added, "I think most people would say Dan Gable's story was quite a success story."

"So, it is about winning. You're about winning."

"No. I didn't mean that." I took a deep breath. "I don't know Dan Gable well enough to make that determination. From an outsider's view, yes, his story appears to be one of the greatest success stories in the history of sport. I'd want to know more before I said it was true success."

"True success. What the hell is true success?"

Coach Pfitsch quietly stared at me. Again, he seemed to genuinely want to hear my answer. He was talking "sport psychology" now, my language. Definitions. Concepts. It was a simple, straightforward question. A good, simple question. But like all simple questions of definition and concept, it possessed a very heavy weight. Definitions ruled the research world. Surprisingly, I didn't feel threatened, challenged maybe, not threatened. His voice was unique, even and strong, a constant start and stop, test and go.

"I think true success is determined by each person themselves. When an athlete—a scholar-athlete—strives for and obtains five shots on goal or five stops per game or maybe just stays alert and supports teammates for an entire 90 minutes, it could be defined as success—by that person—the person involved, or persons.

Winning might be one of those things, one goal. But it's not the only measure of success."

Coach clears his throat. "So you're thinking success is more like 100% performance."

Was this a rhetorical question? I looked at him intently. It wasn't. "Well—" My mind raced to consider the term 100% performance from a research perspective. Had I heard the term before? Did I know the concept? "100% performance sounds pretty good. It sounds really good actually. I mean, as a term." It was different. Unfamiliar. It resonated well, like "all you have to give" or "what you're capable of on any given day." I couldn't resist. I liked it. "100% performance sounds like a good measure or definition of success, true success. Yes. I think it is."

Coach turned away from me for the first time, twirled a nearby chair around and sat down to face me at eye level. He leaned forward and said, "Tom said— Tom has a good impression of you. I thought you could teach me. Like Tom. He can coach and teach; he can do just about anything with a soccer ball. I'm not sure— I don't think I'd want to coach without him. I didn't know shit from Shinola when I first started coaching soccer. By the time— When Tom arrived— He was wet behind the ears. He could do anything on the playing field. He was a Captain two years." Coach stopped, opened his mouth as if to consider something important. A second later, he continued. "The first day— The day Tom came into my office— I knew he'd be an asset…"

And so began our physical journey together, that is, physical in contrast to metaphysical. Coach and I, having satisfactorily passed unconventional inquisitions of our own inventions, moved forward. Mostly I moved forward to listening. Coach moved forward to story-telling. Coach's ability to spin a tale, connect multiple tales together for one extremely long tale became apparent at the onset of our relationship. Eventually I attempted to interrupt Coach, something I found quite uncomfortable. I had questions to ask and he seemed to avoid answering them as he spun on and on. These were important questions, at least to me, important enough to sacrifice good manners. I was never very successful with my well-intentioned interruptions.

Thankfully, his stories were interesting and humorous even to this serious researcher. And, I can honestly say I strived not only to understand where he was going with them and where answers were to be found in them, but to tolerate the long, impatient minutes I spent with him, sifting through the familiar yarn, organizing the complicated web in my mind, and hoping, whether I found an answer or not, I'd learn something along the way.

Today—almost 15 years later—it's another Fall, the Fall of 2014. Coach Pfitsch is gone. Sort of. His physical being is gone. But, it happened again today, and, I decide, this time will be the last. It started with a thought about Coach. More than a thought, really. Yes, he inspired me. Yes, he frustrated the heck out of me. Yes, he taught me. But I'm determined to make this the last time I begin to write on an unrelated topic only to find myself pondering the "72 Hour Rule" or the concept of "2+2=5." It's bordering on obsession. These distractions must be a sign, a sign I can no longer ignore. Like "thought stoppage," I think they're telling me, "Stop! Write about Coach. Convey what Coach wrote and taught. Quit thinking about it and do something." Crap. He's beckoning me from the grave!

In the next few days I change my mind again and try to ignore his voice—again. My perfectionism, pessimism, and a few other isms I have a harder time admitting, assist me. I didn't know Coach that well. He wasn't a celebrity or my superhero. He didn't find the cure for cancer or establish world peace. I'm not sure his fame extends far beyond the Grinnell College Community. But yet, I think about him and his ideas on a regular basis. I think about his wife, Emily, his family, and his life. Before long I find myself discussing ideas with Suzanne Kelsey, Kit Wall, Jim Powers, all people involved with his first book, *Pfitsch Tales: 50 Years of Grinnell College Athletics*. I think about Jim George, the special role he played in the production of *Pfitsch Tales*, his devotion to

9

Grinnell College history, and his love of story. In their many and differing ways, they encourage me.

Maybe that's why his life and ideas are worth writing about, that is, besides the creepy "beckoning from the grave." Coach was a "George Bailey." He affected people. He was a not so common, common man with a not so common, common family and community. His impact reached well beyond the length of his arms and his physical life on earth, beyond what even he or I can imagine. Coach was a coach in the broadest and best sense of the word. He taught his scholar-athletes how to navigate the challenges and obstacles of life. Maybe in some indirect way, because of the kind of man he was, he will have a hand in finding the cure for cancer or establishing world peace. Regardless of where this project takes me, I decide it's time for yet another "conversation" with Coach. My overactive imagination brought him back to me. I'm going to embrace this opportunity to help him tell another story. Besides, I still have a few questions for him!

Mine is a simple purpose: polish. I figure I'm dusting off and applying polish to the work John Pfitsch, coach, athletic director, and Professor Emeritus of Physical Education, began and held such a passion for. I vaguely remember the quirkiness of his theories interspersed among the more salient story lines. They might have had some validity back then. What would they look like now? I need to find them, translate them, expound on them, and refute them, if necessary. Ha! In a way, this project is my ultimate interruption. Right now I offer a sweeping apology for speaking over his voice here and there. These interruptions might be my revenge on the old man for going on and on as I tried to make my way to class or practice. Poetic justice!

With a little squinting on the part of my mind's eye, I see him smiling. I smile back. His is a knowing smile with a familiar twinkle. I truly think if he were here in the flesh, he would feel joy in this moment. Although, if he were here in the flesh, he'd insist on finishing the Tom McCullen story. Just in case you're wondering, the Tom McCullen story morphed into the story about

10

playing St. Norbert College by automobile headlights, landing on Utah Beach on Day 3 of D-Day, a lengthy and respectful description of Mr. Carl Menger, his high school coach, and Coach Phog Allen, his mentor at University of Kansas, and heaven only knows what else I've forgotten. Eventually Tom came back to let Coach know it was time for soccer practice and I was left with a very firm handshake, an invitation to come back, and a bit of confusion as to what it all meant.

Confusion is the only way to describe my understanding of Coach's mental training theories. I truly loved his stories, but what did they mean when it came to the theoretical basis of sport psychology? I remember Coach wrote about mental training, specifically the mental training of Grinnell College scholar-athletes. His writing turned into a manuscript which he used as a textbook in the 1970s and 80s. In a frenzy, I begin searching for my copy of the manuscript.

My memory is foggy at best. I'm thinking, certainly his theories have been tested by now. I remember bits and pieces. I remember taking the time to scan the manuscript. I used word recognition software to digitize the words into a word-processing file. I spot a manila envelope on the floor next to a box labelled *"Pfitsch Tales."* In my hand-writing, "Pfitsch Tales 2" is written on the front. I've struck the proverbial treasure chest with my shovel.

Or have I? A different message bubbles up from the deep recesses of my mind as I pick up the envelope, and it's much more frightening. I hear it often, daily, in fact. Despite the many notes and audio recordings I have from interviews with Coach, despite having his manuscript in my hand, I'm beginning something more mine than his, or am I? Do I interject personal anecdotes and thoughts about Coach and his theories? Do I dare put words in his mouth? Dangerous business, especially for someone so different from Coach. I bring a researcher's perspective to his work. Analytical. Perfectionistic. Boring. I want to understand what he hypothesized and prove him right or wrong, follow his direction to the end of the road, wherever it takes me. But where will it take me?

Therein lies the greatest source of my angst as I pull pages from the envelope. In *Pfitsch Tales: 50 Years of Grinnell College Athletics*, Tom McCullen described Coach as, "ahead of his time" and "the greatest man I've ever known." So many others thought highly of him, as I did. What if I reread his manuscript and find his theories off-base, out to lunch, unfounded? No doubt they will be rough. But will I be polishing pearls or sandstone?

Like Coach's apparition, the decision comes to me without argument or battle. I decide to read the manuscript again. I decide to begin a conversation with this elusive apparition. The manuscript will help keep the conversation on track. Right. Stay on track. Tune in to his actual words, I'll cut and paste and highlight them in *italics* right now. They can be enjoyed like his story-telling, unless of course they run on a bit. But, I know if I give him a chance, pay attention, and see it to the end, just like a long, tough season, the experience will take me where I want to go or at least help show me the way at some later time of life. Isn't that what great coaches do, and great story-tellers?

I swear sometimes I actually hear the old man's voice. He breaks into my thoughts. He wants to express himself one more time or tell one more story. Or maybe he knows someone else is about to tell one of his stories and he just wants her to get it right.

"Why the hell are you worried?"

I recognize the serious, good natured chiding. I smile.

"It's not brain surgery, you know. You can't— Who's going to give a hell if it's true or not."

I laugh at his curse word, a purposely less offensive one.

"Can't hurt me now. What's truth anyway? Have you spent time considering that? Maybe it was true then. Maybe it was true for me, at least when it mattered. Like the number of Grinnell College students who go on to—well—in some cases—real brain surgery. The group of kids in 1962—the Midwest Championship team—this team, maybe more than any team I've ever had the privilege of coaching, produced physicians, attorneys, well-educated, service-oriented men, great husbands and fathers. When they played Coe that year—"

I shake my head to stop the voice before the familiar story begins to take shape, a story found in *Pfitsch Tales*.

The manuscript is heavy in my hands. Some people thought Coach a little odd for pursuing the mental side of sport. I chuckle. Some people still think we're all an odd bunch. If nothing else, he was courageous, a genuinely unique individual who dared to be himself, to think and act outside the box. Am I rationalizing now?

I have to admit the one thing I remember: "Coach, your ideas were unusual." I hear a familiar grunt.

I leaf through the 100 or so white 8 1/2 x 11 pages. "Firstness" catches my eye. I smile. Catchy name. Interesting idea with definite research support, that is, if it is what I think it is. I must study it now. Study all of them. I worry. Will they simply be entertaining? I remember the day I met Coach. Am I still battling my own arrogance, my bitterness about gender inequity? Stay open to his ideas. Give them a chance. Give him a chance. I see "Bucket Theory" at the top of a page and laugh out loud.

"Don't take everything so seriously."

But—

"No buts."

"Okay, Coach."

I shake my head. Maybe I should listen to him, especially now that I can interrupt him! There's some beautiful irony. I can speak, really speak to him with no hesitation or reservation. I can ask questions and let him—or his manuscript—answer them.

"I want to find more than a story, Coach. More than the same stories. I want your theories to be interesting and valid." I stare at the manuscript in my hands. "I want them to be wise."

"Hmm. You don't have to— It's not important— Take them for what they are," he said. I'm startled by the ease with which I understand and converse with what I can only describe as a supernatural vision, my vision of him. Despite the weirdness, his message isn't lost on me. Tackle the manuscript with an open mind. Take them for what they are, good, bad, or ugly.

"And keep your knees bent."

I chuckle at his most recognizable words. In the world of physical education and athletics, "keep your knees bent" means be prepared. On the court or field, stay ready to jump, catch, throw. On the court or field of life, Coach's parabolic classroom, it means prepare for what life has in store for you. Be ready for anything.

"Very wise, Coach. A great metaphor. But I'm not sure I'm ready for this. What if I find your ideas, um, not just unusual, but, what if, what if they're wrong by today's and yesterday's standards?"

"What if I was 'out to lunch?'" His voice sounds strange. Clear. Maybe it isn't really him. (Of course it really isn't him.) It's comforting to know my imagination has a sense of humor.

"I'm scared. I'm scared to put so much work into something that might not be of value in the end."

"Can't be that scary— not as scary as—"

"Right." For a moment I'm lost in thought. Eventually, I hear myself say, "D-Day."

There's no fog or eerie music; nothing so dramatic. But his voice is clear. His message clearer. A vague and undefined representation becomes slightly more defined. His mouth forms the thin, straight line I remember. He coughs and clears his throat. His eyes shine with a little less twinkle, possibly a reflection of the discomfort he was in near the end of his life. I try to bring him into focus, form the details of his face, the face I want to see, the one I want to remember.

I softly say, "Not as scary as matching dog tags to names on a list. A world at war."

"Hell of a business." He takes a deep breath. The twinkle dims. Coach had grisly and sobering duties after D-day.

I love the twinkle. I want to see the twinkle again. If his words are my own creation, maybe I can produce the twinkle, distract him.

14

"By the way, I've always wanted to ask. Why do you swear, sometimes at the oddest times and in the oddest ways?"

"People don't listen."

The apparition clears further and his long, ashen face appears, the face I remember. Thinning, light brown eyebrows atop hazel eyes behind large, thick lenses. A hint of self-amusement pulls at the edges of his mouth.

"People tend to pay attention more when a person talks a little different. I learned that in the Army. Are you thinking—what if— or—do you think polite society might not appreciate it?" He chuckles, then adds, "To get attention, I suppose. My voice has a— It sounds— After a while, I put people to sleep. Stop being so scared."

I smile at him. "You have *my* attention, Coach."

His eyes widen with interest and the twinkle brightens. I notice the soft gray hair on the sides of his head. He waves an arm in front of his chest as if to capture my attention further and says, "I don't use— I don't like some words. They distract more than—" He pushes himself upright in the chair, the chair of my imagination. "As a youngster— When I was at camp— As a young boy, a counselor once let me teach some younger—"

"Coach." There I've done it. I interrupted him. He seems undaunted. "I want to thank you. Before we go further." I'm smiling now because I'm interrupting without guilt and speaking to an apparition. It seems more appropriate now for some reason. "Strange. You're really not here."

"Why do you think that?"

True. Why do I think— stop. I don't want to be side-tracked. I take a deep breath and begin again. "I want to thank you, maybe because I didn't thank you before or enough. First, I want to thank you for your contribution during World War II. You landed on Normandy! You transported lifeless bodies, matched dog tags to a list making sure there were no mistakes. You never said it, like so many veterans, but you paid such a price so we, I, could live, study, work, prosper, be free. Thank you for your service and the

15

sacrifices of your family and friends." I want to say, "and the sacrifices your wife and family have made throughout their entire lives so you could do what you do," because that's what happens when a good soldier becomes a good coach. He works long and hard with similar diligence and dedication.

Coach looks away. Is he embarrassed? He says, "It was a different business then." The gravelly voice is steady.

"Your experiences make me ashamed to be scared or bothered by anything. I'm afraid of such little things."

"It wasn't bravery. You could have done better."

I smile. He's still Coach.

"It was mostly— Maybe I should say it was only luck. I was lucky often, often enough to come home, when— We were on ships going over to England. We were escorted by aircraft on our way across the Atlantic. They could only fly during daylight. I noticed we didn't have lifeboats. I remember them telling us, don't worry. There'd be no one looking for us if we got sunk by the German submarines anyway." He chuckles. "That's the way it was. I was lucky."

For a moment the frightening warning comes back to me again. I won't do justice to this work, his work. No matter what his manuscript says, I won't—

"Couldn't be worse than the Great Depression."

I laugh.

"What's so funny about the Great Depression?"

"Sorry, Coach. But, you're jumping into my mind now. I'll try to stay on task. I have questions for you. For example, right here." I point to the page I'm reading. "You use the term 'negative reinforcement.' Are you referring to negative feedback or are you using the technical term from operant conditioning meaning taking something away to reinforce a behavior?"

He laughs hard and long. I think I'm going crazy or he is or we both are. He raises a white towel to his eyes. "No. Nothing technical. Nothing so— In the Army, General Patton and most officers would let you know if you weren't doing something

16

correctly— They would let you know in not so sweet terms, so you wouldn't do it again, so you would do it better the next time, so you wouldn't—" He sighs and becomes serious again, as if remembering a distant memory, another story, possibly when General Patton spoke to his officers in the middle of a field when a German attack could have commenced at any time. Coach was in awe of Patton's ability to lead. "It could also be something you're told so you— When you hear it, even though it might be critical or hard to hear, you are motivated to do something you haven't done yet. Patton stood in front of the troops, pacing back and forth, talking, commanding us. We were just kids some of us, but, we knew what we had to do. We were links in Patton's—in the United State's—chain. None of us wanted to let him down. Spring of '44 was when—"

"Coach, what do you think about trying to answer my questions with simple answers, not stories. Not that you can't tell me a story. But maybe answer the question first. Hold off on the story. A simple answer, well as simple as you can make it, kind of like what you just did."

He shrugs and grunts.

"I'll take that as a definite maybe."

A hint of a smile crosses his lips.

Maybe impossible, I think. No matter how my imagination rules our discourse, Coach is still Coach. But this moment in time is different. I feel no fear of a rambling story with no end in sight. I remembered testing him once. I let him talk, and talk, and talk. I learned, given enough time, and it was a LOT of time, he returned to the subject at hand! If I was patient and contemplative, the answer to the question would be revealed, that is, if he or I could remember the question.

I wasn't the only one who came face to face with his or her ability to wait for it. People closest to him heard the same stories many times. It might be a short one, 20-30 minutes or more, on a busy work day. His long ones, well, I'm not sure anyone ever really found out how long Coach could talk. I heard they actually

17

pulled him off stage at the athletic department banquet one year. He had to be physically removed from his ideal limelight: talking about the scholar-athletes he coached.

One person or 300, all anyone had to do was say, "Mornin' Coach." Those who stuck around and paid attention were able to place another pearl on a string. That's what I hope to offer: a string of pearls, well, maybe a short string, but naturally produced, honed and polished by the grains of Coach's experience, joy and sorrow, blood and sweat. In his manuscript I hope to find the biggest and best pearls he ever produced.

The pearls to which I refer relate to the oyster bed called "sport psychology" and the mental side of training for peak performance or "100% performance," as Coach referred to it. Coach was known for his unorthodox pre-game preparation and unique approaches to optimizing performance. His athletes remember him as a crazy strategist and die-hard competitor. He is also fondly remembered for the faith he placed in them even though they were almost always the underdogs: the shorter, the slower, the smaller, the weaker. As you can read in *Pfitsch Tales*, his was a faith that moved mountains.

In the mid-1990s, mostly for the purpose of doing research for what would eventually become *Pfitsch Tales*, I made numerous drives from Iowa City to Grinnell to take notes as Coach filled my head with stories. I drove home, mentally trolling for messages embedded in them. When I moved to the Grinnell area in 1999 and began working for Grinnell College, "pearl diving" became easier, but life more hectic. My office was in the Physical Education Complex or "PEC" where I first met Coach. I taught in the John A. Pfitsch Field House. Coach Pfitsch had become Professor Emeritus and retired from coaching; but having worked as coach, professor, and/or athletic director for 50 years, he was literally and figuratively still very much a part of the landscape of the PEC.

In fact, if a person entered the PEC early enough in the morning, a low, authoritative voice could be heard barking orders in a rhythm much like you'd expect from a sergeant in basic

18

training. The sound came from the Ray "Obe" Obermiller pool, named for one of Coach's colleagues and cohorts. Not being an early riser, I eventually heard the curious sound. I followed the voice, climbed the steps, opened the large steel doors to the pool and peered down. Approximately 20 bobbing heads and waving arms seemed to be following incoherent instructions. I recognized the tenor of Coach's voice. "Huhm, two, three, four, huhm, two, three, four..." I spotted him talking with the life guard. No wonder the class sounded the same every morning! They listened to a *recording* of Coach giving instructions. There was a preponderance of bald and white-haired heads in the group. Participants in the water aerobics class appeared to have aged right along with Coach. According to Patty in the main office, they affectionately called themselves "Pfitsch's Pfishes."

By 8 A.M. Coach was in the Main Office where Patty Johnson and Mary Kissinger worked. I could hear his voice from my office. It was the beginning of his "rounds." He regularly touched base with the coaching staff after big games or before big games or simply to see how we were doing. In the beginning of my employment at the PEC, I'd stop and say "mornin" to Patty, Mary, and Coach on the way back to my office. He'd spot me and bark, "Who the hell are you?" with the familiar twinkle in his eyes. Then he'd begin a new story. I loved it, until I was regularly late or unprepared for my morning class. Eventually, I avoided Patty and Mary's office, hoping to finish my "most important" work before Coach got to my office at the end of the hall. Even Coach's pearls had to wait for class prep and tardy expense reports.

Coach and I met on this informal basis as well as on a more formal one. We didn't have many "formal" meetings, per se, but, like a good researcher, I took copious notes and made recordings. He didn't mind the recordings. In fact, with the help of his wife, Emily, former student, Kit Wall, and his co-writer for *Pfitsch Tales*, Suzanne Kelsey, he created his own recordings, now a treasure trove for the Grinnell College archives. Along with Coach's original manuscript in italics, the pages I present in this book encapsulate years of meetings, chance encounters, and imagined interactions based on those real life meetings and chance encounters. They blend together in the regular font of this book.

Coach was definitely known for his "oral history," but the day he handed me his manually typed manuscript, things changed for me. "One of two copies," he said. "This may not be brain surgery, it's probably old business, but I think it served its purpose for a few of my classes. It was probably the mid 70s when…"

Maybe it was "old business" for Coach. For me, well, I can trace the beginnings of the disconcerting echo I'm hearing today back to that fateful day. Fainter, yes, but nagging even then. What does he want me to do with it? How do his old ideas compare with new? Is this manuscript worth a serious read? What do I say to him and to others if it isn't?

As I hold it in my hands, I realize there were probably only a few research reports and even fewer sport psychology textbooks available when Coach wrote this text. I look for a date on his manuscript and find none. Always a work in progress, no doubt. Sport psychology as an academic discipline was truly a newborn in the 1970s and 80s. Leafing through page after page reveals the most recent reference to be 1983, a year triggering strong resonance in me. It was the year I began my graduate study in sport psychology at The University of Virginia. I'd been admitted to one of the few sport psychology programs in the country at the time. I thought *I* was a pioneer!

By the time Coach placed the manuscript in my hands, I had scholar-athletes of my own to attend to. It quickly found its way to the bottom of my "to do" list. After all, I was just a "kicker," one of many possible kickers. On a daily basis, I worked hard to focus on the task at hand, my task, which turned into another task, and another. Now, many years later, with the ghostly echo too loud to ignore, there's an excitement building in me. I guess you could say the clock has run down and it's time to kick for one last point, or should I say dive into the deep with hope of finding a pearl, polishing it, and offering it to the world to see. This is my adventure. It's a bit scary. But, nothing ventured, nothing gained. Onward with knees bent, as I say now, as we all say now, that is, all of us who knew the man we called "Coach."

Note To Readers (disclaimer):

It's a misguided venture to read this book in order to satisfy a desire for a review of literature, data, methodology, results, and conclusions. I've intentionally revealed few sources. Coach and I are the primary sources, both scientists at heart, in our own ways. Coach approached "problems" with an open mind in a huddle of scholar-athletes. I approached them in a library and laboratory. Regardless of the source, when it comes to research questions involving human subjects, science may never be able to single out all variables and make statistically significant causal connections. This book concedes defeat on many counts. Instead, a greater focus is placed on the people who study these issues, practitioners and academicians, specifically John Alfred Pfitsch and Barbara Teetor Waite, possibly you, the reader, and how immersed, how overwhelmed, and how gratified we are when a little progress is made toward understanding the phenomena we observe in sport. I hope readers see the value in this discourse, because ultimately, in sport, as in life, the greatest progress isn't measured with statistics and results, but moment by moment in the minds and hearts of the participants. A smile there, a grimace here, grunts and groans, sweat and tears, hands raised high. As tempting as it is at times to claim scientific validity, quantify the unquantifiable, or report results as if they were the final word or ultimate authority, please don't take too seriously any attempt on our part to do so. But, to fellow scientists everywhere, good luck and many significant results to you all!

Barbara Teetor Waite, Ph. D.

Chapter I
Coach's *Prologue*

Coach scratches his stubbly beard. "I want people to know where I'm coming from."

"Coach, it's good. It's a good idea."

"It tells the 'why' of it."

"Yes. It gives more depth and explanation. I'd like to ask a few questions, too, fill in some blanks." My imagination is working like a charm. I think I should have had imaginary talks with Coach a long time ago.

Coach looks around and chooses a straight back chair to sit on just outside the kitchen in his home. I pull a similar chair from the nearby dining room table and set up my recorder on the floor between us. The table and chairs are plain and sturdy, similar to the house and most of its furnishings. Evidence of the inhabitants' world travels and well-informed views are found in small items on tables and shelves, books about faraway places, multiple religions and cultures, and handmade and exotic crafts and art. My tablet for notes rests on my lap. I glance down and see the scribblings of thoughts from our previous meeting. Question marks sprinkle the right and left margins of the page.

Emily walks through the kitchen and toward us. I scramble to greet her, but Coach is already speaking. Emily's hand comes up to say, "Please sit." I relax and settle back into my chair. Emily and I have met many times but haven't had a long conversation in a while. It's as if she knows it's Coach's time to shine. But, I want to ask her questions, too. Hers would be an interesting story. Today she stops our conversation early. "John, move into the living room. Make yourselves comfortable." She looks at us both. "Would you like some water, tea, coffee?" I guess I'm more like Coach. I don't think about where we sit or how comfortable we'll be after an hour or so. I wonder: What is it like to be married to John Pfitsch? What was it like to raise children with such a dedicated coach? What did she do during World War II? Did she work outside the home? Questions interrupt my thoughts as they often do, like the subject of another book, possibly the next book.

Coach says, "I don't think anyone cares to know about my— What it was like—"

Emily touches Coach's shoulder, her silent way of insisting. He abruptly stops speaking. He understands. I understand. We resettle ourselves in the living room, he in what I assume to be his favorite chair, one that allows him to be upright and alert, me on the nearby sofa with soft upholstery. I send a grateful glance toward Emily before turning sideways to face him and place my recorder on the coffee table in front of him. Coach continues.

"I just want them to understand— What it is— Why I put these ideas together. They can decide if they mean anything or maybe just a lunatic telling stories for—to hear himself talk."

"I think you should go for it, Coach."

He shoots me a look like, are you sure? You're actually telling me to talk, to repeat this old text? He chuckles quietly to himself while shuffling pages of the original manuscript on his lap.

"Although, fair warning. I reserve the right to interrupt. And, I'm recording."

He keeps grinning the hard-set and contemplative flat grin, letting me know he'll continue, although reluctantly, under my set of rules. Apparition or not, at least for the moment, I'm feeling in control.

His face turns serious and focused, as if beginning a lecture in a room full of scholar-athletes. His voice, clear and controlled, strikes out with confidence and literary sophistication. I am every bit as eager as the young minds at Grinnell College, yet more wary. I haven't forgotten my ancillary duty to critique and guard the answers, to provide the authoritative response of science.

Having spent a lifetime working with sports and athletic teams in particular, I have in the last few years had a strong desire to review the 'bidding' in my career. I would like to capture in my words my longtime experience in motor skill learning, particularly

23

with regard to team sports, and on the psychological group dynamics which help produce near 100% performance. Here then is a review of my athletic experience which should give you an idea of 'where I'm coming from'—to use a modern phrase.

I chuckle. He stops. I raise my hand. "Sorry."

My first organized athletic experience was playing for the Alamo Heights, Texas, Jr. High School Football C Team in seventh grade in 1931. That year Coach Carl Menger coached all three teams in the football program, classified ABC. Students going out for the teams were placed on the team which best fit his physical qualifications of age, height, and weight. In general, the younger and smaller boys ended up on the C team, the larger and older boys on the A team, and those that fell in between, filled the B team. Because I was very small, at eleven years of age, weighing only 65 pounds, I was definitely C team 'material.'

In 1931 the Alamo Heights C team had nearly as much prestige as the A team and certainly, in my eyes, it may have been better. I was to understand and learn many years later that Coach Menger was a solid fundamentalist. He was also a good psychologist and the program flourished, with his athletes being motivated to their top performance. It was at Alamo Heights that I first became aware of the old dictum 'it matters not if you win or lose, it matters only how well you played the game,' loosely interpreted: playing and or practicing 100% regardless of the outcome of games.

To me 100% became a symbol for trying hard, and as far as I know that translated into 'maximum conscious effort.' Little did I realize that the concepts and questions raised concerning athletic motivation and performance would become the problems which I would grapple with the rest of my life.

"Coach, I understand the 100% reference now, but I kind of cringe whenever you use the word 'problem.'"

He looks puzzled.

"I think the word used in sport psychology today would be 'challenge.'" His face remains still as stone. "A more positive word."

24

"You probably also think—" He stops in mid-thought. "I see your point. 'Challenge' is more positive. It's the same thing and it doesn't matter. But, the important thing is they were— There were things presented to us without answers, easy answers. We needed to figure out how to tackle something to bring about what we hoped to have happen, what we knew could happen. It's one of the greatest challenges a coach faces. Every individual is a bit different. Every team is different. But, even after saying that, I have come to believe there are certain things you can and can not do to draw out the best in them. And that's the problem."

I laugh. "Got it, Coach."

He nibbles at his lower lip. "Are you going to stop me every time I say something—"

"Politically incorrect?" I tilt my head toward him.

"—or even slightly—?" He mimics my head tilt, raises his eyebrows and waits for an answer.

I look down at my notes and smile. "I'll try my best to refrain." (Lordy, what am I getting into?)

He takes a deep breath and exhales with a huff before continuing.

The C teams at Alamo Heights on which I was fortunate to play were football, basketball, and baseball. I say 'fortunate,' for it was and is unusual for a program to be constructed where boys who were as small in stature as I was at 12-13 could play committed, organized athletics on a recognized and prestigious team. Our teams were quite successful. We played full schedules, as other schools had similar programs in San Antonio.

"Coach, these programs sound amazing." I'm thinking of the countless boys who don't mature as fast as others. When all the boys play on one high school team, even excellent athletes have a hard time competing due to sometimes temporary size and weight differences. "It can be scary, too, watching smaller kids on the same court or field with more physically mature ones. And, kids can only sit on the bench so long before they lose their drive."

"I often wonder how the system I knew, the one I was fortunate enough to grow up in— I believe it would have changed the lives of many other young boys."

"And girls."

"Yes."

We sit quietly for a moment before Coach says, "Did I ever tell you about Cindy Root?"

"Yes, Coach. The world-class badminton player, a student at Grinnell. But right now you're telling me where you're coming from."

"It's an important story, the Cindy Root story."

"Yes. I think so, too. It's in *Pfitsch Tales*."

"Right." He pauses to sip some tea. "You're doing a good job keeping me on track."

"Coach, you know there was more than one good female athlete at Grinnell College before Title IX. They might not have played intercollegiate athletics, but they existed." The accusatory tone of my voice frightens me. I remind myself how he fought to gain financial support for a physical education complex accommodating women's "interest" in sport. Where had I read that quote? "When you knew players like Cindy Root, did you and your cohorts realize women wanted to play sport and would benefit from playing sport as much as men?"

"It was a different time. We struggled to support sports already in place."

I feel tears build up in my eyes. I'm not sure if I'm angry or sad or both.

Coach looks at me and inhales audibly. "It was my honor to play badminton with Cindy. She showed us all a thing or two. I knew women were playing sports."

"They just didn't have the equipment, facilities, and financial support for intercollegiate play."

"Yes. But the women had their own facility first."

"At Grinnell College. Rand Gymnasium. It was amazing. But, it burned down in the 1940s and wasn't rebuilt. For years afterward it seems like women took leftovers and hand-me-downs."

"I think it took us— We needed to begin working closer. We didn't realize we were, that we had similar goals. Some women didn't want to join with us."

I sense the presence of a can of worms. "I'm sorry, Coach. I don't mean to place blame on you for the entire history and state of women's athletics."

"That's a relief." He situates himself deeper, more comfortably into the chair. "I think we needed to be hit over the head, and we weren't, or at least we didn't really feel it, that is, until the late 60s and 70s, with Title IX. Even then, Grinnell College moved— We were moving to the forefront. It might have taken us time, but we moved quicker than most schools. The PEC was built with women's sports in mind." He stops to take a deep breath. "In the Fall of 1967—"

"I know the story, Coach. It's a good one." I purse my lips. "Let's get back to your early days, okay? Tell me more about Texas."

I hope the word "Texas" acts as a cue, but he still seems far away.

"It was a Grinnell connection you know—in Washington."

"Yes. Your trip to see the Assistant Secretary of Education." I knew of his trip and his triumph: building the PEC with the help of a government grant and low interest loans. He was proud of his accomplishment. "Let's try our best to stay on topic. Mi culpa, tambien."

"Si," he says with a grin.

I smile, too. We simultaneously say, "Texas!" and laugh.

His countenance sobers as he picks up his manuscript and slips back into lecture mode.

My father moved to Ft. Davis, Texas, in the summer of 1933, during the Depression. My family moved later and I started high school in a school system containing 33 students, 15 of them male.

I went out for the Ft. Davis High football team which was highly respected in West Texas. Mr. Bart Coan, who was Superintendent of Schools, had also earned a fine reputation as a football coach in the area. Ft. Davis played 11 man football, and with only 15 players it was mandatory that all contribute.

When I reported to Ft. Davis I weighed 70 pounds and was 5 feet tall. I left Ft. Davis two years later at 5 feet 1 inch and 85 pounds, having played again, three sports: football, basketball, and tennis. The experience was amazingly different from Alamo Heights, but excellent for me. We were undefeated in football and I played backup quarterback and safety.

"Did you fight it?" I ask.

"Fight it?"

"Did you fight the movement toward women in sport?"

He brings his hands up in exasperation, then together as if to pray. The pause gives me time to regret my impulsive question.

"No. When it came time to— I fought for it, especially when it came to the athletic conference. But, I know— I admit, it wasn't my first concern in those days, the early days."

"It wasn't many men's first concern."

"Yes. I suppose not." He takes a long, slow breath. "Why do I suddenly get the feeling I want to stay on topic?"

I close my eyes and shake my head. When I open them, we both smile. He clears his throat, straightens his back, and begins again.

My fundamental learning from Alamo Heights held me in good stead at Ft. Davis even though my size and maturity disadvantage was significant. The athletic teams of Ft. Davis, particularly football, were outstanding. The talent of the players was excellent and the motivation of those players was superior. The coaching was first rate and the traditions built up over the years seemed to hold forever.

I wonder if he knows how I feel hearing his story, how I identify with the passion he held for sport, how I felt as I ran headlong into the wall of prejudice preventing me from pursuing my passion? I look into Coach's eyes and see the innocence of a young boy loving sport. His life was spent playing, competing, and coaching with and against boys and men. I realize, if I want to make progress, if I want to hear and understand his philosophy and theories, it's time to set my still very deep-seated feelings aside.

I notice his slight nod as he continues.

My father's CCC Camp was than moved to southern Texas and I found myself a senior at the little town of Pflugerville, Texas, ready to play again. The high school size was 60 some students and the athletic reputation was as weak as Ft. Davis had been strong. Again I played football, basketball, and tennis. At 16 years of age I stood at 5'3" and weighed 100 lbs. 'wringing wet.' I played quarterback on the football team, guard on the basketball team, ran track occasionally and played tennis.

This time, on a football team with a tradition of weakness, I learned for the first time in my career how it felt to lose and lose steadily. I found out that playing 100% individually was not enough to pull the team through. I learned the experience of continual negative reinforcement, of doubting oneself and one's ability, and of low morale by the group and the resulting performance loss. I also learned about athletic performances which were above normal for individuals and yes, even teams on occasion, making me wonder about how these performances came about: could they be 'arranged,' possibly through coaching or brainwashing?

Coach's sly glance catches my stifled laugh and head shaking disapproval. The corners of his mouth turn up ever so slightly before he continues.

It was my first, thorough taste in wondering how a poor team could 'put it together' to win 'in spite of themselves.' In fact I was not just wondering about it, I was occasionally 'doing it' and always 'trying to do it.'

It was also my first real understanding of the adages: 'You will be a better man for your efforts' or 'You may get your head knocked off, but you will be a lot bigger man when it's over.' Even though the seasons at Pflugerville were not 'winners' and I had not grown very much physically, weighing 105 pounds at graduation, I grew a lot psychologically.

At 5 foot 3 inches and 16 years old I reported to Coach Keiffer of Texas Lutheran College, a junior college, for football. He decided my life was more important than playing varsity football, so I played as much as I could in practice, filled in as manager and trainer for the team and saved all my energy for basketball.

I spent two happy years playing junior college basketball on a team that in my sophomore year earned state runner-up honors, a considerable feather in Coach Keiffer's cap. The team had one exceptionally talented player, a few normal junior college caliber players, me, and some others similar to me. The organization and motivation of the team produced steady near 100% performance, a tribute to Coach Keiffer, as well as interesting evidence for me as I continued observing the motivational phenomenon of 100%-ism. I also played tennis and finished in second place in the finals of the State Junior College Championship Tennis Tournament.

University of Texas was my next stop—way over my head as far as talent and ability went. However I did play a little on the varsity basketball team and the tennis team. But the values received here were growth—from practice and observation—plus a very big break: my introduction to Phog Allen, the great basketball coach of Kansas University. Dr. Allen made it possible for me to attend K.U. as a graduate student upon graduating from U.T. and thereby giving me a chance of a lifetime: to be part of the K.U. Jayhawk basketball organization in the 1940-1946 era during which there was a war to be fought. I was a part of the organization for three basketball seasons, the first two when I was co-coach of the freshman team, the last season, 1945-46, when I was assistant varsity coach.

"You fought in World War II in the middle?"

"Yes."

To be able to coach at K.U. and specialize in basketball with the K.U. reputation under the tutelage of Phog Allen was gratifying and inspiring. Coming to me from my vantage point of lowliness as far as ability, knowledge, and experience, it was a miracle.

I laugh. "Coach, you're being too humble."

"No. I believe I started mastering the art of 'winging it' even before then. I became quite good at it. But I was lucky. And, I'm grateful—for my luck.

The Kansas experience is long enough for a book in itself, but for purposes of this effort let me say that my interest in psychological motivation of athletes was aided and enhanced 100 times over by my association with the 'Old Man.'

History has proven that Dr. Allen was one of the last of the 'emotional motivators.' Knute Rockne, Dr. Allen's close friend, likewise has gone into history as one of this mold. Both coaches strongly believed in the Kantian philosophy. They continually preached the dictum: 'A man can do anything he wants to do, if he wants to do it strongly enough.'

Dr. Allen believed that it was possible to elevate any mortal's motivation level by preaching, talking, and manipulating the environment. The goal was 'arousal' of athletes and the technique was inspirational talk: stories, anecdotes, and challenges, the 'negative challenge' in particular. Dr. Allen's results were spectacular and his records speak for themselves.

"I'm not sure what you mean by 'negative challenge.'"

"Well, I wouldn't— I'm— It's nothing technical. Like negative reinforcement. You would probably say— It's maybe— A more popular or current term is 'reverse psychology.'"

"Ah."

"When you— If a player wasn't giving his best, Dr. Allen might say something like, 'You aren't strong enough, fast enough. Don't worry. We'll find someone else who is strong enough or fast enough.' Before long—and it wasn't very long—that player was strong enough and fast enough."

"Got it. Challenge with a little sly manipulation thrown in. Something we might not get away with today."

"Hmm. Maybe not." He shrugs.

"Some of Phog Allen's inspirational speeches sound like they might have been a bit over the top."

"He was a master, a unique— a very intelligent man. But, back then, even then, the hand writing was on the proverbial wall." He looks past me for a moment. "We saw it. We'd progressed from Knute Rockne's 'win one for the Gipper' to more evolved thinking, or so we thought."

I imagined young men returning to school after fighting a war in another part of the world. They must have come back changed, mature, toughened, in some cases, traumatized. Part of the team might have learned to cope with the greatest forms of stress a human being can experience while others stressed about grades, paying tuition, and getting a date. How would a coach begin to design a practice or prepare for competition? It was no doubt an interesting time to coach and be coached.

Shortly after the war, sports writers and coaches began explaining to the outside world that inspirational 'fight talks' were passé, and that the modern youth were too smart to be 'conned' into good performance by diatribes, emotional garbage, etc. In 1946 I helped Dr. Allen's team go to the finals of the NCAA. While sitting on the bench, I listened to some amazingly simple exhortations and then saw Allen receive superior responses from U.S. Armed Forces WWII veterans. Responses of the K.U. team usually were performances near 100%. I then watched my colleagues, including myself, nearly universally drop the technique of inspirational fight talks and develop other techniques hopefully to produce better results with the 'new thinking' of the modern generation.

"You don't sound convinced that the 'new thinking' was any better than the old thinking."

Coach says, "I'm not sure the new thinking— It might have been the new thinking only because things change. It wasn't better so much as different for different times."

"So, by new thinking, you're referring to the Inverted U Hypothesis or Catastrophe Theory?"

Coach squints. I turn to a fresh page of my notepad and begin to sketch. "I think by 'old thinking' you're referring to Drive Theory, what Coach Allen based his early approach on. As a person becomes more highly aroused, he or she performs better. So, as a coach, you're charged with revving your athletes up to get the most out of them. It basically looks like this." I turn my tablet around and point to the top of the arrow. "Peak performance with high arousal."

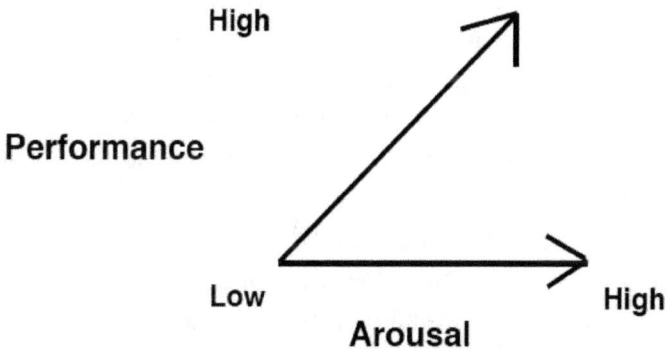

High

Performance

Low   **High**

Arousal

Coach looks at it with an expression of recognition. He nods. "Yes. Most of us felt the same way. But after the war, they didn't have much fear. You had to give 'em bigger and better pre-game talks. Most coaches saw the change coming. We had to be more creative."

He seems to remember something, a memory with a good feeling attached. He smiles. "Phog Allen was one of the best at preparing his athletes to give their all."

Emily enters the living room carrying a stainless steel carafe and places it next to us. "Phog Allen coached in a different era, John. Maybe Barb doesn't know who he is." Emily leaves the room without another word.

Coach's face lights up as he pours hot tea into our mugs. "Yes. Well, Dr. Allen—he was a doctor of osteopathic medicine. He actually worked on many of his athletes as if they were his patients, manipulating their knees and ankles when there was a problem. And they'd get better! He was one of the greatest coaches I've ever— I was honored to be an assistant at Kansas. A lot of people might say it was a case of the right person at the right time. He was effective because he worked with a certain group of athletes during a specific time in our history. But if you knew him at all, you'd say he was a phenomenon. And he didn't mind making changes. If he dealt with this new generation, he would have figured out how to motivate them. He was innovative and creative. He would tell his players the darnedest things. He'd quote the classics or make up his own glory stories, some cockamamie story about overcoming formidable opponents. He'd remind the players they were fighting for their honor and pride or the school's honor, or their family's. He had great speeches and they would do anything for him.

"Today—" Coach sips his tea. "Today athletes are more anxious. 100% performance doesn't happen when they feel more pressure. They're anxious and fearful. You can't hype them up further. Most of the time, maybe all of the time, they need to be calmed down. Most of them already want to win. But they need to stay focused and that comes when there's less stress, not more."

I move to the edge of my seat. "Yes. That approach we would consider the 'newer thinking.'" I quickly draw another graph on

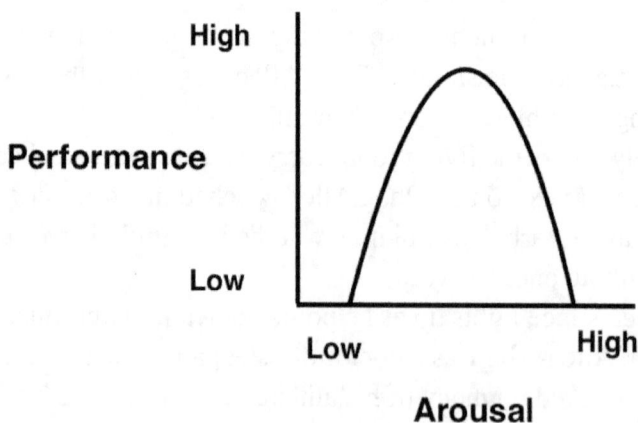

High

Performance

Low

Low   High

Arousal

the same pad of paper and turn it around so he can see the "Inverted-U Hypothesis."

He looks at the diagram. "'We,' meaning 'we' as in professors of higher learning?"

"Coach, these theories, at least as they apply to sport performance, were not being written about so much until the 1970s and later, not so much when you were coaching with Phog Allen. But they're good theories and practices, yours and academia's. They eventually came together." I laugh. "Kind of like we are now."

"This—" Coach taps his stubby strong finger on the diagram of Drive Theory. "This is what we all realized wouldn't work anymore and I agree with this." He taps the Inverted-U.

"Which makes sense, Coach. Drive Theory captured the truth of the time, so to speak. But we began to realize there were limitations to it. When pressure builds, at a point, performance begins to drop." I draw an invisible line with my finger over the top of the Inverted-U and down the other side.

He shrugs his shoulders and grunts behind the smile. "Don't misunderstand me. I have respect for university studies, but when you don't have one, you don't need one. See? That's pretty simple stuff, stuff we knew. We were just doing our jobs as well as we could. I'm not sure— Do these names matter? Inverted-U or upside down cake."

I laugh. "I suppose it doesn't matter, not for a practitioner in the field. But in the lab, a theory or concept needs a name. Terms need definitions, clarity. How can we measure something and study it, if we don't clearly define it?"

"I suppose you're better for naming it and drawing pictures of it."

"You figured it out, though—in the trenches."

"Probably. Undoubtedly. We figured it out first." He smiles. "Which is why it occurs to me. Why do we need you—you researchers?"

I grin, then sigh audibly. "Better tell me more about where you're coming from."

His eyes twinkle as he continues.

Needless to say my experiences with Dr. Allen and a little experience in the Army with General George Patton in between affected my thinking a great deal and provided me with ideas which started me on my career as a college coach. My ideas described here are mostly experimental. They are concepts which were derived from actual games, the reactions of my teams, and others that I coached.

My career past K.U. has been in two institutions, both small liberal arts colleges of the Midwest: Midland College in Nebraska and Grinnell College in Iowa. I coached, taught, and administered at Midland for only two years, for I was head coach of all sports (7), athletic director and chair of the Physical Education Department which offered a physical education major and required P.E. courses. I had no assistants except for a part time football assistant and a student trainer. The load was enough to send me in search for a new job. I found that job in Grinnell, Iowa, where I would reside, struggling with athletics in general, as Athletic Director, and coaching many teams, by now 97 of all types.

The important thing about those 37 years of experience at Grinnell and Midland, is that both programs were, for different reasons, 'underdog' programs; that is, to win, one had to do the unusual. And so I have been entrusted with the never ending challenge: how can I take these kids and help them make winners out of themselves?

My mind spins with the potential impact of his last statement. "Sounds like you're placing the ultimate responsibility on your athletes."

Coach ponders for a moment, then says, "It didn't matter what I did. They're the ones on the field. How else do they— How can anyone perform their best? They might learn skills, good technique and strategies, but if they don't think they at least might be winners

36

in their own right, they might never be. On the field or afterward off the field."

"So, by giving them the ultimate responsibility, they reap the ultimate reward. They attribute their success to what they did, not luck or what someone else told them to do." I'm thinking out loud now. "Sounds like Attribution Theory. Sounds a bit altruistic on your part, too." I grin. "Making sure they take credit for their progress and success."

"Of course I know what I've done and haven't done. Sometimes it works out and I'll be— I can celebrate, too. As far as public opinion, if I give a hell what it looks like for me, what good does that— I like to hear someone praise me, like most people; I believe they do. But it doesn't work well for a coach to concentrate attention on it. It makes more sense to establish a working relationship, a good relationship, but that would not include athletes relying on you. I might— I often help them set it up; but, they're the ones doing it, pulling it off."

"You know, Coach, research suggests that internal attribution for the cause of success is extremely helpful if you're pursuing significant and enduring positive growth, self-efficacy, and peak performance."

"Ha! More intellectual enlightenment from research. You're not as dumb as—"

"Don't be making fun of me now, Coach." I chide back. "I think it's important your approach makes sense from a research perspective, too."

"How could I ever make fun of you? You're the expert. You know everything."

Ouch. That stings a bit. "I don't mean to—" Then I realize, I did mean to— "Coach, I'm sorry for my arrogance. I really don't mean to come across—"

"Yes you do. Don't you?"

Who is controlling this conversation anyway?

"John." The voice is Emily's. "Show some respect for her position at the University and her professional training."

Coach's mouth snaps shut as he smiles. He looks up as if the words came from Heaven above.

I suppress a smile and quickly say, "So, if you beat your chest and announce to the world how great your coaching ideas are, you take something away from athletes, you negate or discount their feelings of empowerment and self-efficacy. You want them to know they caused their own success: believe in themselves. Don't you want to take credit?" Okay, now I'm baiting his ego.

He grins from ear to ear. "I've coached a lot of teams. I've seen them do remarkable things. And then they go on to do remarkable things after graduation. I'll beat my chest then."

He's the coach I never had. I bet Emily is smiling now.

It occurs to me there is an even more important question: "What did you do when they weren't good enough to win? What did you do when they made mistakes? Big ones?"

He jerks his head back and to the side as if I'd given him a shove. He makes a smacking sound with his lips and sharply inhales before saying, "When was that? Every athlete at Grinnell had the potential to be successful. They weren't state champs in high school. They weren't going to the pros. But, they were ballplayers and they wanted success during their years in college like anyone else. We did our best to find a way. It was a minor miracle sometimes."

I chuckle. "How did you do it, Coach? I mean, how did they do it?"

"Win? You mean win?"

"Sometimes win. Play their best. 100% performance."

"I love to win. I've told you, you can teach everything you know, all the techniques, but there's nothing better than a win, or a loss, at the right time to teach a lesson. We sat around, coaches, captains, talking for days, months before we even played a game to figure out how to win. Sometimes we needed the Almighty's help. Reminds me of—"

"Coach, you told me about the Coe game. Before we get into that, why did you write this manuscript on the mental aspects of coaching?"

"My book? This book? I'm not sure it's worth much today."

"I'd say you're off to a good start—telling readers where you're coming from and revealing a most powerful strategy by any standards, yesterday's or today's: letting athletes take credit for success whenever possible."

He smiles. "I'm glad to hear it. But—" His eyes wander. "Phil Jackson wrote a very interesting book. I once met—"

I lower my gaze and look sternly at Coach. "What did you hope to accomplish with this manuscript, Coach?"

He takes a deep breath and clears his throat.

The overriding motivation for writing this book is the hope that it will be interesting reading, first to young coaches in the early years of their careers, and secondly, to athletes who might be able to understand the concepts discussed here and use them to better themselves in their athletic careers. Some of the concepts I discuss are not clearly understood if understood at all by the athletes who graduate from our educational institutions, even though most of them have had a great amount of experience in learning the games they want to coach. I have tried to sort out the concepts which seem after a forty year career to be the most important and to point out which seems to me to be the best way to apply them. I do not claim that they are scientific facts, not originals, merely that they may be explained from a different point of view then before. The stories which I relate are true stories which occurred during my coaching years. My analysis and conclusions may not be totally accurate; however they do provide an interesting way to attempt to understand what actually took place in the complex psychology of human nature.

I am hopeful that these stories will provide another group of readers the enjoyment of re-living their escapades on the fields and courts of Iowa and Nebraska. I say this recognizing that there is a big risk at relating events in which so many participated with so much emotion and commitment. Each story can have dozens of versions; this is only mine, a coach desperately trying to achieve and learn from the experiences.

Shame on me for thinking I might not learn from this white, privileged, older man, this Division III coach. I shake my head and grimace at my arrogance. I need to start with a little humility of my own. It's obvious to me now: it's up to me to learn, and to behave myself. If I do, who knows what we'll come up with together?

One more point to remember: the concepts which are labeled 'firstness,' 'visual imagery,' and 'positive reinforcement,' may be applied to both the individual learning process and to the team learning experience. Most emphasis is on the team aspect, as I have devoted most of my career concentrating on that aspect of coaching. The fact that the concepts are originally applied to the individual, in all cases seemed to necessitate comments regarding that, prior to the team discussion.

Lastly, I want to reiterate that I am not in any way claiming that these concepts work absolutely as described. They are experimental and theoretical under any stretch of the imagination, and limitations can be found in them rather easily. The problem is to determine as accurately as possible what conditions, stimuli, or psychological dynamics can a coach use in order to guarantee near 100% performance from his players' combined potential every time they are tested. The following pages describe the concepts which I have used in my long career and which I believe are worthy of careful consideration by all coaches attempting to produce consistently excellent or top performances.

"Coach, I like your willingness to see through the reader's eyes. I think it's a testament to your sincerity, your convictions, and values." I have his attention now. "You talk a lot about performance on the field and court, but I think it would have been nearly impossible for you to view performance in sport apart from human development. You didn't sacrifice the valuable lessons for the result. The result, no matter what it was, became a part of the lesson."

I try not to pause too long between thoughts or take a breath—
"It makes me sad to contrast your philosophy with many others, especially so many so-called 'elite' coaches today. Coaches *can* be all about winning and results. They can use selection and attrition to maximize chances on the field or court. If athletes don't produce, others form a long line waiting to step in to take their place. And when there's not such a long line, some coaches end up coddling players instead of letting them learn through tough lessons. What do they learn? They need coddling forever. What a disservice. I don't think you had it in you to work that way."

"It didn't matter what was in me. Back in those days youth and young adults played sport because they wanted to. They played because they were needed to fill a roster. Especially at Grinnell College, a Division III institution, they played for the team, for the social interaction, for the exercise, for just about every reason other than because they were the best or because they wanted to win more titles, accolades, or have a career playing sport. They taught me winning wasn't the most important thing." He pauses to reflect and that thin familiar grin spreads across his face. "I still love to win."

"So, how did you win, Coach? Sometimes. How did you maximize performance? We've established you gave them responsibility for the outcome. On a theoretical level, that instills confidence. Was maximizing performance simply a matter of instilling confidence?"

"I was C team material for sure, an underdog, all my life. Short, skinny kid, growing up in a small town. But I knew how to scrap for every advantage and tried to play smart. I fell in love with playing sport and teaching. My parents sent me to Y Camp when I was seven. That's where I learned I could play. Everyone played. It didn't matter if you were good or not. You played and you probably enjoyed it. Someone gave you a chance. One day one of my counselors..."

"Coach, you told me about Y Camp. But you must have been like a blast of heat under a skillet of underdogs at Grinnell College. They were all pretty much underdogs, weren't they?"

"No. Not everyone."

Not Cindy Root. I bite my lip to keep from speaking the thought out loud.

Coach hesitates, then says, "I worked with some fine athletes. But, as a whole, we definitely couldn't do what others were doing. We would have lost a lot, maybe all the time. We did lose a lot. Some years we had to do a lot of convincing, convincing players to play in the first place or talk their friends into playing. We had a physical education requirement back in the early years. We could see in class who could play and who couldn't. Even Edd Bowers had a heck of a time in football."

A distinct image of Coach Edd Bowers jumps to mind. Similar to Coach Pfitsch, Coach Bowers, isn't easily forgotten. Even in his older years, he commanded a physical presence. His hulky frame, slightly stooped from age and discomfort, would straighten as he spoke, and straighten when he cheered for Grinnell athletes. Sometimes it just takes one observation to know a coach is special. On one such Saturday, it hadn't been a close football game. Down by multiple scores, a seemingly insurmountable deficit, I remember watching one of the most miraculous, yet purposeful and methodical come backs I've ever witnessed. The Grinnell College Pioneers worked and worked, grinding out each yard, playing good football, making few mistakes, doing their jobs. Finally a kick clenched the win in the final seconds. I was sitting close to retired Coach Bowers, who, like me, was vicariously living every high and low during the game. But there was nothing quite like the emotional high after the game. We stood cheering together, almost in tears. It was time to leave when a player walking from the field saw Coach Bowers in the stands. His eyes immediately lit up. He pumped his fist in the air and yelled at the top of his lungs, "That's what you're talking about, Coach! That's what you're talking about!" Yes. That's what he talked about.

Graduating from Grinnell College in 1947 and coaching there for over 30 years, it was said Coach Bowers bled scarlet and black. He was one of Coach Pfitsch's long-time cohorts, colleagues, and closest friends.

Coach broke through my reverie. "We knew who could play. We'd corner guys in the dining hall and convince their friends, other members of the team, to put pressure on them to come out for the team. At times even the faculty didn't want students to play or our teams to do well. There's always been a strong sentiment at Grinnell College to keep athletics 'in its place.' Brain versus brawn, or some such— It doesn't make much sense to me now. A smart kid can't play ball? Or, a kid who plays ball can't be smart? Or having a good experience in athletics doesn't prepare you in life to use your brain for better things? We almost came to blows one day in the South Lounge. Somebody was upset because the football team was doing too well." He chuckles. "All these people were afraid Grinnell was going to become a 'jock school.'" He shakes his head. "Professors thought too much emphasis was being placed on sport, football in particular. There were articles in the school newspaper and people convening to talk about it. It was like a protest from the 60s, but this was 1980, and we'd only won two games, one the year before, and the other the first game of the season." He laughs hard making me laugh, too.

"How did you do it, Coach?"

"Do what?"

"How did you coach underdogs to be winners?"

Chapter II
Coach's *Umbrella*

There are five group dynamic concepts on which I will dwell. However, fundamental to all is a general condition which I choose to call the 'umbrella' or environment, for lack of a better word.

It means that in any athletic group, there must be established and maintained an environment which is 'positive' in nature. The coach's principle goal must be to understand this and to develop a program of techniques and mechanisms which can assure him or her of accomplishing this goal.

I smile and say nothing.

Coach-player relationships are basic to this goal. Secondarily, player-player relationships are also basic to this goal. Any experienced coach and or player will tell you that a player's attitude is an absolute to success of the team. Good player attitude is dependent upon the positive environment, which the coach must provide.

The elements of the positive environment umbrella are: (1) common sense, (2) honesty, (3) high motivations of the players, and (4) the Captain System. These elements depend upon good knowledge of relating to players by the coach, good knowledge of the game by the coaches, fairness in dealing with the players in the competitive situation, and success in the execution of skills and tactics as the season or years go by.

Bear in mind as we discuss the concepts of firstness, visual imagery, 72 hour game plan, and seasonal game plans, that each of these are dependent upon the development of a sound umbrella to work under. A discussion of the first points of the umbrella should be attempted prior to leaping 'into the fire.'

First, common sense stands a coach in good stead in accomplishing the goal of a positive environment, which ultimately means positively reinforcing lesser players.

I'm all ears hearing this different take on "common sense." I don't believe it's so common.

It is impractical to create an environment where athletes aren't reinforced for what they can do. And impractical to not cultivate lesser players who might contribute to your team in surprising ways. If a coach has good common sense he will make decisions which will positively reinforce lesser players and that is the end of it. If he does not, he will fail, and that might be the black and white of it. I believe that some coaches seem to 'have it' and others do not and never seem to get it.

"Coach, this seems opposite of what many coaches do. I'm not sure I'd call this common sense: 'positively reinforcing lesser players.'"

He raises his arms and lowers them before he speaks. "Yes. I suppose you're right. But, the point is, if stronger players are positively reinforced, a great deal of your time and focus will be lost on them. Whereas— It's a sad— Many outstanding athletes become coaches. It's my belief that if you learn from mistakes— If you weren't necessarily the fastest or the biggest, but you were brought along by a coach or a parent or by whatever it took, a counselor— You can see the obvious advantages. You learn to follow this common sense approach."

"Positively reinforcing lesser players."

"Yes."

"Because if you do—?"

I was one of those in the middle, like many will be. I was not natural and I was not a total waste of time. I have learned a lot and have been able to apply some techniques after learning the hard way from mistakes of poor common sense.

"You're talking about learning the hard way—you learning the hard way—and, that's how you know it's beneficial for coaches to reinforce lesser players."

He shakes his head. "That's what I said. And maybe I want it to be common."

I smile. "Yes."

I have found that basic motivation is usually found in our athletes. The total athlete environment is strong enough for most of our athletes to be sufficiently motivated. In other words they want to play and make the team, so the desire is usually there and strong enough to carry them for awhile.

"So athletes are naturally motivated to do their best; but the lesser ones, even more than the better players, need positive reinforcement to grow and eventually excel. That's where the winning comes in, sometimes."

"Yes."

"Seems simple enough."

He takes a sip of tea. "It may be simple, but not altogether easy."

"You're saying coaches find it difficult to positively reinforce lesser players?"

"That is when it's difficult."

"Simple. Not easy." I shake my head in agreement. "You mentioned honesty. Is that simple, too?"

He clears his throat. "Yes. Simple, not altogether easy."

In player-coach relationships, I have learned that honesty, or truth, dealing with players is by far the best principle from which to function. This is basic to a positive environment. This means be above board about everything. Explain your program as it is. Teach as you believe, explain your actions from the actual truth of your feelings, thoughts, and theories.

If you prefer speed over size, say so. If you prefer intelligence over experience, say so. If you want a rigid system over freedom of action, say so. Let them know what you are up to and sell your program honestly and fairly.

I thought of the years and years of study before the research community came to this realization: no leadership style being best for all situations, except authenticity, integrity, honesty.

However the perennial problem of the coach of team sport athletes is to teach and organize the group in a way which they are satisfied sufficiently to continue to work hard and 'grow' in the competitive situation they find themselves, that is, trying to make the first team.

"Coach, before we go further about motivation: you said 'Motivations' not 'Motivation.' Was that intentional?"

"Athletes respond differently to the same stimulus, but they want to win, generally. It's probably something we could assume, for different reasons. Some schools, Grinnell College for example, consider athletics secondary to academics. I think some of the most well-respected faculty think it's a sign of intellectual weakness if you are athletic. We had a lot of 'motivations' at Grinnell. I think participation in athletics, the process itself, at Grinnell especially— We weren't strong and fast so much as— The process had to be worthwhile or valuable. But I've always thought that. You have to make it fun and fun is different for different people."

"Fun could be winning and wanting to win could be motivating, but fun could be a lot of different things."

"We, the Captains and I, once stayed up half the night preparing for a game with Coe. That was fun. We worked on new strategies for soccer starting in the Spring. That was fun. If I thought it was only about winning, well, I'd have probably quit. Winning feels like, well, it is good—with many positives— I can't deny it. If we don't have winning, we have to have something of importance. Something must hold our fascination, give us a reason to stay up late and fight our battles on the field when it's raining and cold. If it's not winning, it's all that winning requires of us, even if we fall short."

His last words touched a nerve. "So you think winning and success are tied to measuring up, to testing self-worth, what we're made of, so to speak?" Having studied self-concept, I wonder if Coach ever gave the "be a man" speech or motivated an athlete with, "Show us what you're made of!"

Continued motivation seems to boil down to a coach's ability to inspire enough confidence and trust in the players by demonstrating that his criticisms of techniques and of failure to execute assignments are criticisms of those techniques or of blown assignments and not of the players personalities.

I lean forward.

If the athlete understands and believes that the coach is basing his judgments on technique or assignment alone, the athlete will continue to be reinforced and the umbrella or environment will remain positive. If not, the umbrella will leak and morale will erode and attitudes will become poor and all the psychological theories will go down the drain.

I hold up my hand, asking for a moment to digest what I'm hearing. I can feel my heart picking up speed. "This idea is a big one, don't you think?" It was to me. Maybe the biggest. So fundamental. Like the foundation, the core. "Coach, I think you're describing the biggest mistake coaches can make." I'm literally on the edge of my seat. "And, the greatest source of their power." My mind is racing along with my heart. The concept is one I studied for years, establishing an approach I believed in. Yet, through the years, it had to be the most controversial and poorly received talking point when it came to coaches.

"Right. Yes. You might be right.

In today's society many young people have been conditioned to think that any criticism of themselves or their actions, regardless of the reason, is an attack on their character. For whatever reason this is a fact as far as I am concerned, and coaches must be able to deal with this conditioning.

Communication to the group that is criticism is leveled at non desirable behaviors, poor techniques, or assignment executions and not leveled at their personalities involved. Judgments regarding quality of execution and play likewise are meant to be based on the actual execution and not personalities.

Strong positive reinforcement should be provided for good techniques and good execution. Since most of these judgments and decisions are subjective, it is totally important that coaches devise a good system or organization to ensure best possible success.

"By 'personalities' and 'character' you mean the core person in contrast to their behaviors on the field. Personality and character equate to self-worth, identity, or self-concept." I struggle to find an appropriate term.

"Yes. I believe I agree with that."

We are on the same page, literally and figuratively. I stare at him in awe and hear myself say the word out loud. "Awesome." For a few moments, the only sound is a clock ticking.

It occurs to me that intrinsic to the player-coach relationship is the attitude of the coach toward humanity if you will. I do not think it is possible for one who does not appreciate, like and trust young people to establish or perpetuate a positive umbrella for a team. For no matter how good the material the coach is dealing with, he or she will not be successful in the long run if he or she does not 'like' people.

Many problems must be solved with subjective judgments during any season, particularly with highly motivated and competitive people, to say nothing of people conditioned for continual positivism. Without perseverance of the coach, I believe failure is assured. Without strong positive feeling towards the value of your team members and a sincere and honest personal liking of them, success will be limited.

He appears so certain. I've studied the theory for years, questioning, being questioned, knowing its potential yet never proving it. When a concept is fundamental to everything about us, it readily becomes complex, difficult to measure, difficult to control with scientific methods. He's lived the concept. He lives by the philosophy naturally sprouting from the concept, his insight, his way of life, treating fellow human beings with a basic respect and compassion. I exert control of my excitement with fidgety movements. "Coach, sounds like you're talking about a concept called 'acceptance': caring about people whether they catch a football in the end zone or not."

"Acceptance? What the hell is acceptance? I'm not talking about acceptance." He seems to be talking to himself now, trying to decide what acceptance is. I've distracted him with a new term, a mistake, possibly, a confusing and distracting mistake. He adds, "We weren't accepting much of anything. We weren't good enough to accept it."

I can't help but laugh. It's a mistake I've made before. "I don't mean approval. You might be thinking I mean approval. The word acceptance has multiple definitions and it's confusing. The concept I've studied for many years is all about valuing the person separate from the behavior. I think you would say 'behavior separate from personality and character.'"

"Then call it disconnectness or dissociance."

I laugh.

Coach continues. "We were taught not to accept. Never accept. Strive until the bell rings, or someone rings your bell."

"Yes. You have a point. We might need to use different language, so people readily understand the meaning of acceptance, the concept I'm talking about. But acceptance is what it was called 100 years ago, in research literature. Self-acceptance: the ability to take in information about yourself without getting all defensive about it, valuing yourself warts and all, so-to-speak, mistakes and all. It's synonymous with mental health. Back in the day it was also called adjustment or being well-adjusted.

"You teach that?"

"Yes. Acceptance relates to so many things in sport, I can't help but bring it up all the time." I drive people crazy with it. Give them headaches. I hesitate to say more. It's acceptance, the concept of acceptance, I've wanted to discuss with Coach all these years. "Your Umbrella includes acceptance. I'm so excited!"

"Me, too. Sounds like this could help my golf game."

"Coach, what are the odds?" I'm shaking my head in dismay. "Your fundamental tenet, your Umbrella, is based on acceptance, my line of research." I marvel over the coincidence. "Can I describe acceptance to you?"

"If it will help my golf game."

I grin. "Of course. That's the point, right?" We share a smile. "It's really just what you said. Athletes listen and are motivated to make changes and improvements when they don't feel threatened, when their egos or self-worth or self-concept isn't threatened. Kind of like, I tell you you need to work on your golf swing. You might hear what I have to say or you might block it out immediately because all you hear is 'You're not good enough.' If athletes are accepting, if the coach treats them with respect, accepts them no matter what, they tend to hear the criticism without jumping to the conclusion coach is criticizing them as a person, their personality or character, their self-worth. If coaches are accepting when it comes to their athletes, they convey the idea that their criticism is about technique or strategy or skills not the athletes' self-worth. It's huge! They listen, really listen."

"This might help my golf game. It might help Bowers help my golf game."

"You can't take Bower's criticism?" I'm grinning.

"Bowers can dish it out pretty good." He grimaces.

"He doesn't separate your personality from your behavior?"

"I'm thick skinned," he says. We both smile. I have a feeling it's all pretty good-natured chiding on both their parts.

Coach stops talking for a moment. Somehow I know he's thinking hard about acceptance, or maybe Bowers and his golf game. I'm fidgety with impatience.

He finally takes a sharp, deep breath and continues. "Some athletes aren't. Many athletes. You have to be careful. But, I agree. That's essential. Give a damn about them, not just how they kick or pass, they'll listen and probably do anything you ask. If you have a group of down-in-the-mouth athletes because they don't think you care about them, they won't care for you either, fight for you. Athletes would do anything for Bowers. Like the most incredible game I ever saw played—"

"Coach, I remember that game, the one you played under car headlights. This is big, Coach. Bigger."

"I'm not sure I agree."

"This idea of acceptance, well, you said it yourself, if you fail at this, everything you work hard to do falls apart. No matter how good the athlete is, if they don't feel you care about them as people, what good can come?"

"There's always a bust if you touch a nerve. If it hits them hard. You tell them— You give them just how much they need to know. Play it safe. Over the years, it's been my observation, most of the time they know it anyway, what they did wrong, what they need to know. But the game. The headlights and cold that night. Playing on and on. That is the biggest…"

I remember the story, a story of perseverance. Playing through fatigue and cold and dark. Coaches philosophy is based on events and people, mine on theory and science.

"I also remember the story you told about taking your freshman football team of 16 to play Coe College, a formidable opponent with three times the number of players: larger, more powerful players. It was a challenge you wanted them to confront. The way you told it, if I remember correctly, you wanted them to decide whether to play or not, but you couldn't help but suggest they would feel better about themselves if they played the game, that they'd be 'better' men for it."

He drops his head, deep in thought. The sides of his face tighten.

"Were you emulating Phog Allen, or General Patton?" As I speak, I sense a growing fear inside me. I don't want to show disrespect. I swallow the fear and ask the question. "You wanted them to dig deep, rise to the occasion. Was this your strategy to get them to do it? Did you suggest playing a game equated to being a man?" My thoughts take a dark turn. Like being a soldier? Like going to war? Sometimes a coach goes too far, suggesting an athlete who doesn't embrace the challenge is somehow "less than a man." Sometimes the challenge is senseless. Damage is done. Wars are fought. Lives are lost. My mind was racing. I put on the brakes.

Coach seems far away.

We sit in silence for a moment.

"How did they know you cared, especially if you cared so much about winning? How did they know you cared more about them, more than winning?"

"I don't know if I ever really knew." He stopped, once again deep in thought. After a moment, his head tilts forward with a serious expression carved on his face. "Can I tell my story now?"

I think, it's probably not important whether he knew it or not, but whether they knew it. "Sure," I say, while my mind continues to reel with the notion and importance of acceptance, real life acceptance.

"I was going to tell you about the Frosh game against Coe, the day I asked them— The one you are so concerned with. We played that game, 16 players against 34. I remember it now because I motivated them to play to prove something, to prove— I knew they'd feel better about themselves. And, they played. Maybe that's what they needed— What I needed to do to motivate—" He pauses. "—to take boys into battle."

I look down at a blank page and imagine the heart break and ultimate exhilaration of taking young men, boys, into battle with the notion their fundamental worth is on the line, and their lives. A supreme test. Coach isn't saying it, but I sense there was more to the moment, more than a test of manhood. I begin to speak from my heart, from my heart to his. "If you talked to them and listened to them, and you showed them you're interested in them, why wouldn't they know you care? Even if you asked them to go into battle."

He remains quiet, but I feel his heart responding.

"Coach, you said they would do anything for Bowers. You once told me Coach Bowers was a 'class' coach. What does that mean?" Coach Bowers died before Coach Pfitsch. He spoke of him in the present tense. I wonder if they are playing golf in—

"Bowers really gets along with the people: number one. Don't misunderstand. He also knows football very well. He's not a specialist in that area. He doesn't really, uh, that's kind of interesting in my opinion. He's not near as interested in football

53

techniques and stuff like that as he is in golf, for example. So, that's not one of the reasons. I would say there are a lot of people who know as much football as he does. But you don't need to know a lot of football, what you really need to be good at is, to take a group of kids and get them to play at a top level of performance, to play together and work together, to sacrifice their personal self for the good of the team. Everybody says they do that, but he did that better than anybody I know in the football business. I think Young did that in track. And Obermiller had it."

Dick Young coached track and cross country at Grinnell College in the 1950s and 60s, long before my time at Grinnell. His name was immortalized by the Grinnell College Hall of Fame and when the College's largest track meet was christened the "Dick Young Invitational." I knew Ray Obermiller. He successfully coached the Grinnell College Men's and Women's Swimming and Diving Teams for over 30 years after being a very successful diver in his own right at Iowa State University. I saw him make a gutsy dive after the swim team won the 2011 Midwest Conference Championship: a forward 1-1/2 pike off the 3 meter board at 82 years of age! I might not have been the only spectator dialing 91— in the tense moment before his face bobbed up through the bubbles.

"It's very simple to say." He smiles when he says the word "simple." "This business of getting along with people, respecting people whether they play at 100%. The difference between Edd and other good coaches is that Edd got along with 99% of the players, to where they had great respect for him, and would do almost anything he'd ask them to do. He didn't ask them to do abnormal things. He had good judgment and he was a fine person in that regard. He had the ability to get people to play, practice harder, work harder, and play better, together better, enjoy the game, he was extremely good at getting them to enjoy the game. Almost all football coaches that I know of besides Bowers, that is not true. They don't— They have a very difficult— There are people who can work you harder, do all kinds of stuff, but they always do that to the point where they make it either boring or cruel, and not any fun, certainly not any fun: what most people call fun. Bowers really had kids that— His kids always had fun playing football. And he had a lot of people who learned how to play football for him that didn't play very—at all— So he fit it into Grinnell's business. Some kid would say, 'I always thought I'd like to play football, but I'm too little or this or that,' and he would almost always take that guy and later on you'd find out he was just having a hell of a time playing football. Because Edd has a great knack to do such things."

"Coach, I think I got it. It's not just the tough talk, it's the combination of that tough talk and the way you always took time out of your day. Bowers did the same thing. He talked with athletes, recognized them as people. It might have been an effort to separate personality from behavior." I shy away from calling it "acceptance." "But it was also— You really did love people, win or lose. Why not win, if you can? Make it as fun and rewarding as possible. Fun, hard work, and win or make character-building mistakes, either way, you cared. That's how mistakes are character-building in the first place. We learn we can pick ourselves up. We learn that a coach still cares. We learn how to be braver the next time. Coach, I think you and Bowers lived the concept I've been studying."

"This thing you call 'acceptance'— You're saying we must have been in the forefront about that, too." He grins.

"Well, kind of. The concept of self-acceptance has been around a long time, before you or I studied sport. But the concept of self-esteem, not self-acceptance, was the concept of choice in the 1950s, 60s, and 70s. Teachers were being taught to spare negative criticism and only provide positive reinforcement to boost self-esteem. It's real life 'spare the rod and spoil the child' and undoubtedly the 'conditioning' you've been referring to."

His eyes widen.

"If you studied how to parent or teach or coach during your coaching years, it was probably all about promoting self-esteem. I think we all see the good in promoting self-esteem. But, without also promoting self-acceptance, it becomes easy for kids to believe 'good job' and 'good boy' become one and the same. Boosting self-esteem encourages people to achieve as much as possible and to feel good about themselves based upon those achievements. Who wouldn't work hard to prove their worth? Self-esteem is powerful stuff. But, it's a disaster waiting to happen without self-acceptance. People make mistakes. People aren't perfect. If self-worth is based on achievement and you make a mistake or a series of mistakes or you just can't do something you want to do, where does that leave you? Self-esteem can't take an athlete to 100%. Fear of making mistakes grows. It becomes a fear of losing self-worth. It can be paralyzing. Self-acceptance gives an athlete freedom from the fear of making a mistake, from the terror of making a big mistake, from losing self-worth. Full potential can only be met when athletes perform without this fear." I'm talking, but he isn't listening.

The proverbial lightbulb has lit up his face. "You're explaining my theory of— It's more important to take pressure off. They can't take as much now as before. They were spoiled!"

"Well, some—" but I get it, too. He's talking about the relationship between arousal and performance and the part acceptance plays. As we light up together, the feeling overwhelms me. My hands fly up as if in thanks to a higher power. I shake them. "Don't you love this?"

I'm not sure he understands until our eyes meet. The twinkle twinkles brighter than ever. He opens his mouth, pauses, and just as quickly, our minds move foreword. I sense a story coming on. I quickly add, "You know, acceptance isn't taught to coaches. As important as it is, it usually isn't taught, period. Yet, here it is, in your theory, right here under your Umbrella."

He says, "We're on the same hunt."

"Yes." Different paths, I thought, I through academia, he through coaching, both in pursuit of 100% performance. "Coach, tell me more about the Umbrella!"

Coach takes a long sip of tea and begins describing the fourth element of his Umbrella.

In my experience in small colleges, I have coached with limited professional assistance partly because I learned peer group leadership can be effective and develop a good umbrella, and partly out of necessity. I have developed a pecking order with elected captains, which helps me in this regard.

I recognize that there is nothing unusual about an elected captain system since they are probably traditional. I expect what may be different about my organization is the amount of responsibility I give to my captains. The pecking order may be old fashioned but it still works in our culture. The captains in my organization are only one part of the system, but because of the great amount of luck I have had with many great boys, I tend to think of the system as the 'Captain System.' Let me explain the whole set up and then tell you a story of the 1981 soccer team to exemplify the Umbrella.

The first so-called principle which I use as a guide is: upperclassmen are always given first priority over underclassmen in all situations as we go through the season.

That is, seniors have priority over juniors and juniors over sophomores, etc. A more definitive description would be that senior lettermen would be given priority over junior lettermen, junior lettermen over sophomore lettermen, and sophomore lettermen over freshmen. This ladder is the pecking order. It needs to be communicated to freshman and justified to them, a big job of the captains as well as the coach.

"So the pecking order starts with senior letterman. If you're a senior and not a letterman, you don't have the same seniority on the team?"

"That's right. There probably— It wouldn't normally be a concern of mine because of the low number of seniors who haven't lettered, maybe none. But that's important."

"It prioritizes performance to a certain extent."

"Yes. As a basis for who is making decisions for the team. For example,

The pecking order becomes a base for the evaluation job of picking the varsity team. The principles here are something like this:

Principle 1: if a senior is even in ability and value to the team with an underclassman, the senior gets the job. The same principle is applied right down the pecking order. The underclassman must be clearly superior to an upperclassman to take the spot.

Principle 2: players select the positions that they want to play. Players may change positions whenever they desire but changes are subject to the pecking order principles. If they change position, they start competing at the bottom of the pecking order for the new position.

"But Coach, you mean a very good senior would have to start behind a first year, if the first year was there first?"

Coach looks dismayed. "What? No. It didn't work like that. If there was a senior wanting a position a freshman wanted, the senior would probably have already taken it."

"But Coach, what if the senior hadn't already taken it? What if he wanted to make a change?"

"You're thinking a lot about this, aren't you? These rules are the kind of rules I never liked. You should write them, make them air tight. But, this is the way it was, or at least the way I wanted it to be. All the better players played. That was it. Seniority mattered when two players seemed approximately similar."

"So, the player didn't go to the bottom of the order when he moved positions?"

"I can tell right now, you would be a very good policy maker. What the hell are you doing talking to me? You're the writer. You figure it out and write it down. I can't remember exactly how it worked. But it worked. And I believe it worked well. Every now and then, I suppose, not very often, if a senior player wanted a position and the players were pretty well matched in ability, the one wanting to take the other's position would have to start in the runner-up position. At some later time, if the player, the senior player, was clearly a match or better, that player could play because everyone wanted that player to play. But it just didn't happen, or at least I don't remember it happening. I wasn't aware of it happening. It was my understanding, my recollection, that the better players played all the time, that was our goal, at least that was what we tried to do. We all wanted the better players to play no matter what year they were, and it was up to them. Maybe we had some problems, but that was dealt with by the captains. The captains dealt with those problems, unless of course the problem grew to be— If it was a bigger problem, I might have dealt with it."

"They must have done a pretty good job."

"They knew the rules as well as I did. Hell, they made the rules." He chuckles. "Everything seemed to go pretty smoothly along those lines." He pauses. "The most difficult times as I recall, were when new players, lower underclassmen, came onto the scene. These players were sometimes well and above the players who had established themselves."

"How did they work it out?"

"I think they must have just known. We were able to practice many days before the season, the competitive season, began. And scrimmages. That's plenty of time, and drills of various kinds— Players worked it out, usually by the first game, if not soon afterward."

"That's really kind of amazing."

"What?"

"Well, that you basically let them determine their own lineup."

He smiles. "Most of them knew more than I did about soccer. Even if I knew soccer as well as Bowers knew football, I think they did a better job than I could have done. I believe I stumbled upon it out of necessity. And it worked well in many different situations. For example, when Doug Rowe—"

"Coach, what was number three?"

He shoots me a look of exasperation and takes a deep breath.

Principle 3: captains are elected using open nomination, but with a strong recommendation for election of senior or at least junior candidates. Experience in the system gives continuity, wisdom, and real value of captains' leadership. Good players who have leadership capability are obviously preferred over poorer players, however there are exceptions to the principle.

"As long as they lettered."

"Yes. I believe so."

I chuckle.

"Do you want me to continue? Don't you want to know these, whatever you call them, pearls of wisdom?"

I chuckle more. "Yes. Please. No. 4. Is there a No. 4 pearl?" It dawns on me I never told him about "diving for pearls."

"Of course." He pauses. "I might be able to reduce this list."

"Maybe the part about going to the bottom of seniority when changing positions."

He shoots me another look of feigned disgust and rolls his eyes upward. "We can edit this thing, right?"

We both know he can't edit it. "Do you want me to edit it?"

Suddenly he seems deep in thought. He opens his eyes wider and says, "No."

I smile as he continues. No offense taken.

Principle 4: have captains represent positions on the team, that is, a captain for forward line and a captain for defensive line, etc. With this representation you can have great help in the organization and execution of practice drills since drills are often done by position.

You like that one?" he asks.

"Yes, Coach." I can't suppress a smile as he quickly regains momentum with every word.

Principle 5: organize freshmen into a unit as soon as practice begins to give them attention, positive reinforcement, a positive climate, and particularly to overcome negativism often assumed by freshmen due to the pecking order. In other words they may think there is no 'light in the tunnel' for freshmen. They want to be sure they are going to get to play and play before they are seniors.

The formation of the frosh unit immediately serves two purposes: to give them peer group reinforcement and to give the varsity immediate and spirited competition. Of course the freshmen are told if they clearly demonstrate superiority they move to the varsity. One can see that by extension of this system that the freshmen team evolves thru the season to a junior varsity, a mix of frosh and upperclassmen.

Now this system provides a working mechanism. If all players understand it, it gives a mechanism for evaluation of performance and rewarding superior performance as well as justifying personal decisions. If the captains work positively with the coach it can provide a sound umbrella.

My career as a soccer coach was relatively young at this point and came after approximately twenty-five years experience with football and basketball. Most of these ideas came from experience from the other sports. The big difference has been that I had no personal playing experience with soccer and therefore had to overcome a weakness in knowledge of the game. The captain system enabled me to learn the game while coaching because of some tremendous young men whose knowledge of soccer was obviously superior to mine. Their understanding of the necessity for organization and motivation helped them work with me instead of counter to me in developing a good soccer program for Grinnell.

I've picked the 1981 season to describe because it was our most successful not only because we won our division and were runner up in the conference championship, but because in so doing the problems which we overcame and the tactics which evolved were in my opinion largely due to the program I have just described.

Coach looks at me. He seems to be asking permission to continue. I smile and nod. Do I really have control of our conversation now? The sense of control I'm feeling might be part of the illusion. Contemplating this point seems like a bad idea.

Our 1980 season was fairly successful from the standpoint of win/loss record. We finished with an 8-1 record, second place in the Southern Division to Knox College, losing to them by one goal in the championship game.

Our team was a good defensive team with a limited offense, limited almost entirely to the scoring talents of one player, a junior named Doug Rowe, who had established himself as an excellent scorer in his freshman year and consistently thereafter at the rate of about twelve goals per year or at little better then one goal a game career-wise. From my experience with soccer that is excellent and a coach or team is lucky to have such a scorer. But the handling of one star scorer in soccer is likened to the handling of one star scorer on almost any team. The attitudes and morale of the team, the nature of the environment or umbrella, and the common sense decision-making regarding strategy, tactics, and emphasis on defensive and offensive strategy all can hinge around the relationship of that player to other players and to the coach.

Doug Rowe was a fine scorer, but he played with a great deal of ego, according to his peers. He was not the most popular player on the team and his style of tending to keep the ball and work individually for goals was not looked upon with favor by some of his teammates.

This coach was taxed with the problem, but learned long ago, from basketball, to preserve a good shooter. I built my offense around the offensive ability of Doug Rowe. My job became one of selling that concept to the team.

Doug Rowe had already been selected All Conference the two previous years and was elected captain in his senior year in spite of a lack of support from teammates for his style of play. The team also elected two fullbacks as co-captains: Dave Furth and Dave Morote. Both were All Conference performers the previous season. The election was immediately after the season ended in 1980, so we had the entire spring to plan and visualize the 1981 season.

Coach and captains meetings were held periodically during the spring and we were prepared for the season's tactical planning when we started.

The basic tactics called for a similar offense to the previous year. For best scoring possibilities we used a short pass, conservative control game in the front field with emphasis on getting the ball to Rowe. We emphasized defense, one that we felt was good enough to limit scoring by opponents to no more than one goal per game.

I silently notice their objective was not perfection. Their approach appears challenging yet doable with the potential to preserve or enhance motivation after setbacks, i.e. acceptance. This was good goal-setting.

Captains and coach set up practices intended to condition the team as well as possible, including twelve hour pre-game plans, visualization and concentration exercises, plus the season objective of a conference championship.

With captains working in practice as position drill leaders and freshmen providing early season competition, we moved into the season. We increased the quality of the opposition by scheduling stronger non conference games to help us toughen up.

The season went pretty much according to plan. We successfully won most of our games and were undefeated in conference play. We scored just enough, mostly Rowe, for our defense to hold most opponents beneath our total. It was those games that provided anxiety all the way. The problem with Rowe's individuality and my continued support for his style as opposed to attempting change for a stronger offense or for other players to have more of a chance to score remained a sticky problem as far as morale was concerned. In other words the positive environment umbrella was always a bit shaky.

In my opinion, results showed the good effects of the system. Rowe learned more from being captain than he had in earlier years. He learned how to be a better team player and he learned the responsibilities of being a team leader as well as an outstanding player.

All other players learned that your game plan, which exploits the capabilities of the best players, can work, if everyone stays with it. I do not say we did that all the time, but we did it well enough to be generally successful and to accomplish everything we really wanted except the final game of the year, the championship game. We lost to Lake Forest. It was a game in which Rowe was shut out from scoring and our defense gave up one goal.

We were far from perfect, but we had an excellent year. We all learned quite a lot, much of which was apart from soccer techniques.

I might add that Captain Furth and Captain Morote did much during the season to communicate and influence both team members and coach on decisions of importance to keep a positive umbrella. Captain Rowe also unselfishly gave much to the team's effort all along the line. Furth and Rowe were selected All Conference and Morote probably would have been except an injury forced him out of action the last month of the season.

In discussing the positive environment I have made reference to a condition which I think many modern day athletes develop. I characterize it as the eternal quest for positive reinforcement.

Here it is again.

Sometimes I characterize the products of the syndrome as spoiled kids.

The effect of nurturing only self-esteem without self-acceptance.

I believe that this condition is more prevalent today than at any other period in our history and it is difficult to describe and attack. At least partially, it is due to the misunderstanding of the differences between a challenge, negative reinforcement, and reward.

Interesting.

He looks up. "Do you have something to say?"

"No." I'm loving this.

All athletes—

"Aren't you loving this? It's what we talked about."

He looks at me as if he's waiting for me to catch on. And then it hits me again: he's not really here. He's been gone more than a year. He's a figment of my imagination, because he's—he's omniscient! That's it! Of course he's loving this. He knew what he was going to say before he said it. He knows what I'm going to say before I say it. Then again, maybe he's not omniscient. After all, this is his book, too. He knew what he was going to say, he knew our conversation would travel along with the words he'd already written. I'm about to ask him if he's omniscient when he clears his throat. Twice he clears his throat.

"I'll be quiet," I say.

All athletes learn better from positive reinforcement than through negative reinforcement. But a challenge such as a strong schedule of games is not negative reinforcement. And many athletes seem to think that if you present them with a difficult goal or obstacle to overcome, you give them negative reinforcement. Therefore they resist, instead of using the challenge as a reason for accelerated positive response.

"Just so I'm clear, Coach." I'm treading on thin ice. "'Negative reinforcement' doesn't mean taking away something that causes a behavior to be repeated."

"Yes. Whatever you just said. It is very confusing. It's the reason— Only smarter people can— But, negative reinforcement — If I was to— It is a challenging message. Didn't we already discuss this?"

"Yes. I just want to be sure we're still talking about the same thing. The goal of negative reinforcement is not to punish or put down?"

"No, but critical, with an emphasis on the technical side. They don't have a skill or the knowhow or the potential of some kind to do something. Agitate them in an attempt to motivate them to prove you wrong. It was— We would knowingly shake them up, not too much."

"Got it." I settle back into my chair. He seems to sit up straighter. I sense another story coming on.

Clear demonstration of the challenge to the team is a must. Challenges historically have been the inspiration for the successful. On this basis I would like to tell the story of another Grinnell athlete—

Ha! I'm omniscient! Coach sneaks in a disapproving look before continuing.

—an athlete who I believe epitomizes one who used the challenge, negative that is, to inspire himself to great heights. This, too, is part of the umbrella of a positive environment.

In 1955 a young man enrolled in Grinnell College by the name of John Copeland. He had been sold on Grinnell by a good friend who had played on my varsity basketball team in the years previously. John's story epitomized my thoughts on positive negative reinforcement and I believe to recount will help clarify the muddy thinking regarding the concept.

Positive negative reinforcement. I chuckle to myself. He says the language of researchers is confusing. I make a mental note to tease him later.

John was 5'6" tall and weighed 140 pounds—not very big for any college program in 1954, but especially not very big when you hear that John's college ambition was to make the varsity basketball team.

John had had a very successful high school athletic career competing in football, basketball, baseball, and tennis. He had been an excellent football player, particularly as a runner and kicker and he had been a good basketball player. I do not know what his record was as a baseball and tennis player, but I am sure they must have been better than average.

I was coaching both football and basketball at the time and was interested in both sports equally, however we had more need for football talent than basketball talent as both the number of the team and the win/loss records would indicate.

Because of John's size and quickness I really thought he would be able to play football and I doubted that he could make our basketball team. The basketball team at the time was in the upper third of the conference and we were blessed with good members with better than average talent.

Freshmen were not eligible by rule then, so we had separate freshman programs in all sports.

As John's freshmen year commenced he did not report for football. He took a physical education activity class that I happened to be teaching, in which we played touch football. His abilities, speed, quickness, and talents in passing, kicking, and running impressed me greatly and I tried my best persuasive arguments to get him to come out for frosh football.

He told me 'no' in no uncertain terms many times and also told me that he had decided to make the varsity basketball team before he would consider playing football again. He also said he thought that he would play tennis since we did not have a baseball program at that time. Since we had a year to argue the case before varsity football competition I let up on the pressure to get him to play football. However, I remained concerned that he would be very disappointed if he could not make the varsity basketball team, so I maintained my 'game plan' to convince him to play football by the time he was a sophomore.

He came out for freshman basketball and was successful at being placed on the starting five by Coach Booth. I watched him carefully, and although the frosh basketball team was quite successful and John was very much a leader, he was not a very good scorer and remained unconvinced that he would make the varsity team. So I continued to talk to him about the possibility of playing football and to putting too many 'eggs in the basketball basket.' I must say that I do not believe that I changed his mind one iota. You might say that I was positively reinforcing his football potential challenge and down-grading the basketball; but John was continuing to reinforce the opposite and was personally visualizing his basketball goals very specifically and very strongly.

67

John made me understand the power of visualization, which I will discuss in detail. Another example of the coach learning from observation of the athletes.

In an era of skepticism, Coach made a name for himself with his pioneering use of visualization. I chuckle to myself again as I recognize the need to "wait for it."

Well the story continued as projected by John. In his sophomore year he again did not play football and now November was upon us and the basketball team reported for action. We had eight returning lettermen, a squad of fifteen upperclassmen and ten sophomores reporting, among them was our 5'6" guard from Keokuk, Iowa whose expressed goal was to make the varsity.

I had visualized his situation as one in which he might be able to make the first team by his senior year as his best possibility. I was to learn very soon that that was not his game plan.

I should have been able to understand that sooner, for in our many conversations about his athletic career in the year previous he had asked me to tell him specifically what he needed to be able to do to make the varsity team and I remember telling him that I liked my guards to average 10-15 points a game and also to hold the opponent guards to fewer points than that. This served him as something to visualize.

I was to be reminded of that conversation many times after the first game of the varsity season. Our opening game was at home vs. North Central College of Illinois. North Central had a good team and I remember that the game was closely contested with us winning in the last few minutes. Because of North Central's reputation I was fairly pleased with the results.

I was able to play some reserves in the final minutes of the game and John was one I got in for a few minutes. He scored four or five points. At this point in time I had him positioned at about #5 guard. I could see he had possibilities which I had not realized previously.

He came into my office early the following week for a 'talk.' To summarize the talk, he wanted to know exactly what he had to do to make the team and by the 'team' he meant the first team. He also was quite insistent and he upset me somewhat with his overconfidence bordering on arrogance. He pushed very hard and I pushed back just as hard explaining that most sophomores do not make the first team until they demonstrate leadership and other characteristics which showed their obvious superiority to the upperclassmen. In other words, he would have to pay the price to play and he must earn the position. I told him he would not play because he was insistent upon it or because he could intimidate the coach. As I recall we put most of the cards on the table; but in the end, John continued to ask for specific, measurable objectives to work for.

I had no trouble giving them to him. As I remember they were: (1) to score consistently or to average fifteen points per game (assuming he played the majority of the game), (2) hold opponent to half that number, (3) lead the fast break, (4) be more than effective point man in the press, and (5) be the team quarterback in setting up our 1/2 court offense.

I thought that I had given him a big order even for his big ego. Our next game happened to be with Drake University. Drake was playing us in their early season as a warmup and 'cheap' game; we were only fifty miles away. We were playing Drake because I liked to challenge the team early, hoping to mentally condition our team to a higher level than we normally had to play, and for a matter of tradition. Drake and Grinnell had years before been members of the original Missouri Valley Conference.

"A challenge, but not negative reinforcement."

"Yes."

This Drake team had a legitimate all-American player on its roster by the name of Morrell. So the game was to be a really tough challenge for us. I hoped to give them enough of a game by not using many substitutes.

"Maybe a little negative reinforcement for John Copeland."

"Maybe. Yes."

I see a hint of a smile on Coach's face.

The game did not develop as planned and we were intimidated or not well prepared, and we found ourselves twenty points down at half time. I realized the first team's percentages of improving its position in the second half, so decided to play several second team people to give them a chance. Among them was my friend John Copeland. John played most of the second half.

He passed and pressured effectively; he set up the pattern offense; he guarded his opponent better than average; and, he scored fourteen points. I did not take him out. I was impressed, especially as to the effectiveness that he performed the specifics which I had outlined for him earlier in the week.

I began to consider John for first team duty, if not starting.

"So, it was an effective negative reinforcement for John, but not for others."

"The experience wasn't— I suppose it was my misjudgment to think it would be, and, it furthered my belief in the spoiled condition of many Grinnell athletes, even those who played quite well."

"They were spoiled."

"Not that they were— It was different, a different time. Not like pitching fits, having tantrums. Just not responding to adversity by raising their game."

"100% performance. Like John."

"You're catching on." He smiles.

Our first conference game appeared on the horizon. We were to play Ripon College in Ripon, Wisconsin. I didn't start John, but I was ready to use him early if conditions seemed right.

I'm thinking John's greatest challenge might have been contending with his coach's "visualization."

Coach lowers a dour gaze on me before he continues.

We had a 'flat' first half, one of those kind that the 'guts' of this book is dedicated to preventing. So flat that I was furious with ten minutes to go in the first half, so furious that I decided to put John in the game with a strong statement like, 'Straighten out the team John. See if you can reverse the situation!'

70

The record shows that that is exactly what he did. His leadership showed up in setting up a disciplined press and resultant fast break. We stabilized the score down ten points at half time and slowly gained control in the second half with John showing 'the way' in nearly all phases of the game. He even scored 15 points. We were able to go on and win the game.

As we walked off the floor to the dressing room, John arranged to catch up with me and walk beside me and I remember very clearly his poignant question, 'Do you think I'm getting the idea, Coach?'

I laugh out loud. Coach shakes his head and says, "There's more."

I should add to this story the career finish for John Copeland and point out the important elements regarding the psychological phenomena of visualization and positive reinforcement. As I reflect, I realize that this and other stories painted truths which were not very clear to me earlier.

John started and played the great majority of the possible games in basketball the rest of his sophomore year. He was selected All Conference Second Team his junior year and All Conference his senior year. Our team placed in the top three of the conference all three years.

Incidentally in his junior year John came out for the football team and made first team quarterback. He was a very impressive football player as I had predicted.

Score one for a coach's visualization. Coach sends me another stern look. I forget he's possibly, maybe, omniscient.

He also played on the tennis team in his sophomore and junior year and switched to baseball, playing centerfield on the first modern day Grinnell College baseball team in his senior year. It is also interesting to note that John took a pre-med course load at Grinnell, majoring in chemistry, attended University of Iowa Medical School, and is now in general practice in California, enjoying a reputation as an MD comparable to his athletic reputation.

In retrospect, I think the phenomena which were working here were dependent upon John's strong goal orientation. His single minded objective of playing varsity basketball over other goals recommended to him. The second factor was a negative challenge made by the coach who sincerely believed that John would get more out of football than basketball. I would describe my efforts to convince John of the desirability of playing football and the negative challenges—not purposeful ones on my part—but in fact that is the way it worked out. John had convictions strong enough to withstand the pressure and obstacles. Also I believe the continuing obstacles and numerous discussions gave him continuous motivation to become a good college basketball player. His visualization was somehow 'internalized' by him and was reinforcing if not causative to his later success as a basketball player.

My positive reinforcement after he performed fairly well no doubt helped some. However I discovered that John enjoyed a reputation of overcoming obstacles naturally and thrived on the challenge.

"What do you mean by 'internalize,' Coach?"

Coach looks down. He rubs his ear lobe for a moment. I fight back a smile. It isn't just academic curiosity behind my question. On the one hand, using words inappropriately, words like "negative reinforcement," make it more difficult for me, for academicians, to use them appropriately and communicate with the same audiences. I'm not very fond of the frustration. I'm not fond of people making fun of academicians as they attempt to remedy the situation. We each have our own goals and jobs to do. I have a good reason to ask the question, but this time, I'm poking a little fun, too. We both know what he means by "internalize" even without verbalizing a definition. It is a good word for the two of us, for two people trying to communicate about something so complex and mysterious it defies definition. But, I couldn't help myself.

Coach rises to the challenge with a twinkle in his eye, albeit a focused, serious, twinkle. "I don't know how you would define it, but I think it's making something I might call a thought or a series of thoughts and the actions attached to those thoughts become automatic, without thinking, without cognitive processes, when athletes make whatever it is a part of them, a skill or a habit. If it's internalized, they don't think about it anymore, which is what we want in sport." He looks directly into my eyes. "Too much thinking can make fools of us."

Ooo. Who is poking fun now? I grin.

He says, "When the thing is set in motion, you want to do what you have internalized. And you hope you've internalized what you want to do."

"Nice, Coach."

He smiles and nods at his cleverness.

"Hence the need for mastery rehearsal: imagining what you want to have happen over and over, or coping rehearsal: imagining what you want to have happen in situations which aren't easy, where there are obstacles." I look for his reaction.

"Rehearsal—visualization—imagery—mastery—Does it matter what we call it?"

"Yes, Coach. But, before I forget, let's talk more about athletes being 'spoiled': not being able to take criticism or 'negative reinforcement.' How did you deal with it?"

"It wasn't the Army."

Silence fills the room. I'm not sure where he is going with this.

"Positive reinforcement was better than negative reinforcement, but much less expedient at times," Coach says. "And, I'm not sure I was very good at— Talk to Coach Freeman or Coach Hurley. Most people don't know it, but Ev is one of the best coaches in the business. And, Coach Hurley, well you know—" He chuckles.

I do know. Many times I'd observed her saying the darnedest things to athletes. They always seemed so attentive. Half the time they were laughing or smiling by the end of the coaching moment, even when the moment included some form of criticism. And her dedication, like Coach Freeman's, the long hours, open door— It was easy to see how much they cared.

"I think I get it," I said. "It was easier in the Army when you could just tell someone what they were doing wrong and they had to listen and do what they were told. Telling athletes what they need to do without it being perceived as demeaning, without attacking their personality, as you call it, it's not easy. They're— We're all so sensitive."

He nods. Again, we are on the same page, the next page. I want to seize the moment.

"This is where my training might help, as an explanation." I recognize the look of skepticism as it spreads across his face. "For years academia promoted self-esteem. I know I've already mentioned this." He might be grinding his teeth. "But I believe acceptance, not just esteem, is an integral part of your Umbrella. And, it doesn't only involve positive reinforcement and separating technique from personality. I *know* it wasn't only those things for you. Heck, you make fun of my name and you tell it like it is, which is not exactly positive or reinforcing." He opens his mouth as I raise my hand. "The kids are 'spoiled,' you said. They don't respond well to negative reinforcement. Simply put, it's just too scary for them." I might have his attention now. "If a person's worth is based on esteem, it rises with achievements and falls with mistakes and failure. Not meeting a challenge can be crushing, not just a setback."

"That's not—"

I hold my hand up again. "When athletes put themselves out there and make mistakes or fail, they potentially learn the most, and not just about sport. Learning how to fail and still have worth is like learning how to become fearless, or less fearful, in the face of a challenge."

"100%."

"Yes! Like runners finding their potential. How do they know how fast they can run, if they don't go all out, sometimes gasping for breath or falling down before the finish line? Mistakes are inevitable. Being fearless—sometimes in a moment of intense competition—it isn't easy. Striving for 100%, when defeat and diminished worth are possible—"

"Yes, but—"

"It's scary! We're scared, not spoiled. Well, maybe spoiled, too." I lean forward. "That's why self-acceptance allows us to reach 100%. When we feel of value as people 'win or lose,' it frees us up to try our hardest without one of our deepest most powerful fears: loss of worth—or personality or character."

Coach grunts. There's a long pause. "Is it safe to speak now?"

I take a deep breath. "Of course. I'm sorry. But, there's so much to this concept. It wraps around and through everything about 100% performance. I don't want us to overlook other important aspects of the concept, maybe the most important." I grin and chuckle. "Now you can speak."

"Well, you're right." His voice projects more energy. His body straightens and he begins to move his arms excitedly. If he hadn't already passed, I would be worried about his heart. "We spoil them and want them to be tough later, when they face greater challenges. If you're a kid who's been told how great he is whenever he's accomplished something, anything, when he makes mistakes, even silence or encouragement on the part of a coach can send the message he isn't good enough or you don't like him."

"Yes! Which is a serious blow, more serious than a coach might realize."

"Teachers and parents and coaches are afraid, too. They're afraid to say something critical. We can't prime athletes with this business of all positive reinforcement and expect them to handle setbacks and criticism later on. But that's what they need, at least that's what they need to get to 100% performance: setbacks and criticism, constructive criticism."

And someone to care about them as they experience those setbacks.

"Especially when their 100% isn't someone else's 100%, their mistakes aren't someone else's mistakes."

"So knowing each individual, something important about each individual's path to 100%, where they are and how to challenge them appropriately is key."

"Yes." He says, "Mistakes might be the best teachers, but they often aren't the best motivators."

"Athletes get down. They get down on themselves."

"Yes. I believe I was better able to teach them if I stayed relatively positive, but at times I couldn't do it. And, I don't think they responded well as the years went on. I don't think some wanted to hear the truth of it. The ones that did, we got along best."

I hold my breath (and tongue) while he continues.

"In the Army, if you gave an order, it was followed. In a way they had it easy, easier, like having students all the time, not just an hour or so a day, and if you said someone wasn't doing their job, they didn't go sulking or pout about it or talk back. They might test you or not be happy about it. Maybe that's why we were careful about the orders we gave. Everyone—these people—had guns." He smiles a thin smile.

I laugh. "Sorry." I grimace. "So you learned that positive reinforcement was better, more effective, and you used it, but you didn't always use it."

"Well, I wouldn't say I used it only because it was more effective. That was a good enough reason. But it was— That's what I meant by Umbrella and liking people. I grew up with a good set of parents, a great set of parents, and good teachers. They taught me to look at other people the same as I would anyone."

"And if *you* didn't perform well?"

"In sport?"

"In anything."

"My father was an interesting man. He was a doctor, a physician. I was born in India because my father was a medical missionary for the Lutheran Church. And he joined the CCC, so we moved more, like in the Army, from base to base. He probably wanted me to be a doctor." He pauses. "I think he did want me to be a doctor."

"But you went into physical education and coaching."

"My father never did give a damn about athletics. My mother, she went to all my games, but we were very close friends."

"You and your father?"

"Yes. He was a really great guy, a helluva person. He did a lot of great things. They both treated me very well, but they treated everyone well. I would have liked to have played football in college. But I think my father knew. He wanted me to go to Texas Lutheran because of academics and religion. But it was also a place I could play ball. At 5 foot 3 inches and 100 pounds, I wasn't going to play for University of Texas or A & M. I had skills and physical coordination, but I just couldn't grow. I tried. I remember eating bananas when I was 15 years old, lots of bananas, because I heard eating bananas made you gain weight. Anyhow, it never really bothered me. I did all these things. I went to YMCA camp and the school I spent much time in was extremely progressive. I was able to play and have a head coach, possibly the best coach I've ever had. His philosophy, that everyone who wants to play can play, is the philosophy I still hold today."

"You're talking about Carl Menger?"

"Yes."

"It sounds like he was very accepting of others, too. I think it's difficult to convey acceptance verbally. He might not have actually said, 'I value you or care about you win or lose,' but I bet he did some things—"

Coach chuckles. "Carl Menger loved sport, but he loved his players more. He might have said that. I can see him saying that."

"Did he say that to you?"

"No. Well, in general, I don't think we talked that way."

"So how did he show you he accepted you, cared about you, win or lose?"

"I don't know. I can't take credit for knowing, for being that smart. I think he just treated people the way he thought they should be treated. I was brought up that way. My parents— He might have — He probably confirmed it was the best way to conduct yourself."

"Your athletes reaped the benefits."

He looks at me inquisitively.

"You nurtured their self-acceptance like your parents and Coach Menger nurtured yours. You haven't studied it like I have, dissected it to figure it out. You naturally did it. Your athletes were lucky to have you. Your acceptance of them placed them on solid ground, so to speak. Their worth wasn't dependent on achievement, performance, and outcomes, not with you. Those things were very important, but, it comes back to—you must have cared about them as people no matter what."

"No. Well, yes, but—" Coach stops talking for a moment. "Emily— This is it. We all loved to win. We all loved it when a player hit the— made a record or goal."

I'm not sure Coach accepted what I just said about him.

"These were important things. In general, it was a touchy business, but yes, I think I bothered some people. Mostly we got along. Emily— She was tough. I know she was tough, but she was the caregiver, the person who showed she cared. If you're asking did I care about them even if they missed baskets down the stretch? Yes. It didn't mean a damn when it came to the banquet, or after. I knew they would be lawyers and professors and run businesses. Why remember missed baskets?" He chuckled. "Although, well, there was a player, a basketball player—"

I think he's trying to remember the player's name.

"He threw his warmup jacket or towel, I think it was a warmup jacket, from the opposing bench, and it wrapped around one of our players, his face and shoulders, and he missed his shot at the buzzer. That was a hell of a way to end a game."

"Coach, do you think your respect for them as people helped? And knowing Emily? I know their relationships with her meant a lot to them. But the question is: do you think your athletes actually played better because of these things?"

"I suppose. It makes sense. Every kid who was on my team, whatever team, my personal kids, my wife will tell you, will still tell you, that maybe it's even a weakness in my personality that I treated my athletes so well. I cared about them. I think it was true; it may have been true that I at least that I— It was easier in the Army. You have them all the time. As a coach, you have them for maybe an hour or two a day. As a teacher, in classes, you have them less than that. I wanted to prepare them to be able to go out to face the world." He slips into deeper contemplation. "My father never saw me play, but he prepared me well. He didn't hold my hand all the time, and you might think that he didn't do a good job, but he did."

Coach isn't looking at me anymore.

"Sounds like you were tough, and accepting."

"I think you're digging deep, deeper than I would. I probably was thinking more about Xs and Os and where and when we were going to play or how to get a player to relax more. I don't think— I didn't think so much about how I cared about them or how I showed them I cared about them. We just didn't do that sort of thing." Coach paused in reflection. "But I did care. I'm sure it made some difference, and I hope it made some difference, to be treated well, to be cared about. But whether it helped them perform at 100%, I don't know."

His hands normally shook as he raised his tea to his lips. This time he begins to raise the mug only to place it back down on the table.

I sense it's time for a break. "Will you excuse me while I take a moment to write?"

"Sure. I'll call Bowers."

I help Coach rise. He seems distant, but his hands are warm. He slowly shuffles into the next room to make his call.

I frantically scribble notes into my notebook. Coach seems to be tiring, or is it I who is tiring? I don't want to forget what he said, and what he didn't say. I don't think he fully comprehends how much his caring for his athletes, the basic respect he had for them, influenced their learning and performing.

Coach enters the room and settles back into his chair. "Bowers will be over in a minute."

"You said you started playing in Texas, where sport was very important."

"I was as nutty as— We all were nutty in Texas. We played all the sports. When I say I played, I played football, basketball, baseball, and track. It was the standard. We played them all. We didn't have this specialization. We played season to season."

"Then you played at Kansas?"

"No. Well, I always played some sport, but I finished my education at Kansas, and worked under Dr. Allen."

"Right. Dr. Allen. Interesting pregame prep. Can you speak more about Dr. Allen's approach from a mental skills perspective?"

"Well, that's it. That's what I'm saying. He loved the fight and winning, but he wanted his players to play for many reasons. He thought winning should never be more important than sportsmanship and character. He didn't want basketball to be big, as if he could predict the abuses of the future once money entered Division I. He took care of his players like they were members of his family. He was a physician, you know. But, very tough and demanding. Very high expectations. He treated his players like they were patients and I heard he treated his patients like they were his players."

"Sounds like he was a very accepting person, too. He cared about them as people, above and beyond the wins and losses. Do you think it made a difference in their performance or confidence?" It dawns on me. Almost all the most important figures in Coach's life have been very respectful and caring people. Accepting.

"Hmm. I think they were motivated, very motivated. Most of them knew— They appreciated what Dr. Allen offered. And it wasn't a pro career, like today."

"They enjoyed playing for Dr. Allen?"

"I think we all— It wasn't— Don't— It was work, hard work; but we liked what we were doing. It was the time of our lives."

"And arousal or anxiety? You said you think athletes became more uptight after the veterans graduated, and fight talks stopped working?"

"Yes."

"Hence the need for multidimensional theory."

"Yes."

I look at Coach. I'm not sure if he means "yes, go on: tell me about multidimensional theory," or "yes, I already know this." I assume the former and he'll stop me if the information is "old news," as he would say.

"The Inverted-U Hypothesis explains the basic nature of the relationship between arousal and performance. But the relationship is a bit more complex. For example, there's positive arousal and negative arousal, so to speak."

"Yes."

It's difficult to read Coach's "straight man" face. Regardless, I'm determined to make sure we're on the same page. "We now understand some of the reasons behind the relationship. Athletes can exhibit signs of arousal or stress like sweating and upset stomach: somatic anxiety; but we know those things don't have to mean pending doom for their performance. They can actually be good signs the athlete is preparing for a big event. The outcome depends more on the athlete's interpretation of those signs. Does he or she worry and expect doom and gloom, which we call cognitive anxiety? Or does he or she sense readiness, maybe uncomfortable readiness, but readiness nonetheless?"

He explodes on the idea like a cat on a mouse. "Well, that's what I've been telling people for years. Some athletes thrive on this business, others are doomed before they— The challenge before the game is too much for them. But, I believe even the best have to be calmed down to perform at 100%."

"So you learned to rev them up and to calm them down?"

"Yes. But most of the time calm them down. It wasn't so much my business to know why they were stressed. I thought it was academics. They're doing a lot of work and they're tired. They blow off steam and don't get much sleep."

"Have I told you about my advisor at University of Virginia, Bob Rotella?"

"No."

"He works with professional golfers and writes articles about the mental side of sport."

"You're saying maybe he can help me with my golf game?"

I smile. "I'm remembering how Dr. Rotella told us to pay attention to athletes, the actual players in the world of sport, not simply teach from scientific research. He used to say athletes are the best teachers. We think we are, of course. You said you learned from athletes at times." He nods. "Rotella said when the Inverted-U Hypothesis gained it's strongest support, some of his best athletes told him how it wasn't true for them. They said their 'over the top' physiological response to being excited before a big competition didn't always mean they were going to tank their performance. They even reported vomiting, excessive sweating, and uncomfortable levels of agitation. They said they viewed these responses as signs their bodies were preparing for the big one, possibly their best performance ever. Long before science explained the difference between cognitive anxiety and somatic arousal, some athletes knew the truth of it."

"Without the fancy terminology."

"Yes. I suppose so." Good point, Coach. "They provided 'unscientific' data for coaches who were willing to listen and observe, like Rotella and you." Coach was listening.

"Somatic arousal?"

"Yes."

"Related to body," he says.

"Yes. Like sweating, stomach upset, headache. Cognitive as in thought or belief or mind." I flip the pages of my legal pad to a

82

fresh page and begin to draw the graph. As I draw, I describe Reversal Theory.

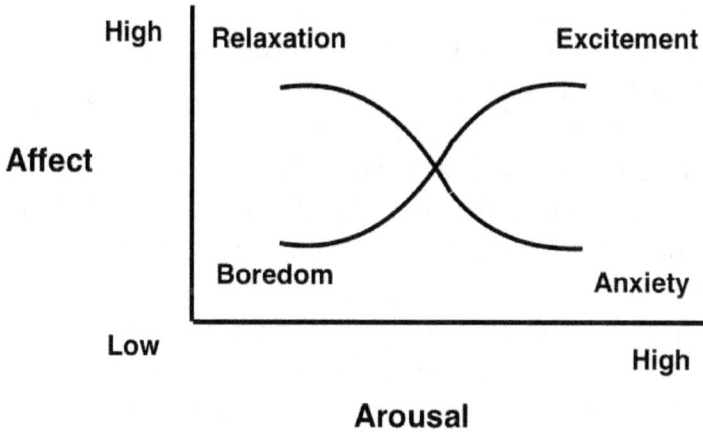

"We sabotage ourselves by worrying about an upcoming event. If we start to sweat or have to go to the bathroom, these are things that happen when we are excited." I point to the intersection of the two lines on the graph. "Sometimes our physiological reactions convince us we're not ready. We think, 'I'm losing it,' or 'I must not be able to handle the situation.' The mind actually becomes the saboteur…" I trace the line going down to high anxiety. "Or, on the flip side, the mind can be the best friend or best coach and we say to ourselves, alright! I'm getting prepared or I'm really up for this one!" I trace a line from the intersection up to "Excitement. Positive emotion despite high arousal."

"Like self-acceptance."

The proverbial lightbulb illuminates my thoughts. I imagine the graph looking the same: excitement rising or dropping depending on how a person views their self-worth. If a performance situation threatens self-worth, the result would be higher anxiety and poorer performance. If a person is self-accepting, the situation wouldn't be as threatening, even with high symptoms of arousal, stomach upset, sweating, nervousness. The situation might just create the high arousal needed to perform at 100%. "Yes!"

Coach beams. "It's easier when you have a very large hammer, professor."

I narrow my eyes to form a question.

"It's just not necessarily the tool you will use in every situation. If all you have is a hammer—"

In unison we say, "—every problem looks like a nail." I laugh. "I need to remember that," especially when it comes to acceptance.

A sudden knock at the door and Edd Bowers enters the Pfitsch home. Coach stands on shaky legs. "Edd, remember Dr. Waite? I'm helping her put thoughts together for a book."

Edd looks directly at me and points to Coach. "Who's he kidding?" I stand and walk toward him as he lumbers toward me, smiling, two hands stretched out in greeting. It's been a while since our last meeting in the flesh. I miss him. His hands are as large and rough as I remember.

With a grin and a wink, he says, "Is that Waite as in Steve Waite?" I laugh and shake my head as he pulls me in close for a big bear hug, just like I remember.

Chapter III
Coach's *Firstness—Habit*

Coach and Edd Bowers play nine holes on the Grinnell Country Club golf course while I type, read, and review notes. When Coach returns, I have his chapter on "Firstness" in front of me.

"Coach, if I buy into this idea of Firstness, how much has habit dictated my destiny? I'm feeling defensive. You compare us to horses."

"Try to keep an open mind." He chuckles. "Be more accepting." He chuckles again.

I notice something a little out of the ordinary: he's grinning broadly without any apparent reason.

He tilts his head, shrugs, and makes a clicking noise with his tongue. "Acceptance cost Bowers today. I couldn't miss." He moves around the room like a kid after riding a new bike.

I love this moment: witnessing someone feeling acceptance, enjoying it. When it comes to sport, one of the benefits can be euphoria, maybe especially when it comes to golf. The euphoria from simply being yourself and then playing well is contagious. Like on Christmas morning, my spirits lift with the swell of joy in the room.

"You're reminding me of my mentor again."

"Bob Rotella?"

"Yes." In graduate school, under his tutelage, I became addicted to the feeling I'm feeling right now. I can't resist describing one more "Rotellaism." "He writes and talks a lot about our desire to gain back the mental freedom we had when we were very young, playing a sport with abandon, stretching out to catch that long bomb, making a winning shot in the final seconds, going for it with all excitement and no fear. Every moment is a 'final moment,' yet no moment is too much pressure. We're excited by the process, flowing from one moment to the next, in the zone, the zone we try to return to as adults. We sabotage ourselves as we get older."

"Bad habits of thinking and lack of acceptance."

"Now you *really* sound like Rotella. I wish he was here right now. He'd love this."

"Smart man—brilliant man—this Rotella! Truth of the matter is: it is about bad habits, and acceptance—" He picks up his copy of the manuscript and looks down at the top page. "—and Firstness!" Putting the manuscript in his lap, he settles into his chair. He sits facing me, leaning forward with both elbows propped on his knees, hands together, and with a shiver of delight begins talking about "Firstness."

Years of experience passed me by before I began to recognize the significance of methods of learning and secondly the significance of the timing of the learning to the eventual effectiveness of performance. Gradually I perceived, mostly by observation and personal experience, that the most important aspect of motor skill learning is what I will call Firstness. That is, the original or first exposure of a skill by action is by far the most important time in the learning process or the training of that skill.

For it is true that human beings learn motor skills much as animals do by copying someone else's action visually or by following someone else's verbal directions. Much attention to the comparison of the 'how' of learning is considered. An equally important point is the importance of the initial effort to learn.

An easy to understand analogy of this can be made to the training of horses. The human's motor skills can and should be trained much as a horse being properly trained. First principle, the original exposure must be correct. The impact of the original exposure is sufficiently strong on the nervous system that the horse will habituate the action creating immediately a habit which will remain a pattern in the animal for life. If a 'wrong' skill is introduced by accident, neglect, or ignorance, the animal will be afflicted for his lifetime with the bad habit. Horses not 'broken' by a good trainer following the principle of good exposure on

Firstness will suffer throughout their lifetime while their riders try to 'overcome' the bad habit.

Since there are many skills which we desire horses to have, the complexity of this principle can easily be imagined. Go to any good horseman and inquire as to the truth of this statement.

—or horsewoman."

I smile.

With the human, the nervous system seems to work similarly. Most normal people who attempt to learn athletic skills spend the best part of their playing careers trying to correct 'bad habits.'

Arguments abound about the idea that 'one can change a bad habit' or to say it another way 'one can gradually modify a bad habit into a good one.'

The opposite position is that 'one can not modify a bad habit but rather must establish a new one.' One must establish that habit effectively enough for it to become dominant. Note all of the tennis players or golfers you have known who seem to spend most of their playing time and concern and money to do just that.

"Coach, I think improving or learning new habits of thinking is what sport psychology is all about. Changing an old one is what therapy is all about, or medicine, what a lot of people call the 'fix it' model. Sport psychology is different. If an athlete thinks a sport psychologist is trying to fix them, it can erode confidence. They think, 'Oh no, I've got a problem!' It can backfire when it comes to performance. But if athletes are presented with purposeful mental training goals, they think, 'I'm striving to do something better, faster, more accurately' or 'I want to obtain the next goal.' The approach can make all the difference in the outcome."

"That's good coaching."

"Yes. I suppose that's the overlap. Sport psychology is coaching the mind." I like that. I think he likes that.

In the U.S. today, coaching schools, clinics, private tutoring and camps abound in recreational centers. Coaches, teachers, and pros serve the public and themselves implementing their methodology and knowledge to thousands and maybe millions of people wishing to be able to hit the golf ball better or a tennis ball harder and more accurately. From an economic point of view a whole new sector of business, recreational instruction, has developed in great part because of the inadequacy of the initial teaching of motor skills in the schools, clubs, or the sandlots. There is plenty of spectator interest in team sports and for the most part the public is ignorant of the basic psychological principles involved in learning of motor skills. Most people seem to think that all we need to find is someone who can tell us or show us 'how to play.' Which way is best and when.

The learning of a motor skill is best acquired at an early age— how early? The answer to that is as early as the athlete has good muscular control of his body. Depending upon maturation, ages differ with individuals; but motor learning is normally best in the early grade levels: second, third, fourth grades, ages eight through eleven.

The later the exposure comes, say after teenage years, the more difficult that learning takes place, but the Firstness Principle still holds for the older student.

Public school physical education curricula are organized to present activities in the best order for student maturation: large muscle games requiring less coordination first, gradually moving to the finer coordination activities.

Program development all over the country for elementary age athletes in Little League Baseball, Pop Warner Football, etc. were usually conducted by parent coaches, many of whom did not understand the Firstness Principle or even very good techniques. Consequently, a wide spectrum of teaching patterns emerged. Unfortunately more bad habits were taught or allowed to develop than good, in my opinion. When Little League programs have good teachers, ones who know fundamental motor skills of the sport and know how to teach effectively, including the Principle of Firstness, that is, they make every effort to teach the skill well at the outset of the program, in these cases, good learning takes place. Athletes develop habits which stand them in good stead for the rest of their careers and probably those communities in which this occurred were provided a string of excellent athletes.

Think of the many communities who started early programs in football or baseball, who did experience success at developing good fundamental teams for years on end. Check on them later and you will find at best one or two coaches who had the insight and ability to train athletes well from the beginning. The habits remained in those individuals, and from that pool of persons developed the athletes who, with experience, became excellent performers.

On the other hand there is much more evidence available in the communities who had early programs of poor quality, meaning poor fundamental emphasis on initial exposure. Without quality initial exposure, what does result?

The results are so mixed it is very difficult to give simple answers. You get a smorgasbord of motor skill abilities habituated. You have some athletes with poor techniques and some with good techniques. Once habituated they are permanent until substituted for or modified, whichever you want to believe to be the case.

Therefore, you have less then maximum potential effectiveness, the degree depending upon the quality of the initial exposure—five or six years previous to performance time.

The fundamental motor skill program that I experienced at Alamo Heights Junior High School gave me an excellent base in team sport motor skills of which I gradually became aware. Alamo Heights High School developed an excellent athletic reputation which held for years, through the 30s, certainly until sometime after Coach Menger retired from coaching.

Similar examples can be made all over the country if one wishes to take the time to investigate. However progress is slow partly because competitive coaches who 'know secrets' such as 'quality initial exposure' often prefer to keep that knowledge to themselves. Very few coaching schools discuss this type of concept seriously.

In Ames, Iowa an outstanding program in the fifties directed by Ken Wells exemplified athletic success for years because of superior initial quality exposure used as a principle. In accepting the Firstness concept, many questions surface. Good coordinated natural athletes seem to belie this principle in that they are better able to modify bad habits or learn new ones easier than their lesser coordinated peers.

Genetic contribution to fluid coordination does make the learning process for such talented persons much easier. However, evidence seems to indicate that the principle still holds for the talented and the untalented. The relative speed of learning and adjusting favors the talented. However since the great majority of athletes are not highly talented, it is far more important for this group to have effective Firstness training, for the process of reeducation is so long as to make the effort a conscious struggle always.

The importance of training the majority early should be very obvious. Other important concepts will be discussed. These are concepts of methodology or 'how to teach.' The importance of the use of each is important, however, the 'timing' of any method is as significant as the method itself. For all methods are faced with much more difficulty of finding success when they are used on a 'horse with bad habits.'

"I really don't like the horse analogy."

He takes a deep breath and exhales noisily. "Think of yourself as a race horse or thoroughbred."

"Thank you. That helps. A little."

The effect of initial exposure can be readily seen in the individual, but there is indeed and perhaps surprisingly the same phenomenon present with regards to initial exposure in connection with team performance.

That is to say that a team's effectiveness relates correspondingly to its first exposure as a unit as does an individual. This is true in the context of any definite period of time, e.g. within the framework of the season or a portion of the season, the principle holds. The element of learning and training practiced first or the earliest portion of any season or the season itself will be the elements of the game most effectively played under stress during the remainder of the time frame. And that which is introduced subsequent to the earliest will not be executed as well as that which was initially practiced.

"What about the stages of learning and the fact that anything introduced first gives an athlete more time to practice and progress through the stages of learning?"

"This is true," Coach says. "Yet, you will find a Firstness effect regardless of how much subsequent practice on the skill in relation to others.

The exception to this rule—and there is at least one from my experience—comes about when the results of the season produce an almost 100% negative experience for the team. Then at that point the team might accept and internalize new elements and produce as effectively as if the material was initially exposed.

"A long, dismal, losing season." I ponder the exception. "Introducing something new might seem like an initial exposure, a new beginning, so to speak, and therefore more potent." I'm thinking Hawthorne Effect. Anything new, but particularly something promising at a low point, might be motivating, capture attention.

"Yes."

Now that the concept is spelled out, let me present some examples so that you may understand with clarity the proposition. In the case of football in my first years of coaching I coached the techniques which I had observed from some experienced coaches. Essentially I gave out a players notebook which included the entire offense, running games, passing games, kicking games, basic defenses, goal lines, etc.

Then I introduced a few plays at a time on successive days with a definite time table to put the entire system in place in, say, two weeks.

91

Forgetting other factors for the moment the schedule was engaged with average to below average results. The first year we were 4-5 and the second year we were 4-5. In analyzing the seasons afterward most emphasis was put on weakness of material, psychological factors involved in the particular situation, etc.

"Weakness of material. You mean the kids themselves weren't very talented."

"Yes.

However, in checking the statistics carefully, a fact came to light which caused me interest in my succeeding years of coaching in all sports.

The fact was that the plays which these two football teams consistently made the most yardage on during the season, game in and game out, were the ones presented in the initial exposure practice. In this instance they happened to be running plays as compared with pass plays.

We had been known to be a running-oriented team by the press, by the opponents and by ourselves. There was no question about that.

This, in spite of the fact that we had a good quarterback, as good in my opinion as our running backs. Our line was good enough to open holes for the run, but could not seem to be equal to the task of 'back up' pass blocking. Almost all coaches will argue that it is easier to 'pass block' than to 'run block.'

The inkling came to me that the timing of the presentation of the plays may be the key.

I had attempted to emphasize the pass attack throughout the season basically to help keep the defense a little more honest to help our so called 'bread and butter offense.'

In general the attempts were not successful. Another fact disclosed by scrupulous analysis indicated that all plays which I had 'put in' after the first week specially designed for tactical surprise were consistently ineffective whether they were run or pass plays.

I'm wondering what he means by "scrupulous analysis."

The only type of plays which I had put in after the initial exposure which we performed well were punts. That I reasoned was because we had an excellent punter as well as a quick kicker and place kicker. I reasoned that the one talent that could produce without very much help from everyone also was a good kicker. At least the results from our punting game made me discount the significance of initial exposure to the extent that I did not vary from my procedure for several years until I had observed much more evidence of the same phenomenon with other teams I coached.

The next evidence of this phenomenon came from my coaching of basketball. There again in my first years as head coach I depended greatly upon my earlier mentors and their procedures.

When I started, my goal in basketball was to have a balanced offense team, balanced, that is, in style of play, having a set controlled offense plus a fast break, combined with hopefully a strong man for man defense. Now to understand how the Firstness theory applies, let us realize we are talking about teaching and team learning: 1) set offenses 2) fast break, 3) drop back man for man defense, and 4) pressing defense.

Here again as in football I started with the set offense, a rather precise set of plays with options off of them followed by the fast break, followed by the defense.

My presentation was never totally 'black and white,' meaning some drills usually included part of the set offense or break, etc. But the emphasis or orientation was presented in the order described.

Since I coached basketball consistently for many years the above procedures were followed for several years. During each season, statistics were kept. After the season, total statistics were analyzed. Up to this point in time, I had not connected the Firstness concept to basketball and of course had not consciously applied the technique to my coaching of basketball.

So it was another awareness that I gained in analyzing statistics which consistently indicated that the good shots that we *got during the season were from the set offense compared to the fast break. The drop back defense was more effective than the defense versus the fast break or the press.*

In all of these cases, the offense taught first was most effective. Similarly, the defense which had the initial exposure was most effective.

Again, I was not so surprised to find out that additions to the offense and defense during the season were also relatively ineffective, with the later additions being the least effective.

Since I coached a varsity basketball team consistently for twenty-five years, I was able to experiment considerably more with my own thoughts than when I coached as an assistant FB coach. In that case I had opportunity to observe results of other methods or similar ones to substantiate or not substantiate my theory.

I was quite fretful about my failure to produce a good fast break to go along with my good set offense in basketball and so I put a great deal of emphasis and time in practice, exhortation and demanding drills from time to time during the early seasons.

Of course the common rational distractions continued to plague me. That is, I did not have big enough rebounders, not good enough speed, not good enough ball handlers or shooters on the run.

"Material."

"Yes. Material." He looks at me like I'm crazy or rude or both.

I explain. "We don't really refer to people as 'material' so much any more."

"Call it a bad habit."

"Firstness?" I ask.

"Possibly."

I smile. "More like a donkey than a race horse?"

"Hm. I see your point about horse analogies." He clears his throat and forces a thin smile.

In frustration and hot desire rather than a reflective decision regarding Firstness, I started a season with fast break drills instead of set offense. In 1950 at Grinnell College we came out

94

firing on the break initially. We had a team which had been very successful as a set offense in the two past seasons. The results were good, especially because we finally had a break which we could run at will, something we had tried to do previously but never with much success. Already established was the set offense and with initial exposure at the onset of the season the team 'inclusively' ran both offenses well.

The results should have been so obvious that anyone with my experience and interest should have seen the real significance of the phenomenon. Nevertheless, other things were always credited for success of the team! For example, individual record performances by Dave Dunlop, one of the most remarkable basketball players I ever had the opportunity to coach, the shooting of Earl Peisner, the ball handling of Glenn Saunders, etc.

"Good material."

He looks at me sternly, and I smile.

I now think that the principle reason for the success of the total offense was the advantage produced essentially by the initial exposure emphasis.

"So, the years with less than stellar results were due to 'material," or lack there of, but the years with stellar results were due to coaching technique, your use of Firstness, to be precise?"

Coach ignores me. He knows I'm baiting him. I know he knows I'm baiting him.

Another facet of coaching basketball shed more light on this phenomenon as time went on. The basketball coach is faced with having a team prepared to defeat a zone drop back defense as well as a man for man. In the fifties there were not as many changes of defenses as there are today, but the zone and man for man were very prevalent, and teams tactically used both defenses for periods of time.

Here I originally thought that if I had a, quote, 'sound' zone offense, and a 'sound' man for man offense, I was prepared. I might have been, but my team was not, I soon discovered.

"You are really on a roll here, Coach. Again, poor performance is due to material."

"I think you need to let me finish before you call foul." He wags his finger at me unsteadily.

"Fair enough." I grin.

Since I was oriented to the man for man offense I always emphasized it's organization first. My zone offense was invariably statistically proven weaker. It produced fewer points and fewer good shots and fewer offensive rebounds. Concerned about this as with the fast break, I reasoned that the biggest problem we had was in adjusting from man for man to the zone offense when the opponent switched defenses. Therefore, I decided the pattern for the zone must in some way conform to the man for man offense pattern and I proceeded to devise a so-called integrated offense, an offense position pattern which could be used against zone and man for man defenses.

"An integrated offense?"

"Yes. Isn't that what I just said?"

Coach might be a little annoyed with me.

It is difficult to get exactly the same patterns, however, on paper I achieved success. On the court it was a different matter. Should I start with the man for man as a base and then add the zone options or vice versa?

"Are you asking me?"

"No! Why would I— I'm trying to—"

"Coach, we're not on the same page with this basketball strategy. You lost me somewhere in the details."

He stares at me, stretches his arms out, and takes a long, slow breath.

For some years I tried different approaches much the same as I did for the fast break. Whenever I started either man for man base I had a good man for man set offense and not so good zone attack and vice versa, when I started with a zone base I had a better zone attack.

"Okay. I think I got it, the basic point, that is, but only the basic point."

"Hear me out."

I rest my chin on the palm of my hand, my elbow on my knee and try to concentrate on every word he speaks.

Finally I achieved an integrated attack with more or less equal emphasis on both facets. I gave it good initial exposure and produced a balanced attack. This may sound like I always had good teams, but all of my analysis in retrospect was a comparison of statistics of our team vs. our team. The win-loss record I attempted to leave out in these considerations.

"You controlled for winning and losing?"

He stares at me.

"Okay. I think we're definitely on different pages now."

We take a moment to contemplate, both staring, not moving. Stillness surrounds us. I wonder if he's spending his silence trying to catch up or waiting for me to catch up. When he begins to smile, I smile, realizing I've glimpsed Coach Pfitsch, the scientist. He attempted to control for important variables: the varying ability of teams from year to year to win games against varying opponents with changing abilities year to year. Granted, the design still lacked the muster to gain academic approval. It had no random selection, no control groups, although, I think in his mind of infinite experience, every team in his coaching history served as a control or experimental group. Regardless of the number of concerns for validity and reliability, a scientific mind was at work in the real world of sport, and I'm further intrigued and impressed to hear more.

Again in retrospect it became apparent that there is an unusual significance to the early training period in any given season.

My Grinnell basketball team of 1962, which won the Midwest Conference Championship and played in the NCAA Regional Championships was perhaps the best team I ever coached. It also was the best example of a team with which I used the integrated offense and defense to the maximum from the beginning of the season to the end. And the results were suspect.

Yes, they're suspect, I thought. Like a good scientist, he observes limitations. As certain as he is about what he knows, he's not adamant his methods are above reproach or his conclusions are the final word. I contemplate the plight of so many scientists: uncertainty about anything and everything. His certainty attracts my mind like a huge magnet without an expected repelling force of arrogance.

There is another aspect of small college coaching which is a continual problem as it is in high school, that is, highly specialized position placement of personnel, building an offense and defense integrated with respect to action, which requires only the special abilities of the team available for each position both offensively and defensively.

The 1-3-1 offense had been a standard offensive pattern to play vs. most zone offensive for years. I had used it or variations of it always. But I had had difficulty with its effectiveness v. man for man because of the timing of its introduction into the season and the difference of movement pattern compared to our man for man offense.

I decided to organize a 'pure' 1-3-1 offense with very little movement for a zone offense and coordinate that with 'movement' offense of the pure 1-3-1 set up v. the man for man—pure meaning static position—each man playing a position of the floor always and only that position, i.e. high post free throw line and lane; low post baseline both sides; wings, flankers to one side, and point guard, outside in front.

I'm thinking, I'll catch up later, maybe on the third or fourth reread. Coach is definitely on a major roll and I'm not about to stop him again before he's finished.

I had excellent material back two deep for each position, but the interesting thing about the material was that there were only two players who were total offensive and defense players, meaning their skills could have let them be good at all positions. John

Sundell was our center. He was 6'8", a good jumper, excellent rebounder, fair shooter on the baseline, not a good dribbler or ball handler in 1962.

Jim Mifflen played high point because he could out-rebound anyone his size or four inches taller. He was a strong man, a good rebounder and shooter, and good free throw shooter with relatively no dribbling or ball handling ability. He drew fouls and shot excellently at the free throw line. He could play any man very tough if he did not move too much, zone or man for man.

Bob Musser played left wing, one of the few total ball players, best outside, but had a fair inside shot. Good rebounder, lane passer, dribbler, floor leader, and was particularly good on the outside shot left side. Musser could play any position anywhere, giving us good reserve strength at the posts if needed.

George Grey played right wing. He was the best outside shooter on the team, fine fast break, fine ball-handler and dribbler. He just could not play man for man defense well, but was good in the zone and he was extremely fast in converting to offensive break.

Gar Smith played the point guard. He was the team leading dribbler and aggressive. He played excellent defense and was a fine outside shooter. Defensively this man's abilities differed also, to the extreme. He was as good defensively as offensively and could play the wing and rebound with the big boys.

John Sundell could play outside defense as well as inside. He was tall and thin and could move by the big men, so we played him on the baseline a lot.

These five boys set up in a 1-3-1 offensive position and a 1-3-1 zone defense, had almost ideal individual talents for an integrated offense and defense. They could play at either end of the floor in the same formation on the floor as wing-wing-high point-high point, etc.

"So success might have been a little bit about material?" I can't help myself.

He seems to ignore me. I'm not sure how my imagination allows him to do that! I smile as he continues with greater intensity and focus.

For the first time this gave us an opportunity to play the game on offense and defense with skilled players at each position.

Our reserves fit in very well. Bill Parsons was not as good a shooter as Grey but better defensively. Denny Asby was not as good all around as Musser but on some nights stronger and better.

Ray Morton could relieve Sundell or Mifflen with only slightly less offensive effectiveness, but stronger defense. Likewise, Horton played one of the points nearly as well as the regular.

Musser could play point guard and relieve Smith and vice versa.

So it was that we had a team with special talents fitted to the offense and the defense. I integrated the offense and defense using the zone set up as the basis, but organized the attack on an integrated basis with equal emphasis as possible, and introduced all of these important facets in the first two weeks of the season. The 18-3 win/loss record reflects to some degree the merits of the plan and the merits of the players.

I'm smiling as I say, "So, success had to do with both material and coaching? You know, I'm just giving you a hard time, Coach, probably because I'm having a hard time following you. That doesn't mean Firstness is a load of doo-doo."

"Right. It isn't a load of doo-doo because you can't follow me."

"Yes. Right." He seems to know I'm about to ask for a definition of Firstness. He holds up his hand, which stops me.

The 1963 season might have been as good or better because by then I understood without a doubt what needed to be done to be as close to 100% as possible. We were 10-0 at semester end only to have our new point guard declared ineligible. We had no other person who could do what Gordon Kincaid had done up to then. And it was interesting how losing one position could make so much difference.

100

In spite of good Firstness, positive reinforcement, visual imagery, etc. our team lost the next 10 games and finished 19-11 for a very mediocre season.

Quality players count. You cannot 'do it all' in psychology. You also cannot count on players to do it all without good organization.

My own experience during the years was so mixed and fuzzy regarding this phenomena that I can readily understand any one's skepticism of accepting a dictum as simple as 'what you do first is what you will do best throughout the season, the year, the week, or the month.'

"There it is! The definition I was—"

"—not so patiently waiting for.

As far as I am concerned this is true for individual and team performance. Team performance fascinated me much more than individual. For me to attempt to explain the reason for this would be too presumptuous, for I am not trained in group dynamic psychology other than by practice.

I'm smiling. "But your practice used data and analysis. You didn't just fly by the seat of your pants or coach how your own coaches coached you. You didn't follow the crowd."

He seems pleased.

My rationale is that we know very little about the power of the individual mind and we know little of the power and complexity of the collective or team mind. The thing I think I know is that if the teacher or coach can achieve a focus of concentration by a group of players on the goal of developing an offensive or defensive system for a long period of time, possibly a season, in the relative importance of the first exposure to any or all subsequent exposures, the initial or primary exposure is appreciably or significantly greater than any of the rest and possibly all of the rest.

Questions may be raised validly on the length of the exposure, one practice, two practices, a week, two weeks, etc.?

101

My evidence is not precise enough to answer that specifically. Rather it is a general concept that says that the original emphasis and orientation by the coach in a given season is the initial quality exposure, and is the significant learned pattern and skill as far as that team is concerned for that particular season.

Many factors other than Firstness run parallel. One which I will discuss is that of the team visualization of the entire season from the tactical point of view at the onset of the season. When the coach is able to apply this situation concurrently with Firstness, results are better from my point of view, meaning the athlete's mental approach and his understanding of the total situation seats his goals and his focus for the season. Without this, the team or he will wander afield and play will be more inconsistent.

If I made another comment regarding the coach's ability to capture the conscious mentalities of the athletes, the dictum should be that to the extent the coach can induce near 100% conscious concentration on the subject, which would be the skill, the pattern, and tactic, to an equal extent, the Firstness theory will be effective.

My opportunities to observe piled up toward a conclusion in my coaching of baseball.

Oh my. There's more.

"Yes. There's more. Sit tight.

When we started baseball at Grinnell we had no batting cage useable indoors and the weather in Iowa is not conducive to outdoor practice until close to April 1. Therefore practice was confined to Darby Gymnasium, a good basketball arena with a wooden floor. My practicing for the month of March, the first month of the season, consisted of practicing the skills of baseball that one could under these circumstances. Our pitchers could throw, our infielders and outfielders could run and throw and could simulate strides but could not swing to meet the ball unless we wanted to take the chance of breaking lights or windows, etc. We should and did set up small infield and we did some sliding on rugs.

*In short we could practice to some degree almost all skills
except hitting. Here we had an excellent opportunity to test the
Firstness theory and test it we did through many years and with the
expected results. Teams produced could throw and field but 'no hit'
as the saying goes in baseball. The hitting skill is accented as the
most difficult to learn and to perform successfully, so this fact
colored the conclusion that the reason our hitting was relatively
weaker than throwing and catching was because of a lack of initial
quality exposure.*

"Why not the quality and quantity of total exposure? You
probably didn't have as much time hitting or when you did practice
hitting, you didn't have a good batting coach."

He looks exasperated with me. "You'll understand in a
moment."

*A gleam of light was introduced when we were able to
purchase and set up a fairly good indoor batting cage for ensuing
seasons. Of course we introduced hitting simultaneously with the
other skill training after that and the results were appreciably
better. Team batting averages for seasons following the installation
of the batting cage jumped 100 points.*

"100 points?" That is amazing.

*Then when my recognition of the Firstness Principle began to
be internalized I began to put nearly 100% emphasis on hitting in
the first two weeks for a 4-5 week indoor program with the help of
a pitching machine and cage. The resultant averages were upped
another 50 points.*

"That's impressive under any circumstances."

*The problem with coming to the singular conclusion that the
cause of the improvement was totally due to the timing of the
practice is very easy to see because of the many other factors that
are present in coaching a team. So the conclusions are vague and
doubtful depending also on the observer's bias. I continued to seek
the answers with no better scientific method than trial and error
and observation. Although, observing similar phenomena*

occurring in different sports was more impressive than if I had been working with only one sport.

"So you're singing to the choir now, Coach. There's a great deal of scientific, that is, there are many controlled studies suggesting your idea of Firstness has merit. But 150 points?"

Coach raises his hand and one finger as if to say, "There's even more."

Before coaching baseball at Grinnell my spring sport was tennis.

You might be able to follow this."

Ouch. I laugh. "I hope so."

Changing coaching assignments and fate again gave me an opportunity to coach tennis. Now I had a chance to look for the Firstness phenomenon in tennis. The second time around I began to use my Firstness theory and apply it to tennis training.

Having played and practiced tennis for years myself, I know the routine and basic practice habits of nearly all high school and college level players. If left to their own desires in practice, 90% of them will step on the court and hit ground strokes for a long time and predominantly will hit forehands. This is more true with unskilled players than skilled. They will move up to the net area and volley the ball occasionally and will only practice overheads and lobs upon request or direction.

If their intentions are to play a set or two just prior to competition they will serve half a dozen and return a similar number of serves. You can easily see what this scenario will do for the tennis player. In theory the players using that basic described sequence of practice will predictably have a stronger ground stroke game with the forehand being the strongest followed by the volley, then the overhead and the serve because of the initial exposure and subsequent secondary and third exposures.

You might say that the length of time of practice is the more important element and I always thought the same until faced with the situation as described time and time again. Although the length of time is necessary to ingrain habit, evidence seems to me to be squarely on the side of practice sequence as compared to length of practice for effectiveness in a given season.

On succeeding occasions I decided to change the sequence of the practice and emphasis, but I decided also to attempt to do some experimenting in the normal fashion, that is, one on one. However, I asked half of my players to use the order of practice as follows: 1) serves 2) return of serves 3) volleys, 4) ground strokes, 5) lob and overhead.

The other half used the exact opposite order that is: 1) lob and overhead, 2) ground strokes, 3) volleys, 4) return of serve, and 5) serve. I also rated the players on a scale of 1-10 on their quality for each stroke at the beginning of the season.

The results could hardly be called scientific but the results were significant to me.

That statement is significant to me.

One boy had a weak service and he was in the second group. His serve was still his weakest component by admission. Another had a good serve to begin with and was also in the second group. His service remained good but seemed not to improve as much as his ground strokes.

"You ran a pretty good single subject design, Coach. Single subject designs were not so common back then. Do you still have your notes?"

"I'm sure the move from Darby— They're probably in some dump." He taps his fingers on the manuscript and smiles. "I'd have been a lot more keen on all this business of note-taking and statistics if I'd known I'd be facing you."

I laugh. "So you think Firstness was operating in tennis?"

I think that it was in coaching tennis that I became more convinced of the significance of Firstness from any other bit of evidence I had seen in all sports. The basic difference for normal tennis players, forehand and backhand strokes seem to tell the story clearly. That is to say most tennis players develop a forehand stroke first and all subsequent practice emphasizes the first technique so that under normal practice patterns a wider and wider differentiation of quality will develop between his/her forehand and backhand strokes.

The obvious remedy for this situation is to put equal or near equal emphasis on all strokes particularly during the early or first practice period of any season or position of the year.

"Or start with the strokes used most often or earliest in a game. If the majority of points are won in the first few shots, I think I like your order starting with the serve and return." I fight the urge to discuss Firstness and tennis. This could be a long detour.

"I believe Firstness deserves one more example in its favor."

"Another tennis example?"

"No. But it's a short one. Well, as short as I can make it." He takes a raspy breath and clears his throat once, then twice.

Back to football and an example which we all see now hundreds of times a year since we can watch so many professional football games on TV.

I refer to short yardage goal line plays or third down and short yardage plays for the first down anywhere on the field. All arm chair quarterbacks are experts on these plays. To remove these situation plays from the game, would remove much of the element of excitement which makes so many thousands of football fans.

What play should the Cowboys use three yards away from the goal line on third down? Do they run their best back over their strongest lineman? Do they fake that play and run a play-action pass? Or, do they accept the theory that they cannot run and must pass to their favorite receiver? Or, do they run a run-pass option so the quarterback has a chance to do either one of the options because he is good at both?

Again, my experience with this football situation helped make me realize the importance of the Firstness theory throughout my career.

After restudying many years of film looking for the answer, I found the answer is that the team will do the best on plays which are their 'bread and butter plays' regardless of the defense, and their bread and butter plays are always the ones which received the original initial quality exposure. They are particularly effective if the coach has been smart enough to have his strongest individuals doing 'their things' on these plays. For example, Riggins running over left tackle for the Washington Redskins in 1983.

"I remember that game. That was a great game. 1-yard to go for a first down."

"He won the game."

"And then Charlie Brown—"

"Right. Charlie Brown." We both smile at the name. "Riggins was MVP that game."

Living in Virginia in the 1980s meant becoming a Redskins fan. I remember watching the Super Bowl, standing in front of the TV, cradling my son in my arms, hoping to God he wouldn't wake up before the clock ticked down. As I recall, Riggins did what we expected, at least, what we hoped he would do.

"Yes."

Did Coach just answer the question I was thinking?

This may not sit well for those fans who assume a well-coached professional team can in fact have a quality performance on a variety of plays to pull out of the hat for these occasions. A pro or college school team can only do things if they are not handicapped by their training.

"Like not using Firstness."

"Yes, among other superior strategies." He seems to consider carefully what he is about to say. "But, therein lies the exception I came to know."

Okay. Here it comes: the reason why Firstness isn't a hard-fast rule.

Certainly the example which I am putting down for you here is an exception to Firstness, that is, a case when a team definitely is able to produce effectively with latent learning. This may happen when a poor enough season lowers morale to almost an exasperating level and total negativism sets in. New ideas prosper in this case, producing a real promise for better days.

107

I believe a group must be naturally ready for learning in cases such as total negativism. There are times during long seasons when the collective is ready to absorb and internalize and produce. Here is one of my favorite Grinnell stories to exemplify that kind of situation.

Bob Peterson was head coach of Grinnell in 1958 and I was one of his assistants. We had not fared well at all that season, winning only two games before we played the final game of the season at Coe College. Coe had already clinched the conference championship and Grinnell was firmly established in last place.

Coach Peterson and I had attended a football coaches clinic the previous summer at Drake University where the New York Giants professional team had put on a demonstration of their offense. The demonstration had been impressive. I remember because it included offensive team running plays in slow motion on the field. I mean they would huddle, come out of the huddle, line up, and then run the play at half speed, with all players executing their assignments dummy or dry against no defense.

This included even the ball carrier running through the hole and acting as if he was tackled a few yards down the field. All players remained in a realistic pose at the end of the play and on a whistle command preserved all actions and retraced their steps backward to their original position on the line of scrimmage. This was like a movie of the play being run backwards. At any rate, the formation and plays the Giants were demonstrating that day were an 'A' formation with split ends and flankers, man in motion.

Oh dear. Here we go again.

It was very similar to the shot gun formation which we see on television when the pros play today.

Okay. That helps.

Coach Peterson and I took the offense down on paper with the interesting impression it left us, and took it back to Grinnell. As we got together for a coaches meeting on Sunday before the Coe game, Pete said to me, 'What do we have to lose by putting in an A formation for this last game?'

His point was we could gain complete surprise. We had a fine passer, John Copeland, who had been quite handicapped as a T formation quarterback because of lack of height. He was a good runner and kicker as well as passer, etc. I told Pete I had my doubts whether we could teach the offense in a week unless he kept the basic blocking similar to what we had used all season; but I argued it could be fun to try. I also knew Coe would take us lightly. If we could confuse them, they just might not recover. So we adjusted the blocking scheme only slightly and put Copeland in the tail back.

"So he set up to run?"

"Yes. In an A formation."

Hmm. "Who was quarterback?"

"Copeland."

Hmm. "I thought you said he was tail back."

"Both. He was quarterback in the tail back position, like shot gun. He could do it. He could run, pass, kick. When John was a first year—"

"Coach. I got it. You told us about John."

He didn't look convinced.

"Great story. Really great story. Sorry, I interrupted."

He looked around. His gaze fixated on the end table next to his chair. I jumped up. "I'll get it." I dashed into the kitchen, put the kettle on, and returned just as he began again.

We developed a shift from the T formation and went on to indoctrinate the athletes. Our team had the idea and were very cooperative and I remember that I felt the change actually helped us get through what otherwise would be a very tough week. We had had enough of the season and negative morale by that point. But the new offense, with the possibilities it presented and the Seventy-two Hour theory, which we will discuss in the future, seemed to give us a brand new view on life and morale lifted visibly during the week.

At any rate we went to Coe, dressed in the Coe field house for an afternoon game, and I could not help notice that the gymnasium was festively set up for a banquet after the game with three very prominent banners stating: Coe-Midwest Conference Champs 1958-Undefeated.

We let our team read the signs, see the dinner table all set up, and we got on the bus and made our way to the stadium.

I had been designated by Coach Peterson to call plays from the press box in this case from a phone high in the stadium and was looking forward to uncovering our little secret. I had lots of confidence in Copeland, one of whose basketball stories I tell.

Yes.

The question I thought was: How well prepared will Coe be and will our blocking hold well enough for Copeland to operate?

The game started and ended on the same note-all Grinnell. We ran the formation as if the initial and early exposure had been superior. We made very few offensive mistakes. We had not moved the ball in seven games except sporadically, but that day Copeland passed easily and ran well from the run pass option. Miller, our one speedy back, made huge gains all afternoon. We ran a T play once in awhile. Most plays, regardless of formation, worked well. The score was 21-7. We had beaten the conference champs, saved the season as far as the boys were concerned, and I do not know what Coe did with their banner.

"Coach, that's a great story, an exception to your theory, but a great story."

"I probably shouldn't take such pleasure telling it."

"There's an explanation there, somewhere." The complexity reminds me how difficult it is to produce quality research with practical results. "One of the biggest disappointments I've experienced in my academic career was learning how the probability of being published, which academicians must do as a measure of success, controlled the direction of my research more than the other way around."

"You thought you were lost," he says.

"If I wanted to follow the mystery, look for answers to difficult questions, I'd most often run into a wall, and most probably because I couldn't measure the variables. In so many ways, the sport experience is unquantifiable. Unmeasurable. Theories become bogged down by the complexity of relationships, the infinite number of variables. It's next to impossible to measure 100% performance as it actually occurs on the field or court." I stop a moment to ponder. Coach fidgets. "Hence the need for some pretty crazy operational definitions." I look up at him. "Did I say that out loud?"

He looks perplexed.

"At one point we were reduced to studying the effects of stress on performance by placing a free throw shooter's foot in a bucket of ice water. That was stress, or at least a quantifiable measure of stress." I'm wondering if he really cares about the plight of the researcher. He continues to stare at me. I take that as encouragement. It doesn't take much. "And there's the motivation of the subject, the accuracy of perception. We've had a heck of a time figuring out if a person's perception was accurate or even an intentional lie."

Coach's eyes narrow.

"It happens, especially when subjects aren't motivated to participate, which brings in the variable of the researchers themselves, how they conduct the study and how motivated they make subjects feel."

"They could coach their subjects, or not."

"Yes. Which brings up the coach: the challenges we face convincing coaches to let us be a part of their system or strategy or even study it. Quite often they think we're messing with athletes' heads, not providing practical information they're looking for."

He chuckles. "But, you can tell us whether a person can shoot free throws when they're standing in a bucket of ice water."

"Right." I laugh quietly. "Blind leading the blind, aren't we? When you were formulating your Firstness hypothesis, research in sport psychology was a baby still learning to walk and talk."

"We didn't stand around with our hands in our pockets waiting for research results."

111

"Apparently not." I thought of the wasted energy and time spent due to a lack of trust and communication between practitioner and researcher. "I wish we communicated more."

"I remember the ice water study." He smiles. "We thought we knew better. We assumed our years of coaching, talking with each other, my assistants and captains, was a better way to figure things out." His eyes are fixed straight ahead for a moment. He shakes his head and continues. "It was camaraderie, what made the job fun in many cases. We developed our own ideas, like Firstness. I loved looking at data, analyzing. We tried to look at things— I suppose we weren't as objective as we thought we were. I doubt you think very highly of our methods."

"I don't know, Coach. I certainly respect your intentions and know how difficult it is to control the variables you were dealing with. You've lived your life in such a contemplative way. Your life has been one huge case study. 'Firstness' was innovative and forward-thinking."

"Well of course I thought so, too, or at least I didn't know how unintelligent it was. But I didn't know or might never know how it all worked."

"We all may never know, Coach, or answer all the questions we want to answer. Can you imagine randomly assigning college athletes to different coaches to study coaching style, or, randomly assigning them to the high stress group versus the low stress group when stress was taking the last shot or falling behind by so many points? How can we do that? It's just not feasible."

Coach shakes his head in agreement.

"That's probably why the phenomenon called 'Firstness' can't be found, at least as you describe it, in the literature. It's all yours, based on your work with athletes. But, similar phenomena by other names can be found in the research literature. The first and probably the most robust is called the 'primacy effect.'"

"Yes. The primacy effect."

"So you know of it?"

"Yes. But remind me."

112

"It started as the simple idea that if you introduce something first in a sequence, it's most likely going to be remembered more than something introduced later in the sequence. It's a strongly supported phenomenon, especially in the lab and with animals. In fact, early research supported the existence and power of this phenomenon to the extent it was often referred to as a 'law.' They don't throw that word around lightly."

Coach's eyes widen. "Well, it was obvious something was happening by whatever label."

"It's no surprise, due to interactions of a multitude of variables and the inability to control the phenomenon in the real world, more questions have been raised than answered about primacy effects. As researchers have measured more variables, over time the phenomena actually lost its status as a 'law,' and other similar phenomena were studied and labeled like 'serial position effects,' 'novelty effect,' 'first impression,' and the phenomenon they study in business, 'camatotic encoding.' How do you like that one? If you went back to school, you might have to study 'camatotic encoding' with rats or pigeons. Maybe no one knows about Firstness, but you studied it in the real world, something most of these primacy studies can't claim."

He smiles.

"Technically speaking, a scholar can only be confident of conclusions like the primacy effect or Firstness in situations in which it has been tested. We have to refrain from drawing conclusions about the 1958 Grinnell College football season and the Coe College game."

"Not if you lived it, saw it with your own eyes. It was just the way things were. It wasn't magic or voodoo. It was what we all did. We tried to be better every year, so we used what we learned."

"But not everyone studied it, analyzed it, strategized about it, and then wrote about it. Because someone wrote about primacy effect and the impact it had in the lab, we have evidence for Firstness. We have Firstness because you did the same sort of thing. It's just that your lab was your life, your teams, your athletes."

Coach tilts his head. "What else do you know about this primacy theory?"

"Well, the initial definition has been refined and new theory produced, but I think the most widely accepted definition still states that when an individual learns something in what would be considered 'first' in the order of many other similar events, behaviors, or tasks, the individual has a tendency to remember or repeat what was learned first more than the other similar events. In many ways, this first event has greater impact than subsequent similar events."

It's at this moment I expect listeners to hold up their hands in protest or try to hide their eyes as they glaze over.

Coach leans toward me and asks, "How does it work?"

"One scientific explanation is that the subject has more time to 'encode' the memory or place it in memory."

Coach is shaking his head yes.

"Some research suggests the first task presented is more distinct, therefore receives more attention."

He frowns and continues to shake his head yes.

"Others suggest the first task takes its toll on our neural network and fatigues it for subsequent tasks. Even after 100 years of research, we still don't know for sure why or how or even if what a coach introduces first is going to be retained and performed best throughout a team's sport season."

"You mean they don't know."

I smile. "Right. They don't know."

"Given what you— How would you— How would research explain the exception, the—?"

"Coe effect? Well, I've been thinking about it. Two explanations stand out: one is called the 'recency effect.'" His eyes widen. "The other is the 'novelty effect.' There are more in depth explanations and the terminology is a little complex these days."

"I like the simple ones."

114

We share smiles. I nod.

"Well, this is just an educated guess, but I think you're right about it being related to the team being in a desperate situation, prime for something new and different. They jumped all over the idea. That's the novelty effect. So the ideas you presented received a lot of attention, like the initial moment of training when you introduce the very first idea. It was like a reset, and a new beginning."

We pause, thinking about it for a moment.

"The recency effect is a simple rule that the last thing you've been told tends to be remembered more than the things beforehand. So, it stands to reason that if the practices immediately before the Coe game were novel and they were the last practices of the season, there might be both novelty and recency effects at work."

"Yes. I believe it," he says. "Which is more powerful, primacy or recency?"

"Uh. I'm not sure. I think they're both pretty powerful." I love his curiosity. "The one thing that doesn't look consistent is that generally the novelty effect raises a person's level of arousal, increasing the stress response. They were playing important games. They probably didn't need—"

"No. It makes sense." Coach lights up like fireworks. His legs begin to move. He quickens his normally methodical speech. "These players were— The season was almost a wash out. We only won two games. After a while playing a game, when you don't think you can win, it can be a real down— They—"

"They needed a rise in their level of arousal?"

"Yes!" His eyes twinkle as the edges of his grin rise. "Mystery solved?"

"Well, not exactly."

"What else?"

"Other thoughts, alternative hypotheses. Were the players just getting better over time? Maybe they just needed time to improve."

"Thinking too much."

"You say you won two games. When did you win the other game, right before the final game with Coe? That might suggest a slow improvement. And there are basic operant learning laws to consider."

"You're overanalyzing, over-thinking."

"If the team experienced positive reinforcement for the skills they were developing or punishment for behaviors you didn't want them to use— If this was the sole explanation, you'd expect the two wins to come near the end of the season."

I'm distracted as I look for a folder in my briefcase. I'm mumbling and thinking out loud. "It would be expected that certain behaviors leading to the win would be reinforced as well as any occurring throughout the season, win or lose. When the team lost some games, it would be expected that behaviors leading to the losses would most likely not be repeated. But when behaviors are changed for the better and they aren't reinforced by winning, eventually it makes sense that the team would be worn down. We call it learned helplessness. It doesn't matter what you do, the outcome is the same, even though you might have been doing a lot of the right things all along." As his voice finally cuts through my thoughts and registers in my mind, I stop and look at Coach. "I'm trying to find out when the other win occurred."

"The very first game of the season."

I find a file attachment I printed from Ted Schultz, the current Sports Information Director at Grinnell College. It's great to have a fabulous sports information director! "My gosh. You're right. They lost four, tied two, and won two. How 'bout that! They won their first game, 25-8, against Lawrence. Either way, Firstness triumphs! The first game had impact, enough to reinforce the basic skills you taught early on. Then, due to being down and out, the athletes— When you came along with a new idea— They saw a unique opportunity, a first. It was like having everything in place, but no spark. The new strategies added spark, a new beginning, and VROOM!"

"VROOM?"

"Yes. You know: VROOM!" I smile. "A technical term. A novel idea, a new approach. Then again, maybe it was just your bubbly personality."

He ignores my chide and says, "I like it. A term for what happens when Firstness saves a losing season. What you're saying, though, is that the Coe game was not an exception, really. It can be explained by Firstness."

"Well, I think research supports the concept and the exception. One other thing we know about research: it needs to be flexible and open. That's why the definition of the primacy effect has taken on so many different looks. It's been taken around the bend and over the hill. But even after it's long and arduous career in academia, it's a solid explanation for many things."

"VROOM."

"You know, if you continued to reinforce effective practice behavior despite the downward spiral of the season, that was powerful, too. Given the times, it might have been tempting to just sugarcoat everything, not be critical, you know, be positive at all costs or kind of ease up on them. I can't help but think your Umbrella, being critical of behaviors not personalities and respecting their 'motivations,' paid dividends, too."

Coach is sitting tall and smiling ever so slightly. Emily sets warm tea on the coffee table. We exchange smiles.

"You were brilliant not to introduce new skills at the end, just new strategies. Skills would have taken longer, too long, to develop—to internalize. It would have been a disaster. You introduced new strategies using skills they already knew, probably skills they'd learned in the first week or two of practice. The team practiced successful execution of new strategies, hence the reset established a positive 'outcome primacy' effect for those strategies. Odds looked better. They believed they could win using new strategies. They were excited, more excited than they'd been, which was good. It's like the perfect storm, the perfect sport psychology storm. Firstness, Umbrella, and VROOM! Athletes played near 100% at the end of a losing season. Firstness and just about every other theory out there working together to explain the outcome, the Coe Effect."

"I'll drink to that!" Coach raises his tea.

I raise my mug. "But there might never be another game like the Coe game."

"Probably not. Not exactly. But, knowing the how of it, we have a chance to recreate it." Coach is speaking as if he's readying to charge out on the field.

"And no rats or pigeons are harmed in the process," I say under my breath. "It's tempting to generalize results from traditional research to explain the very 'nontraditional' 1958 Grinnell College football season like we just did. I'm not recommending it." I lapse back into analysis mode.

"Suit yourself. I like it—what you said."

"I don't think any scholar worth his/her salt would put it all together like that. An interesting, and fun exercise, though." Like a mystery or a puzzle, with a happy ending. I lean forward. "Scholarly or not, knowing what we just pieced together, I have to say, I might have bet money on Grinnell to win that day."

Coach grins. "Me, too. And there's nothing like the excitement of an underdog meeting a rival team. In the late Fall of—"

"Coach, aren't you tired? Let's take a break." I need a break.

Chapter IV
Coach's *Visual Imagery v. Verbal Imagery*

Coach and I took a break: an energy bar and a walk around the neighborhood for me, a few minutes nodding off in his chair watching football for Coach. The houses in Coach's neighborhood were modest in size and architecture, 1950s and 60s without the "ticky-tacky" cookie cutter look. Yards were well-kept and large enough for children to play in. I passed a young woman walking her dog. She greeted me and engaged in pleasant conversation. No need for neighborhood watch. When I returned, Coach was ready to go again. We settled into our comfortable places in the living room, he on his chair, I on the sofa.

The best coaches know enough to 'let their teams play.' How many games have you lost for your team? If I only had enough sense to quit coaching the boys!

Or girls. I bit my lip.

Why do cliches like these continuously turn up in sport stories, in interviews on television, on radio, in newspapers, and more importantly, among coaches when they are letting 'their hair down?'

Does Coach want me to answer the question? I love tackling these questions, but quickly stem my excitement hoping he's about to reveal another one of his pearls, a pearl we can polish together!

All of them indicate some concern over how much advice, counsel, admonition, direction, orders to render to their team, all of them seem to indicate that most coaches do not know how much of such advice is good, or all of them might indicate there is a time and place during a season for advice, talk, and counsel, and there is a time and place during a season for lack of same.

What is the problem here? Why should coaching be rational? What is the fundamental problem? Why shouldn't a coach coach or when shouldn't a coach coach, and more importantly what shouldn't a coach coach?

I've spent hours and hours studying this issue. My silence is killing me. I literally cover my mouth with my hand to avoid jeopardizing my unique view of what Coach is about to say. I guess there's a best time and place for interrupting a ghost.

I looked in vain for anything ever projected from my formal education in physical education or athletics leading to the answers of any of these questions during my career.

For I too realized soon after starting to coach that there must be some rules or guidelines somewhere which could help me. For I am sure that I lost many contests by coaching at the wrong time.

In my mind I felt I knew much that the athletes needed to know, that it was my duty to constantly 'spray' them with the truth. Only to see so often that they failed miserably trying to do what I was coaching them to do. Performance is what we are talking about. Poor performance can be produced beautifully by very well-intentioned and good theoretical coaching.

Emotionally, as many other coaches like me, I had trouble disciplining myself even after I started to realize that there is a natural psychological phenomena operating in this situation that precludes too much coaching. And there are not many specific guidelines out there to help young coaches understand and tackle the problem. Earlier, I tried to give you a scenario on Principle 1: Firstness. Now let us tackle the next one, the phenomenon of Visual Imagery v. Verbal Imagery. I hope that that will help open eyes to some very important techniques of learning and help coaches solve the problem of 'over coaching.'

Over coaching generally takes the form of verbal descriptions —expedient necessity to convey more and more information.

In the learning process the human being absorbs through his or her senses: his or her ears, his or her eyes, taste buds, nose, hands and body.

In our culture we have developed techniques of teaching and ways of learning mostly by verbal and visual transmission of information.

In teaching of motor skills these two systems are used singularly or in combination, and until the 60s and 70s there was no great concern as to relative merits of either one or the combination of both.

However in the intense desire of coaches and teachers of competitive athletes in search of answers to nagging problems, an interesting psychological phenomena has been discovered and resultantly many coaches and teachers of different sports are capitalizing on this knowledge.

I scan my memory for benchmark studies he might be referring to. Before the 1980s there was research in general psychology and education, research that would inform the first theories in the emerging discipline of sport psychology.

The hypothesis simply is that athletes learn motor skills better by visual transmission of information than by verbal transmission. Secondly, athletes who learn a skill originally by visual transmission tend not to hesitate or interrupt their motor skill performances as do athletes who have learned predominantly by verbal transmission. It must, of course, be recognized that probably no athlete learns totally by one method alone. Therefore the theory seems to be that athletes who have been trained predominantly by visual techniques learn faster and also perform learned techniques more effectively than athletes whose skills were learned predominantly by verbal techniques.

Now that should say something to those who are very familiar with the standard athlete 'choke' syndrome and also should say something about the over coaching problem. Over coaching almost always is verbal. Verbal transmission to the athlete usually results in conscious thought regarding the technique or tactic at the very time of performance, which 8 out of 10 times or more produces a hesitation, hitch and/or physical error and weak performance.

He's connecting the dots like a pro, like an artist. I'm still wondering about his sources.

Tim Gallwey's books: Inner Tennis, Inner Golf, *and* Inner Skiing *are the best exposés on this subject that I have read. I recommend them to you for more detailed explanation of the phenomena.*

Agh! Not Gallwey! In many ways Gallwey was a pioneer and forward thinking, just like Coach. But he wasn't a researcher. He had no apparent formal training in research methodology. His life's work was built on his life's experience. But Coach uses his own terminology, not Gallwey's. It's the blind leading the blind again!

When I first read Inner Tennis, *it was referred to me by one of my former tennis players who had continued his competition after graduation and was also continuing his solution to the yet unsolved problems of his own tennis technique.*

It is the blind leading the blind.

After reading the theory of the 'inner game' as applied to tennis, I reflected on my experiences in the team sports in which I was more seriously involved during my career and came up with much evidence that seemed to me to reinforce much of what Tim Gallwey reported. Some of those incidents and stories might be of interest to provide evidence to substantiate the hypothesis and to add to gradual unfolding of the total psychological pattern of athletes' learning and performance.

"Wait, Coach. Just so we're clear, your 'evidence' is your experience, correct, not research reports from peer reviewed journals?"

"Well, I suppose I value my experiences above most things. How can a person not believe in visual versus verbal learning when a young man like Dave Dunlop proves it to you? He wasn't a professor, but— A first hand experience is factual and therefore— I would say you would have a difficult time convincing a person otherwise." He nods his head as if placing an emphatic punctuation mark at the end of his statement.

"I understand how convincing personal experiences can be. But, we have to admit, our senses can be fooled into thinking cold is hot and hot is cold. In particular we are susceptible to defensiveness and relativity. We only see things from one vantage point at a time."

"And that's why you are here with me today."

What can I say? He makes me grin. "Yes. I'm sorry, Coach. There is no limit to my rudeness. I jumped the gun. I'll be quiet now. Convince me, Coach. I'm all ears."

Dave Dunlop, All American Star of Grinnell Basketball in 1946-50, taught me much about coaching. He was a player with very weak early training. His excellent perception of his own problems of learning techniques and tactics produced many penetrating questions for me which pointed up many of these phenomena.

"Sounds like he was very self-accepting. Could he handle your negative reinforcement?" I smile at Coach. He seemed to know the question was coming. He was already smiling back at me.

"To a point.

Dave was the biggest man we had on the team. I played him as center logically for his potential rebound strength. His strength at the early stage however was a soft touch and a highly accurate shot. He averaged over 20 points a game almost from his first competition and that was considered very good in that period of time. One of my concerns with him was that he did not rebound his own shots very well. I remember thinking if I could improve his rebounding, we might very well be the best team in the league. So I approached the problem in my usual pattern, straight on with a strong verbal rational argument designed to convince him of the value of the new skill. I devised new and better drills to help develop rebound habit pattern and I was always around to remind him of his rebound job. We also had some movies to observe of good offensive rebound techniques or visual transmission.

The immediate results were good in practice in as far as rebounding was concerned and I thought we were making good progress. However, gradually I realized that Dave's shooting percentage was not as good as normal. This was so early in Dave's career, I reasoned that shooting percentage drop was caused by other factors or at the worst an adjustment to the added burden of the new enforced responsibility: rebounding.

123

After a couple of weeks Dave dropped in to see me and his message was loud and clear. The quote was something like this: 'Coach, you are going to have to make up your mind about this rebounding thing.' I said 'What do you mean, Dave?' He said 'I think you have to decide whether you want me to shoot to make it or shoot to rebound!'

At the time I knew nothing of the visual/verbal imagery theory, but was startled by Dave's simple statement. I had a lot of respect for his commitment and his perceptions and I felt that he had said a mouthful, a hidden truth, although I was not sure why. He explained that while struggling with adding rebounding technique to his repertoire, he recognized that when consciously trying to be in position for a rebound he actually moved many times toward rebound position which was not necessarily a good shooting position and that his mental concentration seemed to be split 50-50 on shooting and rebounding or maybe even 30-70, favoring rebounding, and in fact he felt that he was 'shooting to rebound,' not shooting to score two points. I remember we had a long talk about it, and although I knew there were some players who I had known who seemed to be able to mix these two techniques successfully, I did not want to gamble on losing or watering down a 60-70% shooter for a questionable number of offensive rebounds, which in fact were not necessary if Dave could continue to shoot at the 70% level.

I said 'Dave let's forget about it. Shoot to hit and maybe you will gradually get more rebounds with continued experience.' That decision was one of my good ones.

I now realize the psychological phenomena present then. Dave had two problems both put upon him by his coach. He was trying to learn a new technique introduced principally by verbal transmission and continually being reinforced verbally. This new technique was being superimposed on his shooting position and technique. It was necessary for him to consciously translate the actual verbal commands at the time of performance. He was continually thinking each time the shooting position developed.

124

This caused him to lose concentration on the shot so his percentage dropped severely.

It was a good example of Firstness technique in the case of offensive rebounding being taught verbally being superimposed upon another more important skill, in this case, shooting, which had been conditioned to a much higher degree previously.

I think if I had continued to insist upon Dave's consciously concentrating on offensive rebounding his own shot, he would have been a very ordinary basketball player; whereas he actually developed into one of the finest offensive players in the history of Grinnell and at the time, one of the best college players in the Midwest, if not the U. S.

If the athlete is forced to 'think' how to do the skill in the act of doing the skill, the skill will not be done well, at least it will not be done as well as it would have been done if he had not 'had to think.'

It is important to be clear that the timing of the thinking is the important thing. Thinking about techniques v. revising technique mentally prior to execution will enhance performance, but the same thoughts during performance tarnishes the product at best and ruins it at worst.

I hesitate, not really knowing what Coach knows and doesn't know, how much he studied or didn't study what I studied. "Coach, we both realize the importance of the stages of motor learning, the importance of practicing to the point of automatic execution. But, there's an hypothesis called the Dominant Response. It takes a lot of hours of practice to create automation and a dominant response. A lot of repetitions." I remember Coach using the term "dominant" in relation to learning a motor skill.

He nods for me to continue as he reaches for his tea.

"When a performer is placed in an anxiety-provoking situation, like a basketball game with winning and losing and very visible stats on the line, by definition, the performer will produce the dominant response, which is usually the one practiced and performed the most: the one that is automatic."

"Or introduced first."

"Possibly." I imagine research questions: firstness versus quantity of hours, quality versus quantity, focus of attention—

Another Grinnell example of this theory was a football story of Ronnie Frank, one of our better offensive guards in the early fifties. In our offense we were running an off tackle play which required the strong side guard to pull along the line of scrimmage and block the opposing end if he penetrated or played square, or pulled through the hole to the linebacker of the end floated, or had been knocked down by the time the guard got there. Ron was a very verbal young man and when he had difficulty, everyone knew about it, including his coach. He had serious problems early on picking up and blocking the correct man: end, linebacker, or halfback. His coach's verbal complaints often were on technique.

One frustrating day, Ron gave his thoughts: 'Why don't you let me just run through the hole and hit anyone in it anyway I can?' At the time I decided that might be a good idea and from the results of just running through the hole and hitting anyone in it anyway he could, I perceived The Inner Game *theory in operation without knowing a name for it.*

Talk about the blind leading the blind. I purposely don't smile or verbalize my thought. But, Coach smiles as he continues.

Ron Frank relieved of conscious thought process at the time of execution, reacted much better than when burdened with execution thought at the time of action.

Football is such a complex sport that there are thousands of physical actions on which this principle is tested each and every play, both defensively and offensively. It is also very difficult to coach with the minimum of verbal transmission, but I am convinced that the best coaches at any level are ones who whether naturally or by training are excellent at the visual approach and very discerning with the verbal imagery approach.

Another example happened in my first year of coaching football at Midland College in Nebraska.

"Wait a minute, Coach. You really didn't have any research to support a visual versus verbal imagery approach? You read Gallwey's book, a self-help book, and based on that, decided to use visual imagery more and verbal imagery less?"

"I believe Gallwey said it wasn't a new idea, just new for many athletes and coaches. He wrote for tennis players and athletes and coaches. He was an athlete. I believe he was a very good athlete."

"And, it's easier to sell a book with outrageous claims and interesting stories than a dissertation with results based on years of research."

Coach's eyes lose some twinkle.

"I'm sorry. I don't mean to devalue what Gallwey wrote or what you're saying or what you were doing at the time. It actually sounds like good coaching."

He tips his head slightly.

"I mean, I don't think there's research contraindicating your methods. I'm just trying to remember if the research was already there for you, somewhere, literature supporting your approach." Not anecdotal story-telling, but peer-reviewed, respected sources of scientific information!

He lowers his gaze and with jaw clenched, continues.

Joe Chrisman was my number one quarterback. He was 6'2" 200 pounds. He was a big strong boy with an excellent arm and with quite a lot of experience.

He stops and looks up at me as if to repeat the word "experience" in a louder, clearer voice. After he looks down, I smile.

His passing efficiency in routine practice was excellent. He could throw very long and he could throw short, but sometimes too hard. He wound up and did not have a quick release, but he was tall and strong enough to stand up in the pocket and withstand punishment. I thought I had a fine prospect for a good passing game. We also had good ends who could catch well and run fairly well. I decided to put much emphasis on the pass.

127

In scrimmage Joe did not complete passes as well as in dry practice, but nobody does, and I thought he would improve with familiarity with patterns and working with receivers etc.

That did not turn out to be the case. In games Joe had serious trouble with completions, especially short, and unfortunately he was prone to interceptions and also prone to not being able to get the ball away.

By the middle of the season it was obvious there was a problem that Joe and or we were not solving. Our offense was almost totally on the ground with a good kicking game. We were doing fair, but with the pass we could do much better.

In talking over the situation one day with Rich Clough, my big freshman from Omaha, he made a suggestion which seemed crazy at the time, but made more sense to me the more I thought about it.

I have always been a bit of a gambler, so I decided to try it. The suggestion was very simple: Clough had said, 'Joe cannot seem to find our receivers, but he has no trouble finding the opponents. If I knew which opponent he was going to throw to, I believe I could out-rebound most of the defensive backs!' Clough was also a basketball player.

I laugh and shake my head. When Coach looks up, I drop my gaze and raise my hand. "Sorry Coach." He continues as if laughter is part of the story.

The first opportunity I had to experiment in practice, I told Joe to call a backup pass, but to go back three, set up and throw directly to the defensive halfback, number 17. I asked him if he thought he could hit him right on the number. He nodded in the affirmative. I told him I wanted to see if our ends were reacting to interceptions well.

He called the play. When the huddle broke I told Clough that Joe was going to throw to number 17. His normal pattern for the play would put him in the proximity of number 17.

Well the play was run accordingly, and the results were as you guess: Joe had no trouble finding number 17. He could see him all the way. Distractions did not bother him. He threw relaxed and well. Rich Clough ran directly toward number 17 and hooked in front of him and 'out-rebounded' easily for an eight yard gain.

We experimented some more running a number of plays at the safety and a corresponding one at the right half. We put in another wrinkle by running the weak side end in a pattern to end up behind the target half back. We modified the target on the defensive back to two spots, one at the belt buckle, the other just over his head. Joe learned to fake at the belt buckles and throw over the head and visa versa.

"Did Joe know what was going on?"

I did communicate with Joe about the system. We had positive results. Those pass plays began to be our 'bread and butter' offense.

I open my eyes wider. "Of course they did," I say under my breath.

Dale Hisch, our left end and the faster and more agile of the two ends, completed many long passes for a total of 2030 yards. Rich Clough, who I credit with the idea, 'rebounded' for many other passes and the 17s received considerably fewer for the remainder of the season.

Unfortunately the winter of '46 came early to Nebraska and we played most of the last half season in rain and snow. Our newly found game was handicapped by the elements. However the lesson I learned was one which helped my future pass offenses for years.

Chrisman in early experiences had never learned to pick up multiple receivers well. For what reason I do not know. He was a senior when he played for me. He had good mechanics, a strong arm, but without good peripheral vision and poise, the arm merely propelled the ball into space and the defense had better chances at it in that situation than the offense.

When he was able to visualize his target all the way, much like a baseball pitcher, he had no trouble hitting the target and did so.

In our efforts to help him find receivers, we gave many verbal reminders such as 'look to the right before you pass to the left,' 'check the line backers,' 'pass to the outside,' 'never throw short,' etc. They caused him, like most normal mortals, to think about how he was to throw and set up while he was doing it. Which, in my opinion today could be classified as a 'cardinal sin.'

The elimination of verbal instructions and the substitution of a single visual target made it simpler for him. And the task of modifying positions for the ends turned out to be much easier than 'teaching the quarterback new tricks.'

This lesson early in my career helped me recognize similar symptoms of other players and helped me to become a much better coach on the spot as the seasons rolled by.

My analytical mind kicks into gear. "If it had been only anxiety causing Joe to throw interceptions, I don't think he would have been able to adjust simply by throwing to the opponent. And, it probably wasn't a lack of practice hours using conventional passing. You were onto something." What exactly, I'm not sure. Definitely out-of-the-box. I look him in the eyes. "Again, you experimented with your coaching methods much like I might use a single subject design." I shake my head, contemplating the problems involved with drawing any valid or reliable conclusions.

Coach looks unmoved. He's heard these thoughts before, seen skeptical expressions on faces before. I don't know where to go from here. But he does.

Somewhere along the line in my frustrating experiences of coaching baseball, another good example of this phenomenon popped up and continued to pop up enough so that when I read Gallwey's book the light really dawned on me.

It came to me as I compared my own ability to hit a tossed ball wherever I desired, at least most of the time, to the inability of most of my players to just get the bat on the ball some of the time, let alone hit it where they desired.

I began to realize that if I thought about where I wanted to place the ball rather than how to hit the ball, I could hit the ball well, and much of the time, to the spot I desired.

I gradually recognized that the mental imagery of the two situations was the key to the solution of the problem. If the athlete thought 'where' to hit at the time of hitting instead of 'how' to hit, he could hit much better. If the athlete was not beset by continual verbal directions and reminders of 'how' techniques, and if he had a good image of his desired target, he could be comparatively successful.

For I knew I was thinking 'where' when I hit to short stop or left field or first base. Whenever I thought 'how' to hit, most of the time the ball was 'ill hit.'

"I identify with that one, Coach." Three years assisting softball will do that for you. "But how do you know if it's choosing a target or not focusing on the 'how' of it or the interactions among those variables and arousal." I stop before my mind spins out of control. "There are so many competing explanations."

He's shaking his head. "I don't think it mattered: the how of it. I'm not sure it matters now. It's like water over a dam. We found our solution then. It made sense and made us better. Why is it important to know the how of it?" His twinkle catches me off guard and challenges me to a twinkle duel. I try to twinkle back intensely. He says, "What are you doing?"

"Sorry." I'm embarrassed. I fight off the feeling. I refuse to give a figment of my imagination power over me. Recovery is slow. I begin to analyze why I wanted a twinkle competition. He laughs. I look at him knowing I've made him laugh, this apparition of a man with whom I'm conversing. "This is starting to feel a bit crazy."

He laughs harder. "Only now feeling a bit crazy?"

I swallow and attempt to get back on track. "It makes sense to me—everything you've said makes sense. But, I doubt I can explain it as easily as you explain it." At that moment I realize it will never be a simple story for me, maybe a simple moral, but never a simple story.

"Maybe you will be the one to spell it out for others," he says with genuine sincerity. "If you can't help yourself, if you find yourself analyzing the how of it all the time, you probably need to do research. For me. I enjoy observing and telling stories." He sets his jaw in determination and begins again.

My observation of professional baseball hitting of the past 30 years seems to bear great evidence to the superiority of visual imagery over verbal.

There are so many different batting styles in professional baseball today, styles which my coaches in the 1930s would have described as fundamentally unsound or poor technique and would have predicted poor performance. Many of these styles and forms are contrary to the 'classic' forms of level swing, not stepping in the bucket, no hitch with back swing, keep shoulders level, cock the wrist on the back swing, etc.

Yet batting averages are far better than in the 30s. There are more good batters than ever and many of the modern day best hitters became good hitters by visual imagery through TV and in person. Many of the best hitters did not have the advantage, or should we say disadvantage, of a verbal imagery coach to inject the hesitation or 'choke' syndrome by verbal transmission.

The same can certainly be said for professional basketball, particularly in regard to the shooters. There is much more evidence given to the adage that shooters are 'born' not made. I am not sure they are always born, but it is quite possible that so called 'born' shooters were lucky to have had visual imagery training, accidentally or not, early in their careers.

Hmm. Another interesting research question. So many alternative hypotheses.

Modern professional tennis players are also overcoming the problems of training by verbal imagery as is evident by the great number of class players in the world.

"You're pushing your luck now, Coach. It's a stretch to say sheer numbers of great tennis players proves anything much regarding their training."

He shoots me a look with the twinkle barely squeaking out between narrowed eyes.

Perhaps for the skeptic I could throw in one more example, which all of us might have personally experienced. It demonstrates vividly the problem of the person who consciously thinks of the technique or the 'how to' during the activity.

As a novice ballroom dancer you may have experienced observing other couples on the floor making moves which motivate you to imitate at the time. You try, which means you attempt to copy the model on hand while you dance. The executed movement on your part and the reaction of your partner almost always breaks your rhythm and pattern, and you know what results: one or two or more apologies.

The point is that at all levels of athletics, this phenomenon is not well-known. At the professional level it has been known and practiced to varying degrees for years. Ted Williams and Joe DiMaggio have known and practiced and have taught the art for years. But professional coaches and players have often hidden their secrets for their own team's benefits so the secrets often are not well known and more often than not are very fuzzy, if known.

There seems to be no question that the translation of information from the brain to the body, if done consciously, is much too slow to effectively execute skill at the moment of performance. Only if the nervous system has been previously conditioned and allowed to react with no conscious help from the brain can an athlete perform at 100%. The type of imagery in the learning or conditioning process plays a significant role in this for all athletes. This is not to say an athlete cannot execute at all if trained verbally or by mixture of techniques. It does suggest that the visual method is superior because there seems to be less 'translation' than in the verbal operation.

"Coach, you talk about learning from *The Inner Game of Tennis* and seeing validation of these principles in your own life and your athletes' lives, but none of those sources of information are scientific. *The Inner Game* is interesting, but, as I recall, there are no references to scientific studies in that book."

133

"When you decide with your own eyes— If what I've been teaching and coaching doesn't have validity, why did it work, maybe not perfectly, but it worked better as I learned these basic— As I formed my theoretical approach."

"A researcher wonders about other explanations, alternative explanations," I say.

"Yes. I suppose there could be 'other explanations.' My explanations might not be complete or scientifically proven, but they are plain to me, or at the time, they were."

"First, let's examine what you've been teaching and coaching. Consider definitions first. You're saying that 'verbal imagery' is verbal instruction: telling someone what to do versus showing them what to do. Right?"

"Yes."

"And with visual imagery, athletes imagine themselves performing a skill while you show them or they see the behavior modeled by someone, is that it, and they eventually do it themselves by imitating what they saw? No verbal instruction to clutter their mind?"

"Yes. I believe so."

I hesitate, wondering if he means, "I believe so" as in "I'm certain of this" or "It's what I believe, not necessarily what is true." Maybe clarity will come with more questions. "You're saying that verbal instructions translate into verbal thinking while trying to execute a physical task, and that's the problem." Did I just say that? I shake my head. "Verbal thought processes interrupt the execution of a physical task. We think this verbal process will guide behavior, but it actually becomes too cumbersome. It interrupts the athlete's flow, so to speak."

"Yes. I believe so."

"This is good, Coach. There's research to support what you're saying. But, what if the initial emphasis placed on the passing game for Joe raised his level of arousal past the point of optimal performance?"

"It did. He was being asked to do something he couldn't do."

134

"Oh. Well, yes. I think so, too, Coach. You're supporting my point. We're in agreement. Heightened arousal was an alternative explanation for poor performance."

"I'm not saying verbal imagery is the only cause."

Now I'm very frustrated. We ponder the complexities of sport in a moment of silence.

I venture the following: "Verbal instructions for already well-learned skills not only ask players to think about already well-learned skills, a recipe for disaster in itself—"

"Yes."

"—they raise arousal to the point players no longer perform well."

"Yes," he said. "And, we didn't usually have 1,000 hours to make the change. Time was something we never seemed to have enough of. I often felt the frustration in that."

"The lack of time, and motivation—"

He shakes his head yes.

"Because if they had wanted to take the time away from academics or social time they could have."

He continues to shake his head yes.

"I think the lack of time, in some ways, made them underdogs in the first place."

The variables for scientific study are infinite, overwhelming.

"Well yes," he says. "They'd been placing emphasis on things other than sport for years. And in some cases, many cases, this was not entirely the way it was. There were many athletes who had spent hours and hours shooting baskets or hitting tennis balls. But more likely they didn't. They came in as underdogs and we weren't going to change them into elite athletes with our verbal instruction. They constantly, well not constantly, but very often, they revealed this hidden truth. I learned, and sometimes I learned the hard way, very often I learned the hard way, to listen to what they were saying, not load them down with new ideas and changed technique, even knowing how much it could help them, but it couldn't. It was a hard lesson to learn. Stop coaching. To coach well, I had to stop coaching, or teaching—whatever you want to call it."

He reminds me of the constant debate at Grinnell College: is coaching teaching? Why or why not? The overlap is clear. I put the brakes on my mind again. "You know I think research supports everything you describe. It's not a simple visual versus verbal solution to create a better performance mindset, but you didn't think it was that simple. You knew it was just a piece of the coaching puzzle. That's why you have more than one theory."

"A no-brainer."

"Good one, Coach!" I smile. "You know your visualization sessions were probably the single most important reason Tom persuaded me to come to Grinnell that first day. Letting athletes play the way they always have played without too much coaching, mostly visual imagery to raise expectations and enhance confidence. The research world and its trickle down effect is stymied by the inability to control the naturally complex environment of a sport arena. I can find a lot of investigations studying the effect of verbal versus visual cues on the learning of a list of names or facts presented in different orders. Progress was being made back in the day, step at a time. You just happened to be in front of that progress, taking long strides."

"Whether I knew where I was going or not." His humility is endearing. He adds, "Learning a list of facts would not have interested me or Bowers or Obermiller."

"But the relevance is there, practical results to be teased out."

He frowns.

"Okay. I bet not." I search my memory bank for research results. "I don't think it was until the 90s." I'm thinking out loud. "Research began to use more complex models to explain what you observed. I guess you could say the trickle down effect was beginning to flow, but not until the 80s for sure. I think." I smile. "There must have been some usable information about reducing what an athlete needed to focus upon, especially during performance in competition, optimizing the level of arousal they're experiencing for the task at hand, sometimes raising it, sometimes lowering it. But, you're right. You were right from the beginning. Coaching sometimes means not coaching. It's against common sense with regard to coaching underdogs, don't you think? Underdogs need the most coaching, you'd think."

"Yes. We think we coaches are the well of all important and necessary information. We don't want to hold anything back. If we do, we're not doing our job, a good job. And these kids need it. We think they need it."

"Maybe a good initial visual image, then mostly acceptance, not approval necessarily, but more silence and encouragement."

"Yes."

"In grad school we studied Bobby Knight." I'm reminiscing again.

Coach doesn't respond. Usually I see people grimace. I think the positive effects of his golf outing and cat nap are finally starting to wear off. He's showing signs of fatigue again.

"I know Coach Knight hasn't been the best role model at times," who doesn't recall the folding chair sliding across the basketball floor, "but some of his methods are worth looking at, and in many ways, he was one of the great coaches, in this way in particular, because he knew when to stop coaching, well, when to stop yelling instructions and criticisms. At least that's what we found from the limited study we did. It was just a snapshot, relatively speaking, but we studied tapes of his behavior on the bench throughout an entire season. He was up and down and extremely animated and agitated in the beginning of the season, yelling, and on his players' all the time for this or that. But as they started into the playoffs, it was as if someone put him in timeout. He was sitting most of the time, just watching. He was calmer."

"Trusting." Coach pauses. "Trusting his men. He wanted them to trust what they had worked on throughout the season. So he trusted them."

"That's exactly what we thought. Engendering trust is a tough thing to do if you're giving verbal and nonverbal corrections and instructions all the time."

"Hmm. I never knew that about Coach Knight. Reminds me of General Patton."

"Did Patton throw a chair?"

He chuckles. "We would have barely blinked if he had."

"Was it necessary, though, throwing chairs?"

"I don't— I think so. They would never have been able to— It would have been impossible to have discipline." He expresses the word discipline with such emphasis, not so much louder, but his timing and tone suggest he wants to talk about this very important subject.

"He held us— Without knowing each of us— He had a very high degree of discipline."

I adjust myself in the sofa, trying to find a more comfortable position, knowing he's about to move on to another issue of great importance, possibly another pearl. I wonder if this one will crumble like sand or hold firm in our hands.

Chapter V
Coach's *Discipline*

No discussion of the psychological elements of coaching would be complete without thoroughly thinking through the problem of discipline. I believe that if you were to ask a group of coaches to review for you their recent season as to general strengths and weaknesses, nearly all of them would comment on their evaluation of the team's discipline. The word would be used to indicate the control the coach had over the team and or the reaction of the team to such control. Discipline might be coached in terms of the attitude of the team in the coaches' opinion. Furthermore, in the cases of teams which did not fare so well win/loss wise during the season, much blame for the lack of success might well be placed on poor attitude or less than desired discipline.

Inferences might be made regarding the value of good individual discipline among the players when they enter a coach's program. Hardly any coach will think of himself as a poor disciplinarian or poor leader. My point is that 'discipline,' whether it is thought of as individual or team, is a large component of the problem of coaching a team.

Since all or most coaches seem to agree that 'discipline' or 'attitude' is a basic problem for the team, we do much to investigate the sub problems to ascertain any factors which can be controlled to solve the problem.

Coach continues to make coaching a problem to solve, like geometry or algebra. I'm curious how he will approach the issue of discipline, an issue replete with interacting and complex human variables.

Earlier in this manuscript I referred to 100% effort and performance. I referred to players' efforts to learn and produce. I also referred to the term 'commitment' several times, referring to the intention of the athlete to learn skills and to produce effectively in competition. Fundamental to learning is the will to learn. For the athletes this means the willingness to repeat and repeat the exercises in order to establish the right habits.

The willingness to repeat, to whatever extent necessary to learn, and then repeat to the extent to condition the mind and body is called 'discipline.' If it is done by the individual without direction from coach it is personal discipline. If it is directed by the coach, it is team discipline or authoritative or leader discipline. In all cases as far as I can tell, the athlete must possess what we call a 'good attitude' which means a strong positive commitment to do whatever is necessary for as long as necessary to accomplish whatever goals that she or he has visualized for him or herself either by him or her or by the coach or someone else.

"Thanks for the definitions up front, Coach. So athletes with discipline must have a good attitude toward repetition. And, this attitude comes from a strong desire and commitment to learn and perform to the best of their ability to accomplish the goals they've laid out for themselves."

Coach opens his mouth to continue.

I quickly add, "The athlete might or might not know how repetition works—how important it is."

Coach shakes his head in affirmation. "We may have overlooked the importance of informing athletes of that fact. Eventually, I believe they understood. But, uh, let's not jump ahead.

The problem then comes down to the fact that to practice requires physical and mental work. Work is an activity which requires physical movement and energy expenditure or mental exercise which also requires energy. Energy expenditure is considered a 'negative' by human nature. Energy expenditure is overcoming some resistance whether it be mental or physical, and the human body naturally resists the idea. The subconscious mind protects the organism naturally by so doing. In my discussion I am going to refer to this subconscious mind as the 'emotional self,' for as I have said, there are at least two selves in each of us. The second as referred to previously is the rational or thinking self.

140

"You're saying there are at least two parts of the self: the 'emotional self' and the 'rational or thinking self' and that they naturally want to resist energy expenditure or work, which is what is required in sport. You're saying we're naturally lazy?"

"Not entirely. Maybe more like efficiency experts."

I tilt my head and squint my eyes. As usual, his theory is resonating with me in a way I can't quite explain.

The athlete then is faced with making decisions regarding some goal, say learning how to play football and then he's faced with strong feelings within him or her self regarding the action necessary, like learning to run, block, or tackle, all of which require much energy plus some rather unusual accommodation of the body to the surroundings, such as being hit, hitting someone else, throwing a ball accurately, etc. The discipline here is simple to see. The athlete must understand what is involved in the action, a rational process, and conjure up enough willingness to repeat the exercises involved until the goal is reached. His emotional self will be resisting a great deal in the beginning and continuously to some extent. If the athlete is successful at conjuring up willingness throughout the process, his or her emotional self and rational self will become gradually synchronized, meaning that as the goal is reached there will be less and less conflict within himself and the discipline will be easier and easier regarding this particular activity.

Wow. I'm going crazy thinking of the research on these topics. Overcoming resistance. Cognitive dissonance. "Right brain-left brain" conflict. I need a minute.

Obviously one of the problems with the practical approach to the theory is that the athletes need to learn skills early, remembering Firstness, and the rational self has not developed sufficiently to totally understand all the action involved. A strong rational decision is not possible for most persons. Therefore, the motivation and discipline, the willingness to repeat, must be provided by the leaders, such as teachers, coaches, parents and other persons.

We have now arrived at the guts of the 'discipline' problem presented to all parents, coaches, and teachers, that is, how to 'lead' the athletes to do the action involved with a good attitude.

Athletes, like all humans, are motivated from outside by either punishment or positive reinforcement. We already have stated that positive reinforcement produces better results in learning. Conformity or action is achieved by reward. Punishment, or a 'negative reward,' that is, the lack of punishment, is based upon fear. Positive reward is based upon happiness.

Coach, you dog. You're using technical terms from psychology, and you're almost—

He smiles as he continues.

There he goes again. I really think he's reading my mind.

Athletes may be motivated or led by example: visual imagery, positive reinforcement, and reward by the coach, which will produce respect by the athletes. Respect for the positive traits of the leader are in turn transferred to the activity for the individual.

"You would have done anything for Patton." I thought out loud.

Coach grunts. "I did." He shifts in his chair. "I did. We all did. That's how— We would have— Some of us— At times it was an ugly business."

I'm sorry I brought it up. It saddens us both. We purse our lips at the same time before he continues.

If this practice is the order of the day, the young athlete will gradually synchronize his fears of failure, injury, and his natural emotional reactions, with his rational desire to play and will gradually, unconsciously understand the necessity for repetition and work, and will develop personal discipline.

"Are you talking about the war or athletics now, Coach?"

"Are you Freudian? This might get more interesting than I thought. I didn't think you were Freudian."

"What nationality is Freudian?"

Coach laughs out loud, which pleases me.

142

On the other hand, if punishment and fear are used as the motivating forces as in control of prisoners and army disciplines, the negativity and negative traits of the leaders may well become the controlling factor in the individual. The athlete may never realize the necessity for repetition and continue to revolt or fight the negativity. Not accomplishing the goal and resisting conformity brings more negativity and the individual may eventually quit the activity.

The key to good discipline is the development of respect for the coach, teacher, parents, etc. With respect, athletes have a positive base for trust. With trust they can experiment, work hard, suffer set backs and some negativity, and continue to persevere until the eventual goal is won. Without respect the individual will undoubtedly flounder, for such an environment, at best, seems to have more negative obstacles than most.

"Suggests Knight's players had respect for him."

"Might have. Or fear."

"So respect for the leader, or fear of the leader, or both, are sub problems."

"Yes. Respect being preferred.

Respect is accomplished by the proper use of the other psychological elements which we have discussed, namely Firstness, visual imagery, and positive reinforcement.

This line of thinking is fascinating. Coach promotes respect over fear, which in turn promotes discipline. Fear would raise arousal, sabotaging 100% performance in many situations. Whereas respect would be motivational, maybe inspirational. So many variables. I wonder if—

In 1961 I had an opportunity to go to Portugal and coach a basketball team for three seasons. As it turned out, this experience taught me much about competitive sports in Europe, particularly in Latin Europe. I learned the effects of the culture on athletics and one of the biggest lessons I received was that of discipline and morale in a Latin culture. Reflections after the experience gave my mind broader insights into the understanding of personal and applied discipline. To recount some of the experiences might well serve to explain my theory of discipline and its relationship to Firstness, visual imagery, positive reinforcement, etc.

I agreed to coach a First Division team which, at the time of my taking over, was in 8th place in a division of ten. The name of the club was Academica of Coimbra, Portugal. The club represented the University of Portugal, the second oldest university in Europe. The club team was made up of players from age 16-42, all of whom had some connection with the University.

Sport was one of few activities in Portugal which had a free press and much interest. Soccer was the number one sport as far as participation and spectator interest was concerned, and basketball was number two with interest increasing.

The government's Department of Sport was very interested in improving the basketball technique of the young people and their tactical knowledge of the game. An experienced American basketball coach was desired, particularly for the knowledge he might be able to dispense and partially for an experiment.

The experiment was to assign me to a First Division team which was doing poorly for a season, to see if my technique and tactical knowledge would produce a significant difference in team efficiency in the course of the season. I was a guinea pig.

I have to admit I had no idea of what I was getting into. My goal was to learn a new culture by sharing my basketball knowledge and accepting the challenge of trying to develop a successful competitive team in a strange culture while on sabbatical leave from Grinnell.

I was greatly handicapped by not knowing the Portuguese language and had an erroneous idea that my very limited Spanish ability would help me. I relate these details so that you better understand the problems of relating to the young men on the team. I attempted to establish a rapport which might be effective toward providing team or personal discipline.

"Okay. Let me make sure I'm getting this. You went to Portugal thinking you could establish a rapport and gain respect from a team, thereby increasing their potential for success or 100% performance even though you couldn't communicate verbally with them, in their language, and they couldn't speak English?"

"Yes. That about sums it up."

"Sounds like more of an experiment with visual v. verbal coaching."

He pauses in what appears to be deep thought. He says, "I suppose in this story, discipline is the subject matter because without it, there is no coaching of any kind."

"Oh." I clench my teeth, an habitual reaction to "all or none" statements.

The one thing I had going for me was 'good press' in the Portuguese media. I was established as an American basketball authority and that held me in good stead until it became necessary to prove myself to my athletes. In fact I found myself facing the problem as soon as I arranged for 'practices' with the 'director' of the club and was assured that the team would 'be there.' The team was there for the first meeting, whereupon I clearly demonstrated my inability to communicate verbally, although I tried.

I should have recognized the value of visual imagery at that point, but it did not sink in until much later. I continued to attack on the verbal level, with translators and with demonstrations, etc. The real problem began to show in the second practice. Two out of fifteen athletes showed up. As it turned out, it may have been a blessing, for at the time I was furious. I really thought that any team, even a second division team with such an opportunity would be eager to learn the fundamentals and tactics I was ready to teach; but, that was not the case.

The two men who did report were Adriano and Carlos Modiesa, brothers, who became two of the best players in Portugal before the season was over and were the core to a very slow revolution in basketball at Corimba and Portugal itself.

These two young men really loved basketball and were most respectful of the USA position in world basketball. They must have accepted without doubt that I was an authentic extension of USA

145

basketball for they came to nearly all practices. The remaining players were less motivated and more typical of the athletic mentality of Portugal, as I was going to gradually discover.

I coached Adriano and Carlos each day and of course anyone else who would show up. I spent the rest of my time divided between trying to figure out how to get the rest of the team there and talking to the directors: young men who were administrators of my club schedules, budgets, trip planning, etc. Adriano and Carlos gradually explained to me that the problem was not serious because this was the way all Portuguese teams practice. So it seemed to me that they thought whatever the players might be able to learn would essentially be the difference between Academica prior to Pfitsch and Academica after Pfitsch. I panicked at the thought, especially after I was able to scout a game or two with my boss, Doctor Silva. I recognized the Portuguese take themselves as well as basketball very seriously at game time.

This was injected deeply into my emotional self when I attended my first Portuguese game and found the military police outside the pavilion and soldiers armed with submachine guns positioned approximately thirty feet apart all around the basketball court. It was the soldiers with machine guns, rather than the officials, who enforced the rules that coaches remain on the bench throughout the contest.

After seeing two games other than my own, I decided the only thing for me to do was to try to effect some difference in defense, since I believed anyone can play good defense if they want and are trained and I had only two men to train who seemed to have respect for me enough to work and condition themselves. With Adriano and Carlos' help, I could then hope to pull some of the rest of the boys into the program.

I taught Adriano and Carlos to play one on one and eventually man for man defense with the hope of developing a good man for man team defense. Man for man was only something the Portuguese players had learned about in theory. They may have also learned it was 'work' and resisted such effort. It gave them

plenty of reason not to play it. It was, in fact, counter culture—
inappropriate for Portuguese to play.

I decided that was why I wanted to play it; it was my only
chance to improve the respectability of Academica, which I was
getting more desirous of doing every day.

Adriano and Carlos educated me daily about the Portuguese,
as I tried to educate and train them about basketball.

Whenever there was anyone there to teach fundamental skills,
the resistance to any new or difficult technique was always great
and any effort at positive reinforcement and encouragement,
usually was answered with 'Usted no comprende Portuguese.' 'You
don't understand Portuguese.'

What usually followed was 'You can do this if you practice.' Of
course the answer to that was, 'We do not work at practice because
we are Latins, and Latins do not believe in the work ethic,' plus
'We are the worst of the worst, so what do you expect anyway? You
are supposed to give us the American miracle of basketball.'

'The miracle is to work to believe in yourself,' I would say.

The answer was usually, 'You are holding out on us.' And so it
went.

"Your first game must have been exciting and interesting."

Our first game under my coaching was at home before a
packed house, all of whom were looking for the miracle of USA
basketball. Before the game I had yet another shock to overcome,
the pregame meal, which the director set up, as was their custom. I
decided not to change too many things too much, and the pregame
meal was one of the things I left alone. The pregame meal was a
two course dinner four hours before game time, complete with
wine and brandy. By my standards, most of my team was drunk
when we hit the floor.

Adriano and Carlos played man for man on their opponents
while the rest of the team played the basic that Academica had
used previously. The tactic worked out better than I had imagined.
We won the game much to my surprise and of course, happiness. I
was intimidated by the machine guns and soldiers. I could not

147

speak Portuguese yet, so I did not screw up the team with verbal
imagery. The normal Academica offense and the reinforced defense
made its mark.

The crowd loved it, as did the directors, and I was over the first
hump.

The next week of practice was somewhat better than the first. I
presume mostly because of the game results, but also because the
Modiera brothers were impressive compared to past performances.
Carlos was the highest point getter. Adriano's defense made an
obvious difference. He guarded ferociously and was able to prevent
scoring; he blocked shots, intercepted passes, stole the ball, and
passed to his brother for easy breaks, etc.

Even though I had not produced the miracle they were looking
for, the 'miracle' of hard work and fundamentals with only two
players had made its mark, and respect was beginning to dawn at
Academica.

A few more men showed up for practice and were much more
interested in learning to play defense. We also practiced shooting,
and slowly, very slowly, my ability to communicate improved. With
all of these factors the miracle of work began to be the order of the
day. A new strategy based on man for man defense mixed with the
zone and eventually the press, gave us a new look.

"Even with better verbal skills, you must have relied heavily on
visual techniques like modeling and physical demonstrations."

"Yes. Out of necessity and natural desire to communicate
efficiently.

It is not necessary to relate many other interesting elements of
the season. It will suffice to say that Academica finished the
regular season firmly in second place, only one game out of the
championship, and good enough to qualify for the Portuguese
International Tournament played in Lisbon, which involved the two
top teams in Portugal and the champions of Angola and
Mozambique in a round robin. Each team played each other twice
in one week's time.

That tournament was one of the most amazing I have ever experienced. To play six games in seven days, all starting between 11 p.m. and 1 a.m. each evening with the championship of the Portuguese World hanging in the balance, was fantastic and difficult.

In the last game of the regular season, Adriano, my captain and the person who was more responsible for our success than anyone else, was ejected from the game. One minute remained on the clock when, during a time out, he left our huddle and jumped up into the stands to defend his wife's honor against a loud drunken fan of the opposition. In Portugal a husband is honor bound to defend his wife's name on the spot. This being the case, Adriano left the huddle, an example of poor discipline, and tried to defend his wife's honor only to be arrested and taken to jail by the soldiers. The investigation after the incident resulted in Adriano being suspended for the entire following year including the tournament for the National Championship.

So we played the big tourney minus our star and our leader. In spite of the handicap, we won four of six games playing about seven men. We finished second in the all around championship, a feat I was very proud of. I think many good things happened as a result of my team and the Portuguese experience.

There was the matter of discipline. Our team developed team discipline very slowly. The factors were initial respect for USA basketball, not for me. Respect for me came when I was able to sell a couple of players on the philosophy of work and good initial visual imagery.

He nods at me and I nod back.

Luckily it was enough for the team to be successful. As the team was positively reinforced by success, greater respect was evidenced. Respect gradually turned to enthusiastic work, which eventually produced a good defensive team, which was good enough for a second place finish in Portuguese basketball.

The Department of Sport in Portugal held a conference upon completion of the season and asked me to conduct a National

149

Coaching School with courses for local club coaches in four sections of Portugal followed by a month of clinics in Angola and a month in Mozambique. I responded as well as my Portuguese language allowed me to and I must say that those three months were amazingly enjoyable. My reputation had been earned and the respect showed me during all of my clinics was great. I will always be impressed with the Portuguese people and the many friends I made there. I also believe that many young men learned a great deal of basketball and most of all they learned that the American miracle of basketball is based on work fundamentals, and of course genetics and food producing giants.

I chuckle to myself. Yeah, that, too. I sigh. More factors to control.

I do not know whether anything can be done about food and genetics, but pound for pound and inch for inch, I learned that the Portuguese were fine athletes, have a fierce competitive desire, and make great loyal friends.

Also the experience spelled out very clearly to me what team discipline was really built upon, so that I came away much better educated than when I started.

Another story about the attitude of discipline, which may throw more light on the subject, started back in Grinnell a few years after the Portuguese basketball season.

I had been athletic director at Grinnell College for ten years. During that time I had coached football and basketball primarily. Grinnell accepted many of its students from the east coast. During the sixties, boys who played soccer in high school on the east coast were at Grinnell in sufficient numbers to warrant organizing first a club team and finally a varsity team.

Our philosophy at Grinnell is to treat all sports alike in emphasis, so we did as well as we could with soccer. I say that because to treat all sports alike meant having a good coach as well as budget, facilities, schedules, etc. The coach part of this package was the most difficult. We had athletes and players who knew soccer, but no coaches.

150

Our staff was composed of the traditional American trained personnel. We had ten sports to coach with a staff of five to seven men, none who knew soccer. We thought we could acquire the services of professors or other personnel with some experience with soccer, and we did. However, this did not work too well. At first the athletes would work okay with part time, poorly trained coaches; but a pattern quickly evolved. The coach became disenchanted with the job, or the athletes became disenchanted with the coach. Thus, every two years and sometimes sooner, I was faced with trying to improve the situation.

My improvement efforts were unsuccessful. We found ourselves in a situation of increasing student interest as well as unhappiness because of inadequate coaching. Our part timers either did not know the game or they could not handle the players or both.

In 1972 Grinnell College hired a professor of anatomy who had been a Division II All American football player. He wanted to coach football as well as teach anatomy. This gave me the opportunity to relieve myself of my football responsibility and take up a new challenge—that of coaching soccer—a challenge I knew would be great since I was aware of all the problems of my predecessors.

Here again I feel the background is necessary to comprehend the relationship of the story to discipline. Facing my first Grinnell soccer team, this was the situation as I saw it.

We had a squad of 35 men on a team, including 16 lettermen, who had won five games during the previous season. The succession of inexperienced and nonprofessional coaches in the years past had left an attitude more or less found in club teams. That is, players oriented toward a spirit of do your own thing, even during the game. Certainly the players had no respect for the coach's knowledge; hence those with a good attitude demonstrated their goodness by 'helping the coach' out with their knowledge.

I had to decide how to deal with this situation. My decision to coach was based on the premise that I would remain as the coach for sometime, that is, many seasons. That fact alone helped in *making another decision, the decision regarding how to gain respect. Should respect be gained personally? Should I try to read, go to coaching schools, in other words, educate myself and then represent myself as a knowledgeable coach, or should I be totally honest about my knowledge of soccer, educate myself as well as possible within the time frame, and accept opinions and knowledge of players, sorting it out and depending upon my personal respect as athletic director and coach of other sports and learning the game as we went along. I chose the latter. It has always been more successful for me to be honest with my team, and this time was to be no exception.*

Nevertheless I was to be tested by the players and tested early. Captains were elected and these captains served as my consultants and representatives to the team. They also acted as if they were going to be the coach. We had arguments about our procedure, and, in this case, what included preliminary planning, formation to be used and tactics, types of defense, break or no break, kick and run or short pass games to name a few.

We also had the assistance of another part time coach who had coached some junior teams in the Cleveland area.

My memory of the agreed upon tactics was that we were to use an all-field, pressure defense. Our rationale was that the opponents, who were as inexperienced or more than we were, would not be able to have good enough ball control to defeat a good pressure defense.

Decisions were made as to starting line up which reflected judgments of both coaches and both captains.

Our first opponent was Coe College and the game was to be played away from home. Coe had defeated us the year before and was supposed to be fairly strong and certainly favored in this contest.

Game day arrived. We traveled to Cedar Rapids with no particular effort on my part to outline player conduct prior to the game. I really wanted to see how seriously these men were taking soccer or how they had been conditioned to behave in the past. I found out very quickly.

When we reached Coe College at 11 a.m., two hours before game time, we unloaded our equipment, which consisted of individual travel bags and bags of balls and a training kit. My athletes showed their knowledge of Coe by starting to walk in all directions from the field house, leaving me with the training kit and the balls walking toward the dressing room in the field house.

I let them go until I was sure of their intentions, and then I said, 'Where are you people going?' The answer was some sheepish looks and no verbal reply. I said something like, 'Come over here, gentlemen. I think we had better straighten a few things out.' After their slow, resistant return to the field house, I said, 'Let's go down to the dressing room.'

A silent squad followed me to the dressing room. During the silent walk, there was enough grumbling or mumbling for me to get the idea that these people were going to be very resistant to anything I might suggest regarding their conduct before game time and maybe their conduct during the game. No doubt I was going to be severely tested.

I said to myself, here are a bunch of spoiled kids, but more than that, spoiled kids who had little respect for me or my soccer knowledge. What was I going to do about it?

Well, this is what I did. When we arrived at the locker room, some of the players tossed their bags against the wall or in a locker and moved towards the door. I stood in the door and said, 'Sit down, gentlemen,' which was greeted with more grumbling, but reluctant conformity. With everyone sitting, I looked them hard in the face and reviewed 'the bidding.' New coach, not much knowledge, old players, lots of knowledge, discontent with general situation, they were treating this game like it was a 'play day' as evidenced by their initial desire to roam around the Coe campus before game time.

I did not claim to know much about soccer. Essentially, I had used their own advice to organize the team and the tactics. But, I

153

would tell them how to prepare for this game mentally in no uncertain terms, and they would confirm or remove themselves from the team. We would then know whether we were going to have a soccer team at Grinnell in 1972. Remember I was also Athletic Director.

I chuckled. "A little bit of position power."

"Yes."

"Maybe fear."

"Possibly.

I said, 'Now here is what you will do. Suit up in you soccer gear now, then lie on the floor with your head against the wall, and rest. While you are resting, which you will do until I tell you it is time to go on to the field, you will think about how you are personally going to play your position this afternoon, when you get the opportunity, which incidentally will be my decision, whether I know anything about it or not. While you are concentrating, I will interrupt with some reinforcing commentary on the subject. Now let's get going!'

The players did as I said. All accepted the challenge to be quiet. All lay down on the floor and stared at the ceiling. I doubt if they were thinking about how they were to play. A better guess would have been how they were going to deal with me.

At any rate it was quiet, and the first round I thought went to me. However I was quite concerned to having discovered the level of discipline shown by the group. Their attitude seemed to be as bad as their reputation around campus--that of 'flakes' just having a ball playing soccer. I became even more determined to coach a so-called Grinnell soccer mentality into a true varsity mentality as I knew it.

And so I pointed this out, verbally, as they concentrated on the game plan of the day, which was to use a full field press as practiced, hoping to break Coe's pass game up before it got organized. Last but not least, I described in detail how we would do our pregame warm up. The significance of this may not seem great to those of you accustomed to the normal basketball and

154

football pregame warm ups. But I had noticed in professional soccer games in Latin America and Europe the pregame warm up follows a pattern of individual stretching, specialized shooting and passing, and a lap around the field to greet the spectators and give them an opportunity to applaud, etc.

The American version had become more informal and gave an image of a game not taken too seriously by the players. I had noticed American club and varsity teams mixing with the opponents before the game in camaraderie. With my perception of my team's attitude before the contest, the last thing I thought desirable was making the contest less formal and fraternizing with our opponents.

So my description in detail of the pregame behavior included specific instructions, such as we take the field in single file jogging around the field Olympic style; there would be no spectators, so just concentrate on getting warmed up; and, pay absolutely no attention to the opponents while running. Then form a circle around the captains and the captains will lead stretching exercises in union. After exercises we will break down in groups by position and practice basic kicks, heads, followed by a huddle, last minute instructions, etc.

Lastly, I warned them that anyone not wanting to follow the procedure or my instruction could say so and could be excused on the spot. Those who did not quit, but did not cooperate, would not be allowed to play and would be asked to check in his gear at the end of the game. With that we broke our concentration exercise and walked slowly to the field. Coe's team was already in the field and some of their players made an effort to greet some of our older players. However, I was pleased to see that our team followed my instructions to the letter.

Now the big question, how would we play?

We started out quite fast and our press bothered Coe considerably in the opening minutes. We were able to intercept the ball in their territory consistently. Although we had very little *organized attack play, we did get a good many shots, among which, two found their way into the net in the first twenty minutes.*

At half time the score was 3-0, and I felt quite successful as a soccer coach.

Halftime is only ten minutes long in a soccer match and I worked hard to follow up on my psychological program for the second half. No let up. Keep the press on and work hard.

I was able to substitute freely and we kept the pressure on in the second half, scoring two more goals and holding Coe scoreless. The only bad thing that occurred was that one of my captains, Mark, broke his leg after making a long run and sliding tackle to save a goal. Mark happened to be a baseball player and had a good varsity mentality. His loss hurt the team. However, he helped me a great deal from the sidelines for the remainder of the season. We incidentally, ended up 9-3 and second place in the Division in which we were playing, the best record Grinnell had had in soccer in ten years.

The point of the story is the same. The players will test the coach in discipline. If the coach cannot pass the test, the season will be anything from difficult to chaotic, and most assuredly, most of the values of playing in competition will be lost.

"That's a great story, Coach, how a coach can be successful with less knowledge than his or her players and the importance of discipline. But, Coach, with all your stories, you haven't described *not* passing the test. We can only take you at your word that it would be chaos and difficult, and values would be lost. What if in chaos and difficulty the players played with 100% performance? How do we know your idea of discipline is the best for everyone and for best performance?"

"Good point, if you're just trying to be logical." Coach hesitates and mutters something under his breath. "One story of chaos isn't proof, or even two or three. But each story is a part of my training in the trenches. I had good role models for leadership. But I have witnessed other coaches failing to gain, or losing the respect of their players. Discipline is the easiest and first to go.

Likewise, it is an important part of a solid foundation. I don't think I want to tell you a story when discipline wasn't established. Although,

I do not want to leave you thinking the Grinnell Soccer team was perfect in discipline after the Coe game. But the Grinnell team picked up some respect for its coach and incidentally for themselves. That respect gave them a little discipline and a corresponding degree of high morale, all of which is positive reinforcement at its best. As the season progressed, each week gave us another opportunity to add to the base. We were fortunate to have soccer material equal and better than most of our opponents, so the solution to the discipline problem discovered here solved to a great extent the problem of having an excellent team.

"So you're saying without discipline, even if you had an equal or better team than most of your opponents, you probably would not have been very successful."

"Precisely. You're catching on."

I laugh and shake my head. "Don't give up on me, Coach."

"Or you, me." He sips the tea Emily brought us, tea I hadn't noticed was present.

Both of these stories—

"The Portuguese basketball team and the Grinnell College soccer team?"

"Yes.

Both of these stories depict a group gaining respect for the leader and discipline as time went on. Circumstances played into the hands of the coach in each situation. In the Portuguese situation, the athletes had limited knowledge of their coach, but high expectations. The different values regarding discipline and work ethic had to be changed. The athletes' respect for the new value needed to be gained before there was a growth of natural positive reinforcement, that is, success, resulting in more success and a very positive total situation.

I wonder how he knows which comes first, what causes what, and therefore what to prioritize.

In the soccer situation we had mature Americans who had more experience and knowledge than the coach who was imposed upon them. They resented discipline imposed upon them by any authority figure. Again respect had to be gained by the authority figure and was gained by a different means than in the Portuguese story.

"How many soccer players quit that year?"

"I don't remember if anyone quit. I don't believe so. Maybe I've blocked it out of my mind. Do you think Freud would agree, I've blocked it out of my mind to protect my ego?"

"I don't know."

"Your memory of Freud is like my memory of that first soccer season. I'm remembering what my ego allows me to remember."

We laugh and say in unison, "Not much."

Coach leans back, reflecting, or resting. I'm not sure.

After a deep, rattly breath, he says, "Despite huge differences in the problems at hand,

The result was nearly the same in each situation. Positive psychological growth permitted a better positive physical growth in technique, strategy and knowledge of the game. All athletic teams write their own history regarding these characteristics. When the situation can be arranged by the coach to provide good earned discipline, learning takes place in a happy atmosphere. Without discipline there can be no good morale, no good Firstness, visual imagery, or positive reinforcement.

There's my answer: discipline first, preferably, but not necessarily, based on respect. "Coach, in research, discipline, as a psychological variable, is pretty complex. Sometimes it's controversial. When is discipline punishment or humiliation? At what point does it become unhealthy and punitive versus something you want, like team building or commitment building. When does it help the team perform its best? When does it hurt? I'm particularly fond of your definitions because, well, first, they address the complexity."

"They do?"

158

I laugh. "Yes. One of your definitions addresses the 'control' aspect of discipline with regard to team dynamics: at what point a coach has control versus the team having control. The other speaks to the discipline the individual athlete or team has to learn and repeat a behavior until the mind and body is conditioned to respond in the desired way. That's discipline, too. It's fascinating to me how you've brought them together. The first translates into team morale and the second into commitment."

"Yes." He smiles.

I smile. "But there's more—"

"More? A punch line? A but?" He looks at me. "A but."

"Well, yes, maybe. But the 'but' is not really a but, as in 'you forgot something,' or 'you're wrong about something.' The but is more of a 'but, coach, you tell your stories to explain how things happened without implicating you on a personal level.' The stories remind me of your humanness, your humanity, your ability to care about athletes and give of yourself to them. How else could discipline translate into morale? How else could an athlete's desire to practice on your field translate into commitment? You said it yourself. It depends on leadership. I suppose it could come from the athletes' teammates or family or friends, even the fans or school pride. It could have been there before you started coaching them, but why didn't they display it in previous years or from the start? Your part as coach is apparent, at least to me. You showed your discipline, your commitment. That makes for a very powerful role model. You showed them you cared, not just about the team or the wins and losses, but about them, even in the face of adversity. I'm sorry if I'm being repetitious with this acceptance idea. It's a part of the picture, too. It relates to everything."

"I get the point."

"There are things at the core, your Umbrella, that must have been there."

He seems to brush the idea away with nervous hands.

"I'm serious about this, Coach. The respect they had for you, you personally, must have been a significant factor, one you tend to gloss over. Except it comes out in your stories, whether you like it or not."

"There's another one, at least one other one," he says.

I squint as if I might see better what he means.

"Another 'but.'" He takes a deep breath. "But, you can only do so much."

"Oh. The players." I sit back in my chair and quietly say, "Material."

"If things don't click, and often they don't, sometimes it's due to not having the personnel, meaning those individuals who have the basic mental and physical skills and of course, the capacity to build on what they have. You can't want it more than they do."

"Sometimes the best program, one with a great Umbrella, Firstness, discipline, and emphasis on visual imagery, doesn't have the potential to create a championship team."

"Yes. That's right. Coaches do what they can in most cases." He pauses. "We did. I think we did." He looks up at me. "The fun of it comes when there is enough material— If there's enough good material, and the performance is near 100%, there's winning, which in turn keeps morale up. Discipline in this case pays off more than if there weren't the wins. I have to say, I like winning."

"Winning is a great reinforcer of discipline and commitment."

"Yes. That's right."

"Even for the underdog," I say, "Grinnellians who might act like they don't care."

"Especially the underdog. Although sometimes we're not the underdog. More and more, Grinnell College is competing against similar institutions. In recent years, Coach Fairchild has built an athletic empire."

"And scholar-athletes are still going on to do great things afterward, after graduation. Sport, specifically, commitment to sport, isn't hurting them, to the contrary."

Coach says, "Well, even if an athlete just shows up every day and gives his best, there will be positive results. Being a champion team might be what a team wants, but there are many ways to enjoy the process and I wouldn't say it was not worthwhile."

"Coach, did you know two of your soccer players went on to become experts in the field of aquatic biology?" I'm not sure why I'm thinking of this example.

"Higgins and Pistrang?"

"Right." I can't believe he remembers.

"Hmm."

"You're remembering the story."

"One of those young men stole the other young man's girlfriend. Between that and the onslaught of capable freshman onto the team— These guys outran, outscored him. He was a mess. Em consoled him. I booted him out of the house."

"I've heard this story, and I don't think that's the whole story."

"What's the whole story?"

"The young man you booted out of the house said you instructed him to stop whining and accept reality, work to improve and develop instead of being defeated. He remembers the time as if it was a turning point in his life, teaching him how to live his life with purpose and focus, and acceptance. Do you remember that?"

"Well, he was a bit dense as I recall. He was all broken up about it. I don't think I kicked him out without telling him about playing baseball in Texas."

I laugh. "You think he got the message anyway?"

"I believe so." He clears his throat. "Not necessarily by design." He looks down and seems to drop deeper into thought.

I enjoy these moments, seeing a different side of Coach, the quiet side, the contemplative side, even if it is my version of his contemplative side.

"Not by design? Or not by your design?" I ask. He looks up and his twinkle twinkles. I think that's a "yes."

Coach recognizes he had help, he had other people, Emily, and possibly a higher power. He's experiencing a humble moment.

"I don't think much of what I did that turned out good was so much by my own design. I was one of the luckiest coaches on the

161

face of the Earth." He stops to contemplate a moment more, and in that moment, I am fearful, as if he might drop into despair for some unknown reason, and I don't want him to. We both linger in silence.

"Are you thinking you did something wrong?" I ask.

"What? No. No. Maybe did the right thing for the wrong reason or in the wrong way. I thought he needed to be toughened— tougher. I thought I needed to be tough on him. But I think it only worked because of the other business."

"Other business?"

"I don't think I could have done it, any of it, any good at all, by myself. Emily— She's more— She did the right thing for the right reason."

"Good cop, bad cop?"

He smiles. "She's the good cop."

"Does Emily know how you feel about her part in your work? I think she knows how much you appreciated her as a mother and homemaker. Does she know you appreciated her as a partner?"

He clears his throat. And clears his throat again.

"You know, sometimes, like your soccer player, sometimes people can be a little dense. It takes some hard knocks, some negative reinforcement." I smile. "Eventually we get it. I think your soccer player got it." I'm not sure Coach is listening. "Like your 'keep your knees bent' saying. It took me a while, but I think, whether you meant it to or not, well, to me it means more than be ready for life's hard knocks." He's looking at me without saying a word. Again, I relish this moment. He's thinking about something we're talking about, not reminiscing, not responding with a story. We're actually conversing and discussing with a promise of good things to come, not the same story heard before, something new is generating in his mind, and I want a good look at it.

"More?" he asks.

I blurt out what I'd been thinking. "Well, I think it implies you can absorb some shock and spring back or spring into action if you keep your knees bent. You're prepared; but more than that. If

162

you're hit hard by life and you actually fall down, if you keep your knees bent, you might even be able to keep moving, maintain momentum, actually move forward instead of getting knocked down and staying down."

Together we say, "And I can't get up!" We laugh. Both of us have seen the TV commercial.

"It reminds me of going for a ball on the tennis court. Sometimes when you go after one really hard and you kind of stretch out, reaching as far as you can, you're in midair and you think—"

"You'd do anything to reach that ball!" He chuckles.

"Yes! And for a moment you're out there, so focused and determined to do whatever it takes to hit the ball, and then you fall. But, if you've stayed loose, knees bent, so to speak, you roll and spring back up and keep playing the point. You're still in the point."

He grunts. "We need to be saying, 'Keep your knees bent, roll and spring back up?'"

"Yes!" I laugh.

Coach grunts again. "I'm surprised you haven't said it yet."

Hmm. How long does one wait for an answer from an apparition?

"Bend, roll, and spring back up— This is the acceptance you've been harping on."

I light up. "I like that! Acceptance is bend, roll, and spring. You think I can I use that?"

He looks at me like I'm crazy.

But I enjoy the moment of realization, his light-bulb, my cognizance.

"By the way, do you have one of those alert things?" I swing my hand in a circular motion around my neck.

He smiles. "I think I'm keeping my knees bent instead."

"As long as you promise to roll and spring."

"I might have done my last roll and spring a few years ago."

"I doubt that, Coach."

Chapter VI
Coach's *72 Hour Rule*

"Break, Coach?"

"I have to tell you about the 72 Hour Rule."

I look at the plate of crackers and cheese in front of us.

"Eat! Keep your strength up. I haven't even— Are you aware
of—."

"You've told me about the 72 Hour Rule. But I have to be
honest. It's been a while."

"I'll give you the executive summary."

I'm not sure if he sees my eyes widen. Then again, he's a
creation of my imagination. He's been gone more than a year.
Maybe he sees everything. It doesn't matter. Suddenly he has the
energy of a large locomotive barreling down the tracks. Nothing's
going to stop him.

*The implantation of specific game play in preparation for any
game will be most productive if it is executed 72 hours before game
time.*

My eyes widen further. I'm impressed with his early emphasis
on definition.

He sits up straighter in his chair. The corners of his mouth curl
up ever so slightly.

*To begin consideration of the problem of team mental
preparation for a game with this hypothesis will give us an
opportunity to look at all the aspects of team mental preparation
for any contest. Soon we will discuss the aspects of continuance of
succeeding game plans, that is, the season, and the group dynamic
psychological phenomena that a coach must follow in that
seasonal context.*

"Coach, I don't think I have a clue what you're talking about."

"The start— It isn't— Give me a minute or two.

164

Remember that as a coach I have always been coming from the position of underdog and that my greatest concern was to get the most out of the psychological aspects of performance as possible.

The 72 hour hypothesis was involved in my experience through many years of coaching mostly by accident. In fact, the first time it occurred was because particular circumstances changed the timing of normal procedures. My reflections for a game might be significant to the mental preparation of a team.

"You're saying you were lucky, like penicillin, and peanut butter and chocolate."

He ignores me. Maybe *I* need a break.

The background of the circumstances will help put the description of this first changed game procedure in context.

By the time of this experience I had coached as head football coach for eight years in two schools and had been assistant coach for eight more years.

Playing in general with fewer numbers and with fewer talented individuals, it was not difficult to discern that in order to win or even play competitively, the team in these circumstances needed 'to play on all cylinders, all of the time.' Whenever we could do that at Grinnell, we could be assured that results would be gratifying, if not always satisfying.

My observation unfortunately, indicated that more often than not that did not occur. Those judgments regarding whether a team plays 50% to 75% or 100% or 25% of potential are always subjective and differ with every observer. The players and the coach probably are in the best position to make the most valid judgments.

Although those judgments are most certainly biased, I do not claim any greater abilities of crystal balling, except that my hypothesis has been formed over years of experience and I write from a long look back and undoubtedly have been able to shed much of the emotionalism connected with observation at the time.

In other words, I think these reflections may well serve to get to the basic truths involved.

Using a trite coaching word to describe a 75% to 50% performance, it is safe to say that we played 'flat' or less than 100% at least 1/3 of the time. Our goal became to search for ways to prevent flat play.

"Coach, let me make sure I'm with you. You're saying there were a few years where the teams you coached played well below their ability?"

"Yes. The athletes during this time, this drought, they became complacent about winning. They didn't expect it, so I don't believe they trained hard for it."

"Low discipline."

"And more. They had no reason to train hard with no expectation for success."

"Learned helplessness. Difficult to overcome."

"Yes. We had many obstacles we couldn't do much about, which I will mention briefly.

In 1964 I was assisting Edd Bowers with varsity football and also handling our freshman squad. Freshmen were not eligible to play varsity ball at the time, so we had to have a separate team.

We had a small squad of freshmen, perhaps 20 or 21, combined with 33 upperclassmen. Coach Bowers and I were the staff.

"It's a lot different now." We share knowing looks. Despite consistently low numbers of athletes, the number of coaches involved in the football program has doubled, tripled, even quadrupled, if we include volunteers, since the 1960s.

We of course, put much more emphasis on the training and preparing of the varsity. The freshmen were organized to facilitate the varsity as much as possible, particularly doing fundamental drills which the varsity ran. We played three freshmen games during the course of the season. We always had a serious problem of lack of numbers for the freshmen games, since it is a fact that it is difficult to play a sixty minute football game with less than 29 players, given the physical nature of the game, etc.

This particular season was only slightly different than the past in this respect. When we were to play Coe freshmen in the first game of the season, in my judgment, we had about 17 players healthy enough to play. I was greatly concerned whether we should attempt to play. I might add, to my knowledge, we never cancelled a game for this reason at Grinnell, but debated the issue and considered it.

I recognize the story.

"Yes. Now let me tell the whole story, particularly as it relates to the 72 Hour Rule."

As difficult as it is, I silently commit to listening for new details.

On Wednesday before the scheduled Saturday morning game, my concern was so great, I asked Coach Bowers for permission to take the freshmen to the dressing room to discuss the problem of playing or not playing the upcoming game. I wanted to make a decision early enough in the week to inform Coe if we decided not to play, and I wanted to remove the 17 players from contact work with the varsity on Wednesday to avoid injury, if we decided to play. Coach Bowers agreed to my suggestion and we proceeded with the new game plan timing.

What ensued from then on became in my mind the germ of the 72 hour theory. In detail it went something like this:

We took the team into the dressing room, sat them down and in general painted a verbal scenario of the projected game on Saturday, contrary to verbal v. visual imagery theory.

I'm glad he notes this, not me.

First I posed the question of whether they wanted to play the game under the current conditions. Basically there were 17 men playing Coe's 55, and within the 55 members of Coe's squad were five or six all-state players, numerous all-conference, and reputable high school players from the previous year.

Okay. Here we go.

For our part, we had tough kids, but none of whom had received all-state honors. A few had honorable mention all-conference and we had more backs than linemen. To play a game you need more linemen than backs. We did have a good punter,

167

place kicker, a couple of good running backs, and a fair quarterback.

I pointed out all the difficulties and explained that there was no point in playing if they did not want to play. I also pointed out that my philosophy was the 'mail must go through.' Meeting the big challenge was the epitome of life, etc. However, they were the ones who had to play the game, and if their hearts were not in it, we certainly had a valid reason for either postponing the game or canceling it until we were healthier.

I'm waiting and wondering if Coach overtly plays the "be a man" card, the ultimate "negative reinforcement."

"No." He pauses. "Although, possibly yes." He pauses again. "Some of them— I wouldn't have faulted them for not playing. Although, it is, I can admit, a point to consider. But I might have thought they were smarter for not playing." He chuckles. "Just because I was the coach, doesn't mean I had all the answers. They had— There were other important things they were doing."

I swallow. "What did they say?"

We had a short discussion, out of which came the idea that 'of course we wanted to play the game.' This procedure I believe to be also significant in the mental preparation for a team. But to get back to the point...

"Wait a minute. By 'this procedure' you mean leading them to believe their manhood was on the line or letting them make important decisions, take ownership of what they do and therefore any outcomes?"

He looks exasperated. I think he is having a hard time keeping his train of thought and I just interrupted again with a serious insinuation. I bite my lip. I might have gone too far. His response surprises me.

"Yes, possibly on both counts." He pauses for a moment. "I believe, or maybe I believed at the time, it was important to put more on the line at times."

"It's definitely motivating." I'm feeling judgmental.

"When more is on the line, there is usually more to be gained."

168

I hadn't thought about it quite like that. Maybe putting self-worth on the line was worthwhile in some situations, some extreme situations, life and death situations possibly, like going into battle or jolting a team out of learned helplessness. I keep my mouth tightly shut and decide to keep it shut, but I can't help wondering if a team ever let him down, and, what did he do if they did.

Once the discussion was made I decided we needed to make our game plan on the spot. At the time I did not want to go back on the field for practice due to the injury factor.

Rather, I reviewed our potential offensive and defensive tools for the game. The problem was we had not prepared specific offensive plays, but rather had used opposing varsity plays. Our freshmen were used as a scout team each week simulating the varsity's opponent both offensively and defensively.

We only practiced a total of 1 1/2 hours a day, and for the freshmen to learn Ripon's or Cornell's varsity offense and defense, and to execute them well, was impossible. Hence we did the best we could, which was to get formations and offensive and defensive sets, etc.

For offense we ran plays often looking at the card board on which the play was diagrammed. I stood in the open huddle holding up the play card I wanted run. The players would check the assignment and run the play as well as they could against the varsity.

Defensively we did the same. Defense was mostly the alignment and reaction to the varsity's effort.

Our armament for the Coe game was an accumulation of various alignment and sets and plays from different teams. We could not have the cards in the huddle to remind us of the assignments, a difficult problem facing us, to say the least.

"To say the least." I grimace.

Coe's problem was quite different and should be touched on to complete the picture.

Coe had been quite successful at attracting large numbers of football players. Their total varsity squad was near 60 and freshman team numbered 55.

They had 4-5 coaches and—

"Now I get it. You needed 4-5 coaches to win in football even back then and you only had two. That's why football has so many coaches. And players. You only had 17 and you needed at least 29. You only had 2 coaches and you needed 4-5. The highest number of coaches and players wins in football!" I'm a bit embarrassed by my sarcastic outburst. Undoubtedly years of frustration over gender bias, major v. minor sport inequities, and current exhaustion combine to form a lapse in good manners.

Coach looks at me through sadness.

"I'm sorry. I need to be quiet."

Coach softens. "This is a good story."

"Yes, Coach. It is." Although, I wonder if we agree as to why.

Their freshmen were organized separately. Freshman were used as a scout team, but their numbers alone made it unnecessary to use their freshmen against the varsity, at least on freshman game week.

So as I saw it, the odds were about 1001 against us. I do not think our players recognized this.

My reaction to all of this was to paint a verbal scenario of the game coming up, which I imagined in such a way that it was possible for us to win. The scenario was as follows, more or less:

'Men, here's the way this game is going to go: concentrate hard on what I am going to say and I believe you people will be able to pull off one of the great upsets of the football year.

Coe College plays its freshmen football games on their practice field. At this point in time it is bare of grass except on the fringes, so it is not a good field. We can take advantage of that even though it is their field. Now if that field is wet, it can be nothing but a sea of mud at best, difficult to run on for anyone.

'We should assume that that is the way it's going to be. I haven't heard any weather forecasts for the weekend yet, but I

think there is a 50-50 chance we will have a wet field, and we can bet that Coe will not have counted on a wet field. In fact, we can count on Coe expecting to parade their troops with all 55 men primed and cocked for a runaway victory. It is homecoming for them and the first game of the season and their personnel is very competitive. The second team thinks they should be first, etc. And their chance to prove themselves will be in the mud bowl against us.

'Now I think they will be very over-confident and we should help make them more so. I will call today and tell their coach we are coming in spite of the fact we have only 17 players and request consideration of shortening the second half, if the game gets out of hand, etc.

'Now for the game itself, this can be called a specific game plan. Here's the way it will go: if it's raining and cold we will not go on the field until ten minutes before game time. We can warm up with calisthenics and running in the field house.

'Our captains—we elected them at that point—will go to the center of the field and decide whether we kick or receive. If we win the toss, we will kick; if we lose, they will choose to receive, I believe. In either case, we will kick off. Our place kicker is one of the best. We want the ball put into the end zone or close to it. As you know, it will be raining and the field will be heavy and slippery.

'We must make every effort to tackle the ball carrier inside of the ten yard line, which means we have to concentrate hard on getting down fast and covering well. It may be the only play of the day when the footing is decent.

'If we are successful on coverage and tackling, the Coe back may fumble and of course we will recover on the five.

'If the back is lucky enough to not fumble, they will go back in the huddle to call a conservative back off tackle or guard, since they will be somewhat concerned about the field position and the field.

171

'We will line up in our goal line defense. You know that defense formation. It's the one we have used from the beginning of the season against the varsity. More importantly we want to force the fumble inside the 10. We will ignore the possibility of the pass on the first down and loosen up slightly with our three backs on succeeding downs. However there should not be any succeeding downs, if you do everything right up to now, because they will fumble, and you will recover.

'Now when that happens this is what we will do: no huddle, line up wing right and use our favorite end run: Ripon's dipsy doodle right!' They laughed at that. I called all end runs dipsy doodles. The best one we had run was the first one we had learned, Ripon's, so, the reason for the call. 'We run it on the hike, no count, fast, and we take it into the end zone and six points. Our kicker kicks the extra point, and we are up by seven and ready to kick off again.

'If Ripon's dipsy doesn't get us in on the first play, our second play from scrimmage we run Ripon's dipsy doodle left on hike, without a huddle, and the third play will be a repeat of Ripon dipsy left. I believe we will have scored and kicked the point and will be in very good position for Coe to stay stunned and confused for the day.

'If the rain holds and we follow the basic principles already set up, that is, kick when we are in the middle of the field, keep Coe in poor field position by place kicks and punts. We'll use eight man defenses all the time, mixing 5-6-8 man alignments, and running offensive plays quickly when we are in good field position inside the 20 yard line. Now you men think about that plan whenever you can during the next two days and report to the gym at seven Saturday morning. Bus leaves at 7:30, game time is10 a.m. 65 miles away. Pre-game meal at 6:30. That's all.'

On Thursday of that week we took it as light on contact work as I could arrange, however in general we did everything we normally would do. We worked team-wise on presenting varsity

172

opponents defensive alignments and ran some opponents' offensive plays against varsity.

I sneaked in some dipsy doodles and some punts and fake punts.

Friday the varsity had their game plan chalk talk and had a very light work out. We were able to review the kicking games, particularly kick off and punt coverage, but we had no chalk talk or mind set review. I only prayed a little and started getting more than normally nervous. I only hoped it would not be a disaster, for there is very little justification for disasters. Everything goes down the drain in such cases.

Saturday rolled around. Naturally I was pleased and surprised to see that we had had a good rain in the night and it was drizzling at 7 am. We followed the game plan scenario to the T.

By the time we arrived at Cedar Rapids the rain was heavier and it was apparent that either the good Lord was listening or I was very lucky that day. It was important to be lucky vs. Coe. They were our arch rivals.

We dressed shortly and I arranged to use the little field house track area Coe had in the gymnasium for a warmup.

Fifteen minutes before 10 am. I sent the Captains to the field. Five minutes later we walked out to the field and completed a warmup on a rain soaked non grass Iowa black dirt football field.

We won the toss and amazingly remembered to kick. I prayed again.

We kicked off. He hit a beauty, deep to the goal line, down the middle; I can still see Coe's new uniforms: gold pants, white jerseys trimmed in red, gold helmets.

The safety fielded the ball expertly and ran straight up the center. He was hit hard on the seven. I could not believe our 7 men. He did not fumble, but we had many men on the tackle, a good sign.

We moved off the ball, arranged our eight man line tight with the secondary no deeper than five yards. Coe huddled and came out still looking clean. They ran an off tackle play right. We met it at the line of scrimmage for a one yard loss, no fumble. They huddled again. We looked confident, if ragamuffins can look confident. Their second play was a dive up the middle with a different back carrying the ball. Our left guard slipped back and hit him yards behind the line of scrimmage leading to a fumble, a scramble, with Grinnell recovering. No huddle. Coe was not ready. Ripon's dipsy doodle right went to the two. Our back slipped and was hit. Quick line up, no huddle again. Ripon's dipsy doodle left went right into Coe's end zone with the ball in the hands of a Grinnell Freshman who was exhilarated on his first touchdown in college ball.

Score after the kick Grinnell 7, Coe 0.

I will not tell you the details of the rest of the game.

"Coach! I want the details!"

"No. I would like— I think it's important to stick to the topic at hand."

Eyes widening, I listen, with a barely perceptible grin on my face.

The score was 13-6 Grinnell and the game followed the plan extremely closely. Close enough to add lots of ideas to my many notions on mind set, visualization, etc.

The rain you will say was the big factor and I will agree with you. I am not trying to tell you that the verbal scenario or the players or the players' concentration brought on the proper arrangement of low and high pressure to produce water on the field in Cedar Rapids, Iowa.

But I am saying that the scenario and concentration by the team on Wednesday before Saturday produced maximum quality play, and that Coe's probable overconfidence and the muddy field all set up a great upset and made the game a great experience, and not even close to a disaster. And, I am saying that after much consideration of the facts, I had guts enough to rearrange the chalk talks for final game plan to 72 hours prior to game time on several freshmen football games, the results of which were consecutive wins over three years and succeeding successful

efforts in the years which freshmen teams were allowed and our
coaching staff was organized as described. The explanation of the
phenomena which played itself out at Coe that Saturday and
numerous times since goes something like this:

1) a change in time for the day of rest proceeding a game;
normal time would have been one day prior to game time;

"So you're saying the day of rest wasn't the day before the
game? When was it?"

"You're jumping ahead. Give me a minute."

2) a Wednesday chalk talk which conveyed the general image
of the whole game with certain specifics spelled out, thereby
causing the team to concentrate on that image; normally the chalk
talk would have been made 24 hours before game time;

3) normal practice on the next two days, meaning there was a
definite load of physical work on these days compared to Monday,
Tuesday, Wednesday formal workouts.

4) not more psychological verbal or visual imagery sessions
were held for the purpose of focusing attention on the details given
in the Wednesday chalk talk due to the negative effect of verbal or
visual coaching just prior to the game. No chalk talk 24 hours
before game time left the athletes with no immediate emotional
push and also no immediate exhortations to remember or refer to
during the performance. You will remember that the theory of
'thinking' during performance causes less effective play. Hence in
this situation the time change of verbal imagery implanted the
scenario in the minds of the athletes long enough in advance to be
totally internalized by game time and removed last minute
exhortations to the conscious mind which would tend to produce
'thoughtful' action which produces the choke or resultant less than
maximum performance.

"So, you basically flipped the visual and the verbal with the
intent of not providing much of either in the final 72 hours, relying
instead on the athletes' independent mental prep—their own
visualization of the game plan—or lack thereof."

Coach shakes his head yes.

"No physical beating up of players early in the week or rest day late in the week; chalk talk given mid week to provide enough time to internalize the plan. Do I have it?"

He grins. The younger mind of his early coaching years peers through the twinkle in his eyes.

In the case of Coe, our opponents' psychological build up was correspondingly as bad as ours was good on game day. The weather helped a great deal, but Coe had an added advantage of playing at home and the occasion was homecoming and a fairly good crowd. There was no audience support for the visitors.

Reflection on this situation and many similar situations demonstrating the same pattern, convinced me to arrange my practice schedule as close to this as possible.

What seems to be valid is that organized teams seem to focus their mental attention on an upcoming game at least 72 hours before game time. If this focus is provided any later in preparation the team will not be able to use the intended stimulus at game time and will play relatively less efficiently: 'flat.' There is definite time needed for the human to internalize a complex verbal or visual image and three days seems to be the minimum time.

I am sure that some will say how about five days? And also say that game plans are usually spelled out on Monday and Tuesday before a Saturday game and then Friday's chalk talk is a review period essentially. My answer is, that is what our procedure was with the varsity for years and the rough statistics of 1/3 flat games were produced with that approach.

Therefore I have concluded that there seems to be a diminishing effect of the game plan if given much earlier than 72 hours. Perhaps three days is the time of ultimate player interest, so they are more receptive to the plan at that time. For whatever reason, the time period of 54-60 hours prior seems to be the most effective. Resistance to the idea of giving up a good contact day in the practice week makes this plan difficult to accept. My gradual acceptance to the idea of 100% performance for a light practice day on Wednesday as compared to a good chance of a 50-75%

performance for a contact day on Wednesday, converted me to the
procedure.

"So, no more than 72 hours ahead of time. No less than 54 hours. Taking time to cover the game plan during the best days for full contact, Wednesday or Thursday, is difficult."

"Yes. Correct. If I had more than two hours of practice time, I'd probably give them a warm up, the game plan, and then work them hard, all in the same day. But we can't. We couldn't."

"It takes that long to give them the game plan?"

"Yes. And full visualization of it."

"So you take them through a visualization session of the entire game."

"No. Well— I would describe it more as describing a scene to them. They provide the details. I paint the basic picture, the outline, like a paint by number. They fill in the color and detail."

"Nice metaphor, Coach." And powerful approach.

He clears his throat. "I'm not dead yet."

I hear my mouth clamp shut, and a chuckle from Coach.

Another good example of the effectiveness of conscious overt concentration on the specific protected action of an individual 72 hours before game time comes from a story of one Grinnell player in the 1960-63 era. Howard Dunn—

"Coach, is this story necessary. I think I understand 72 Hour Rule now."

"Do you know Howard Dunn?"

Despite his labored breathing and intermittent cough, I've decided Coach's energy is endless. My resistance, on the other hand, is waning.

Howard Dunn played defensive and cornerback for us during these years. He told me the story when discussing the possibility of writing this book. The account went like this.

We were preparing to play Cornell College at Cornell in Howard's senior year. The game was always inspirational for us as Cornell was close by and Grinnell and Cornell had developed a strong rivalry in all respects.

We were riding a winning streak and had won the championship the year before, so there was much incentive for us to play well this game. Cornell also was having a good year and the game was considered by most a toss up with the home team being given the edge.

Our defensive secondary, with Howard handling the left corner, was experienced, solid and very proud.

Cornell had a very sound offensive team, particularly a running game with exceptional outside speed. The running back was a young man, who was small, but with exceptional quickness and ability to run to the outside. He was from Iowa, more particularly from Cedar Rapids. Howard came from Columbus Jct., Iowa, and therein lies the story.

Howard had concocted in his head the idea that the game might come down to a person match between himself and the running back from Cornell. He told me that on Wednesday evening prior to the game he had talked at great length with teammate Gar Smith about a fantasy he had of making tackles on the Cornell running back, preventing a touchdown which made the difference in the game. He told me that he and Gar laughingly fantasied over the possibility for quite some time and then he consciously forgot all about it.

Well, Saturday rolled around, as it always does, and the game was played. We scored first. Cornell second, and we again in the second half. We failed to kick one extra point, so the game ground down to the last minute with us grimly holding on to a six point lead.

Cornell, making a final drive, succeeded in making a first down on the Grinnell seven yard line with ninety seconds to go.

Out from the huddle, first and goal, Cornell came out flankered right, a quick pitch to the running back, racing for the corner. Dunn was fast enough you'd think he knew the play. The flanker missed the block and the running back was smothered for a one yard loss.

178

Second down and eight. Out of the huddle this time in motion right, power and swap right running back carrying the ball again. Dunn anticipating better than average. Again, a good tackle and a yard loss on the play.

Third down and nine with 25 seconds on the clock. Straight formation quick pitch right. Dunn again moves fast with an excellent tackle and one yard loss. The clock ran out. Of course we were ecstatic. Our season was one step closer to being the best in history. At that time the coaching staff knew nothing of the 72 hour 'fantasy,' only the two defensive backs.

My analysis now is that Howard Dunn had inadvertently and unconsciously fantasized a situation which consequently occurred almost as fantasized in the game. He had done it three days before game time which I now think is optimum time for the game plan to be internalized, and if the situation does present itself the players so internalized will react much better than if not. That might be considered 100%, since it is presumably impossible to perform better than 100%.

You can probably tell many stories which have the same ingredients and are easily explainable according to this theory.

I do not believe the concentration caused the situation to happen. That is something that some people have interpreted when I have discussed this phenomena with them. I do, however, believe that if the situation does occur the players so programmed will have their 'wires' cleared, the obstacles within themselves will have been removed by internalization of the concentration and the productivity will be natural and clear and appear to be 120%, because we are used to judging a condition less effective in most circumstances as 100%, an example of 2+2=5.

"—an explanation of comfort zone, Coach."

He looks puzzled.

"Encouraging players to move out of their comfort zones, creating a new PR or higher expectations. It's the 2+2=5 phenomenon you just described. Howard was always physically capable of producing '120%,' so to speak: 2+2=5. But he believed

2+2=4. Something had to move him out of his comfort zone, his belief system. In his case, it was visualization and the 72 Hour Rule."

Coach looks pleased. "Yes." He speaks the word quietly and takes a breath. "Moving them toward believing they could do better—" He takes another viscous breath.

"I'm glad you told me Howard Dunn's story. 2+2=5 is great. And, of course, I see a connection with acceptance. The more accepting athletes are, the more readily they accept the new reality, and their improvement. Sometimes unexpected improvement can be scary."

"Yes. I've seen that many times."

"But, I'm not yet sold on the 72 Hour Rule. I can't recall a single scientific study to back up this claim." I don't think more stories will convince me.

"Indulge me.

A game played later in the season of 1963 provides another example of positive results due to 72 hour concentration or visualization before game time effecting visualization during the game. In this case numerous witnesses were on hand who were involved in the original period of fantasy, three days before game time.

To quickly review the situation. The up coming game was with our old rival Carleton at Northfield. The seventh game of the season, two after the Cornell game, which we have just described. Carleton was one of the opponents in our way to an undefeated season and the second consecutive championship of Edd Bowers Pioneers. So the psychological build up was very high.

It happened by coincidence that we had a campus group of faculty, administrators, and townspeople who met socially during the football season and games. This year the enthusiasm was high and a good many people gathered together on Tuesday evenings to view the films of the last week's game and to talk about the next contest. Of course Coach Bowers was there to explain his point of view and to talk about current problems, injuries, prognoses, etc.

On this occasion the subject of the center's ability to pass the ball to the punter was the principle subject of concern for Coach Bowers. He pointed out how many times Kirk Van Rooyan, our very able and tough offensive center, had passed the ball over the kicker's head during the season. He was a senior and this problem had always plagued him and us and we had not solved it to our satisfaction with only two games left in his career. Coach Bowers posed the question to the group of what to do. I recalled we had no other personnel which Coach Bowers was willing to substitute in a pressure situation. Our college Vice President, Merritt Ludwig, came up with a question of his own, half serious I am sure.

He asked, 'Edd, why don't you use a pigtail like we used to do in sandlot baseball if you really got in a jam and have no other alternative.' We laughed and kicked the idea around for a few minutes for fun, when all of a sudden Coach Bowers said, 'You know, I believe you've got something there Merritt, we'll do it!'

I had been around Grinnell long enough by then not to get too excited about different propositions; and I will have to admit, I did not take Edd too seriously.

But the next day, a Wednesday, three days before game time, Edd finished our scrimmage by putting in the 'Grinnell Pigtail.' He described our problem and assigned Art Peterson, a fine defensive back and reserve quarterback and good punter, to the tail of the pigtail, that is, if we called the play.

Art would be inserted in the line up for one of our backs. One of our ends usually split would play tight to add blocking strength to the formation. Peterson would position himself 7-10 yards behind our punter.

He explained that in the event that Van Rooyan passed the ball over the kicker's head, Art should field the ball and make a decision as to whether he should kick, run, or pass, depending on the predicament and the down, yardage, etc.

We then proceeded to practice the play in a field scrimmage situation, reviewing the assignments, and I am sure, hoping we would never have to use it.

We finished the weekly practice and went to Northfield for the big game. I cannot remember how many times on Thursday or Friday we ran the pigtail during practice. I do remember hearing Coach Bowers tell V-P Ludwig and others that we put it in and he was intending to use it if we had a do-or-die situation.

And of course we did. With only 5 or 6 minutes left in the game we were, as in the Cornell game, nursing a 6 point lead, only this time our drive was stopped on our own ten yard line. Again, at this point in the game the momentum had swung around to Carleton and the pressure was on.

Coach Bowers yelled, 'Art, get in there and run the pigtail.'

My heart froze, but I liked his daring and imagination. I just prayed we would not need the pigtail, that our kicker would get off one of his better punts and we could play defense again.

Art was on the field, called the play, and there we were in the strangest punt formation ever viewed from any sideline.

Things were very tense on our sideline and I am sure very exciting on Carleton's. The battle of intellectuals always provided interesting plays and post game conversations.

Van Rooyan was over the ball, our kicker on the goal line waiting, Art Peterson nearly on the end line peering in. Signals were called, Van Rooyan passed a high soaring ball clearly over the kicker's outstretched hands even with a jump. Art fielded the ball as if he had done it many times and ran as hard as he could for the goal line. He was hit as he crossed the goal line but his momentum carried him to the 11-12 yard line.

It was fourth down and we still had the ball. The Carleton bench was in an uproar. Coach Mel Tauke was on the field protesting the legality of the play or rather claiming Art had stepped out of the end zone before catching the ball. The officials ruled in our favor. I am not sure they were right.

We huddled again and called a regular punt, and prayed that with the practice Van Rooyan had just had he would hit the punter on the numbers. He did. Carleton Peterson kicked from the end line out to the forty.

We climbed out of the hole, surged defensively, and played well enough to force Carleton to give up the ball on four downs. We ran the clock out. What a season, and now in retrospect, what an example of the 72 hour theory.

At that point in time the 72 hour theory was not known to any of us, and so it was not something we did because we understood the concept. It is my analysis of what happened and how the elements combined to make it happen.

I think the play was effective because it was introduced three days before game time and introduced in a manner interesting enough and serious enough for all concerned to visualize the event. When the circumstances presented themselves on Saturday it was orchestrated well, particularly by Art Peterson. He obviously had internalized his reaction.

I have often thought that the visualization might also have been the cause for Van Rooyan to snap the ball high. I believe there is every reason to believe this. But the play was sound for the situation and all in all it makes a great story for Coach Bowers, the players, and the sideline quarterback, Merritt Ludwig.

Earlier I alluded to the fact that the coaching fraternity for the last forty years has generally accepted that the day of effective inspirational motivation 'fight' talks by coaches is done with. This conclusion seems to be based on the idea that our athletes' mentality had become elevated to the plane which makes the substance of fight talks seem ludicrous or ridiculous and this produces an opposite form of motivation, mitigating the positive effect on performance.

The other logical conclusion as to the reason fight talks do not work is that the substance of the talks is essentially weak or nonexistent and the total effort is thought to be shallow and obviously an effort at conning the athlete to great heights. In either event the reaction is the same: negative. Hence coaches do not chance a poor fight talk, substituting them with different forms of communication or no communication.

From my experience with the 72 hour theory of game plan I believe I have to say my verbal talks took on the form of old time fight talks at times. Believing that I dealt with the essential truth of the situation, I dramatized the hypothetical scenario well enough to keep the attention of the athletes. The image, when well plated in this manner, did produce excellent results. So, in that context, I think you can say there is a place for verbal imagery in team coaching and in fight talks closely approximating the old time variety made famous by Phog Allen and Knute Rockne.

The essence for success is the interest by the athletes in the subject matter and the viable substance of the talk, that is, the plan itself. If it has substance and is punctuated by emotion and imagination, the image becomes more intense and therefore the performance will intensify. At least to the point of embarrassment or 'flat.'

"I'm confused. You're saying the 72 Hour Rule and visualization will improve performance at least to the level of embarrassment or 'flat?' Don't you mean 'past' the point of embarrassment or 'flat?'"

"No. It's a joke. Maybe not one of my best." He smiles a crooked smile and continues.

I laugh. Once again, I'm struggling to stay with him.

Recognizing the application of the individual and team psychological phenomena already discussed, we could end here thinking we had some of the answers. That is not, however, the case, for any coach who has gone through one season can tell you that there are complicating psychological circumstances when you must play a game a week for twelve weeks as in football or two games a week for fifteen weeks as you have to do in basketball or other variations of game arrangements over a period of several weeks or months, note the present professional schedules for football, basketball, and baseball.

My experiences coping with these situations will be discussed. I hope to shed some experiential light on the good applications of the phenomena already discussed to the season long problems.

"Coach, I'll admit I'm no expert on football and I'm not current on research pertaining to the timing of visualization before a performance, but I've never seen a study address this question. It might be another case of innovative ideas being squelched by practical limitation. I mean, think about it. How does an investigator apply the 72 Hour Rule in a controlled study? You allude to the complexity of variables and the unending challenges different schedules pose to a coach of any sport. I'm really sorry I'm not aware of any information on timing of visualization in football."

He says, "Football was not the place to find visualization techniques, at least not when I was thinking about this business."

I ponder Coach's comment a moment. "You know you're absolutely right. Even when mental training had established positive results in almost every major sport, football resisted. But, I have to say, two studies do jump to mind, one pretty major one."

Coach's eyes widen with expectation.

"In the late 1980s—you might have heard about this one—a very brave coach implemented a mental training program at Texas Christian University. The study stood out to me for two reasons: first, it dealt with a football team, and second, it was amazingly successful. Wouldn't it be nice to know if they followed the 72 Hour Rule?"

"TCU." Coach appears lost in thought.

I think he's preparing to tell a story about TCU. I quickly jump in. "Yes! Isn't that great? I think of Texas as being so conservative. My bias, I guess. Let's see if we can find the study." I pull my computer onto my lap and search for the report on the internet. I find it easily. "Don't you love the internet? Here it is."

"What did they do?"

I summarize out loud as I read. "Texas Christian University had experienced a pronounced decline in football success."

"I remember. They were a top team, nationally ranked."

"Right. Going back to the 60s. They built up all this pride surrounding football and then the bottom fell out. By the 70s, and definitely by the early 80s, they were one of the worst teams in the country. They went from winning records to records with 80-90% losses. As I recall, TCU made coaching changes, but that didn't change the win/loss results. The current coach when this study started had been there one year, with a losing record. He was approached by a sport psychologist named Richard Fenker. Fenker asked him to consider a mental training program, and I guess the general consensus was, they had nothing to lose."

"Now I remember. They used visualization."

"Yes! The athletes were trained to manage their focus and breathing and utilize cues to maximize effective mindsets in the situations they were going to face." I look up at Coach. "Sound familiar? After they implemented the program, their evaluation showed 86% of the starters said it was a positive thing." I look at Coach again. "That, in itself, says a lot, doesn't it? 86% is a large percentage, especially considering the athletes were probably skeptical from the get-go. But the other results, as I recall, were even more amazing. Just a minute."

Coach smiles broadly. "They started winning."

"Yes!" I continue skimming the report. "The team won their first game on the road against a non conference team and their second at home. They lost a close game against a heavily favored conference rival. They won in the final seconds against another rival, a team they hadn't beaten in 30 years. They followed this win with five more, at which time Fenker describes a break from their mindset. They start to feel pressure to win."

"Yes. And Fenker blamed their drop in performance on lost focus."

"Ready excuse. Focus on what? They don't admit—or accept"—(I look at Coach and he nods)—"how important their mental training is. Looks like they lose the final two regular season games and a bowl game. They end with a record of 8-4."

"So what do you see about the 72 Hour Rule?"

"The methodology is pretty detailed." I scan the report as quickly as I can. "The investigator and coaches used mental training techniques on Tuesday and Wednesday and dropped their plan to use them on Thursday. Initially they planned to have position coaches take over training on Thursdays, but the position coaches were uncomfortable leading the sessions, so they dropped the Thursday sessions." I threw up my hands. "Accident or not, it looks like they followed the 72 Hour Rule! Coach! You're going to love this! They began describing and implementing this new approach at the very first team meeting. Firstness! They made sure all coaches, even those who had some doubts, were willing to support it. All hands on board." And at least some degree of trust. We know how important trust is. "Their imagery reinforced positive thoughts and expectations. The Umbrella! Coach, your theories are supported by this study. But as usual, there's a lot of" (I raised my fingers to mime quotation marks on either side of my next comment): "'can't draw scientific conclusions' from this or that thrown in."

Coach groans. "Maybe science gets in the way sometimes."

"Fenker says their methods lacked the high standards of a traditional scientific study. No control group. Subjects weren't randomly selected. They also experienced statistical difficulty. Some of the questions on their survey required yes/no responses, which can be a problem. Even when you have a preponderance of 'yes' responses, there's too little variance to demonstrate a statistically significant effect."

"That doesn't surprise me."

I look up at him. He laughs out loud. He laughs so hard he coughs and continues to cough even harder. Emily walks into the living room. He raises his hand to wave her concern off. She places a glass of water in it, holding on until he has a firm grasp.

As he takes a drink, I say, "There's another study, not as impressive as the TCU study, but it's one I was involved with." I look for the folder on my computer. "It was never published. We didn't even try."

Coach looks at me sternly.

187

"Well, we're talking about mostly anecdotal evidence." I laugh, realizing the evidence in question was more scientifically collected than a single person's recollections, even 50 years of them. "Anyway, I don't know if you remember this, but in the early 90s, University of Iowa went through a year or so when they were pretty frustrated with their kicking game. A few key games had been lost on a kick. The media picked up on it. This was right after Iowa had won a few games due to their kicking."

"Live by the sword, die by the sword."

"Right. But when things went south due to poor kicking, it was like the media started pointing it out, suggesting they were 'choking.' Hayden Fry defended the kickers just so far. Maybe he was desperate. I don't know. He actually approved a mental training program for his kickers. I was so excited. One of my students approached me about using visualization and doing this study. He was a fifth year student, a football player, which was perfect."

Coach shakes his head in agreement. "Players, and I believe all players, can benefit from visualization. But kickers—"

"Right! They're on the sidelines all game; they go in cold. They have lots of time to think about screwing up."

"Then they call time out."

"—so they can think some more! Someday they'll welcome more time to warm up and mentally prepare. But, without a plan, they're almost set up to fail, to tighten up, to imagine blowing it. I was amazed football hadn't done more with kickers' pre performance routines."

Coach shakes his head in agreement.

"Anyway, my grad student had been working with the kickers. He saw they were performing much better in practice than in the game. Because of decent performance in practice, he knew they had it in them to kick well, not great, but decent. He told me improvement would be great, but mostly he wanted to see consistency. He wanted them to start performing in a game like they performed in practice."

"What was his name, the Italian boy—"

"Romano. Todd, I believe."

"Right. He was a good kicker."

"Yes. He was one of the kickers who showed Iowa—Hayden Fry—" We looked at each other knowing Coach Fry's approval was mandatory, "—just how much a good kicker is worth. He tied the school record for the most field goals in a single game. He kicked a 53-yarder that same game. I think 53 was a record, too. He won games for them."

"Your student was a kicker?"

"Yes. I believe so. I remember feeling fortunate to have him implementing the program. He was someone they could relate to and trust. The program he put together used written scripts, which they wrote themselves and, after I made edits or suggestions, he recorded them on tape. That's what we used back then: cassette tapes. The athletes listened to their audio tapes as often as they wanted. It was up to them, and of course, some did it more than others. But, all in all, the results were very positive." I find the research report from so many years earlier and quickly skip to the results.

BEFORE STUDY

Field Goal Performance 1992 (attempted/made)

Practice	Games
80.9%	76.2%

AFTER STUDY

Field Goal Performance 1993 (attempted/made)

Practice	Games
71.1%	72.1%

BEFORE STUDY

Punting Performance 1992 (average yards per punt)

Practice	Games
41.3	36.5

AFTER STUDY

Punting Performance 1993 (average yards per punt)

Practice	Games
42.6	41.4

"I remember we were pleased. Even though they didn't show a marked improvement in skill, they improved their consistency. The coaches knew what to expect from them. 70% success in practice meant 70% in a game. They weren't so up and down."

"That's a good one." He winked.

I laugh. "Unintentional."

"How did it look for 72 Hour Rule?"

I find the method section of the report. "We gave the audio tapes to the kickers on Thursday. Looks like verbal imagery on or before Wednesday, 72 hours prior, and visual imagery—the athletes' own visualization—from then until the game. I don't think they could have done a better job of following the 72 Hour Rule. Amazing." I have to admit, the study provides a small, but interesting bit of confirmation for a very out-of-the-box approach. "It's a little study. Not many subjects."

"Like a normal team," Coach says.

"Right. Yes. A normal team." I continue reading. "It doesn't meet the standards peer-reviewed journals are looking for, but I remember thinking the intervention was a success." I can't believe it used 72 Hour Rule. "The program was dropped when my student graduated, like so many good programs." I look up at Coach. "Maybe coaches who read this book will start blogging about 72

190

Hour Rule. More evidence like this might come to light." I can't believe I just said that. I feel compelled to add, "Or research."

"Blogging? What kind of— What the hell is that?"

Emily comes into the room with plates of sandwiches, chips, and dill pickle spears. My mouth begins to water.

"Thank you so much, Emily." I reach for a sandwich.

She nods and smiles. "The two of you will starve to death if you continue like this." She turns to Coach. "Blogging on the Internet—like posting your thoughts on a bulletin board for everyone to see. People write about their experiences or express their opinions. Sometimes people can add comments."

"You could describe the 72 Hour Rule, Coach, and others could respond with their stories or their own version of the 72 Hour Rule. It's a way to share information. You should definitely blog."

Coach munches on a sandwich and says, "Sounds more like something you'd want to avoid. Blog, bog, fog, sog."

"We definitely need to get you blogging, Coach."

Emily rolls her eyes. "John's been blogging for years, in his own way, one very long blog." We laugh. As she leaves the room, she says, "Help yourself to whatever you want to drink in the refrigerator. I believe there's a little soda, water, beer, some wine left over."

I imagine myself falling flat on my face after a glass of wine. Coach inspires me to stay sharp. Gotta keep up.

Chapter VII
Coach's *Bucket Theory*

We finish our sandwiches quickly. "Want to take a longer break, Coach? Take a rest or walk?"

"We haven't covered Bucket Theory."

Emily picks up our plates and says, "John is a little unsteady on his feet these days." She returns with a thin, white cotton blanket. It reminds me of a hospital blanket. She unfolds it onto his lap.

His hands appear frail, his skin transparent. They tremble slightly as he helps spread and smooth the blanket. Maybe he thinks our time is limited. At that moment I feel a subtle but distinct surge of determination. I'm intent on listening and understanding Bucket Theory. The name makes me chuckle inside.

Coach says, "We used to say things like—

'Play them one at a time.'

'Don't get fat in the head.'

'Don't count your chickens before they hatch.'

'Don't play the game before game time.'

'We didn't take them very seriously.'

'We lost the game before we played it.'

'We were very intimidated.'

I took these quotes from newspaper clippings and radio broadcasters' statements. They reflect coaches philosophical explanations for the results of ball games played or ball games about to be played. They also reflect the substance of this topic.

I have constantly referred to the continuing quest of coaches at all levels, that of how to get your team to play near 100% each time you play. From my experience with many teams, concern over how to get 100% productivity raised the question of whether it is in fact possible for a team to play 100% in any game.

Since 100% team effort is difficult to evaluate—at best, judgmental—an effort to evaluate using statistics, particularly those from two different games, is one way to get an idea. But the problem of evaluating opponents' strength and more particularly opponents' strength on the day which the game was played, makes a scientific examination of this problem vexing.

"I hear you."

Perhaps in the days of the computer, techniques will be developed which can provide more specific answers to these problems.

"You're quite prophetic, Coach."

He smiles.

My evidence is based more on win-loss records and a comparison of teams played one year to those played one year later.

I open my mouth to object.

The other factor in this evidence is the general evaluation by the coaching staff of the attitude and the effort of the team during the course of the season. That is rated on a scale of 1-10 for each game.

The rather vague hypothesis is: for a team that has no organized effort by the coaching staff for team mental preparation for the season as a whole the average percent expectancy level for that team will be about 60%, with the individual game efficiency percentage varying up and down from 60% about 10 points. For a team that has an organized effort by the coaching staff for team mental preparation, the average percentage expectancy level can be as high as 90%.

"60% versus 90% performance?"

"Yes."

"That's pretty ambitious, Coach."

"Well, yes, but this explanation is by no means exhaustive." He clears his throat once, then again with more determination. "Hear me out, if you will." Coach appears fatigued by the thought of yet one more complete and detailed explanation. With a very set jaw and furrowed brow, he presses on, in fact, he seems to pick up the pace.

Now I have introduced some terms and phrases new to the substance, and I hope to explain what I mean by them in the narrative that follows.

The first time I actually attempted to make an organized effort to prepare my team mentally for the whole season was in 1953 at Grinnell, when I was in my second year as head football coach, following four years as an assistant at Grinnell and two years as head coach at Midland.

"Wow, Coach. Now you're impressing the heck out of me. You first formulated Bucket Theory in 1953?"

He nods.

History, I believe, will bear me out in the story I am about to tell. The years post World War II before my first year at Grinnell produced a total of six wins in three seasons of eight games each. The four seasons 1948 through 1951 produced nine more wins. I was asked to coach football as well as basketball in 1952. I agreed to do so for three years only and proceeded on that basis.

My approach to the '52 season was the same as my colleagues' approach in proceeding years. We tried to play the games one at a time. Our goal as far as I am concerned was to win all of the eight games scheduled. As to the techniques used to gain mental preparation, they also were similar to ones I had used personally and seen others use. Essentially they consisted of having co-captains elected and discussing the season with the captains pre season. Most of the discussion was concerned with our organization, personnel and the new system which I was to put in for the year with little emphasis on relative strengths of opponents and ourselves.

I installed a different offense then we employed the previous year. Defensively the concepts of the past held over. We also employed a new assistant coach who was very familiar with the new offensive system.

My mind reels with alternative explanations for what might appear to be Bucket Theory success or failure.

As far as preparation for each individual game, I followed the traditional pattern. The pattern is familiar to all, I am sure. It consisted of: 1) over the weekend the coaching staff reviewed movies taken of the game with the upcoming team the year before and then showed the film to the team; 2) coaching staff reviewed scout reports of the game played the week before by our opponent except game number one; 3) coaching staff developed a game plan for the upcoming game by Monday of game week, dispersed the game plan in written form to the team as well as in verbal form following the scout report review; tactical work in practice drills specifically focused on the upcoming game; 4) we tapered off of physical practices on Thursday and Friday with a chalk talk for review of the game plan and reinforcement of goal motivation, final exhortation, and inspiration etc. 24 hours before game time.

Here again I want to reiterate my personal idea was to communicate the importance of thinking only of the game we were to play this week, giving credence to the idea that I thought there was something to the notion that if the mental dynamics of the group was not somehow correct, in this case focused on the upcoming game, the team might indeed play less than 90%.

The results of this technique as we played the season out were not good from anyone's point of view, that is, anyone but the opposition, for we lost every single game of the season.

"Ouch, Coach."

Now that may have been disastrous, however, the Grinnell team of '51, on which many of these athletes had played, and I had been assistant coach, had been somewhat conditioned to losing. That team had won only one game. So, from the morale point of view, it was not so disastrous, particularly if, like in my case, there's a search for clues in the season's statistics for reinforcement of any kind. The basic facts, which were obvious, were that the team of 1952 had scored more points than any Grinnell team in history, yet its opponents had also scored nearly as many points accumulatively as any opponents in history. As the newspaper put

195

*it in review, the Pioneers had the best offense in history, coupled
with the worst defense in history.*

*Our team scored an average of three touchdowns per game,
but we allowed an average of four touchdowns per game. All of
this is simple enough, but the gnawing question for me was why
could we be so effective offensively and so ineffective defensively?*

*Analysis of that question resulted in personnel problems, partly
because our lack of numbers in comparison with opponents meant
we played one platoon football. Playing the best players both ways
suggested we ran out of gas and were defeated by the opponents
reserve strength or our lack of condition. We weren't strong enough
to withstand superior numbers.*

"Did you typically lose late in the game?"

He holds up his index finger. He was on a roll, and I sensed I
better step out of the way.

*One game in the string was played against Knox College at
Grinnell on a beautiful October Saturday afternoon. The game
score was 27-27 late in the fourth quarter and we were showing
signs of deterioration on defense. While we were trying desperately
to shore up the defense, I felt a tap on my shoulder. Looking
around I recognized the presence of my good friend and colleague
from Carleton College, Shel Maube, who I knew to be attending
the game as a scout and I presumed to be in the press box.
However, with five minutes to play, here he was wanting to say
something to me. His curt words were, 'Say Pfitsch, the West Coast
scores are starting to come in on the radio.'*

*I looked at him, I am sure, curiously, or perhaps with some
restraint and not getting the point, said something like, 'And what
do you want me to do about it?'*

*He smiled and repeated, 'I just thought you ought to know, if
the West Coast scores are coming in, there must be something
wrong with your game clock. We have been here over four hours.'*

*This time I got it. I glanced at the clock, which was an old
fashioned circular face clock with a long pointer indicating the
time elapsed.*

I'm chuckling, then moaning and shaking my head.

Investigation after the game discovered that our clock had a gear box for both basketball and football and the electrician had mistakenly engaged the basketball gear for this game, which of course made the game go nearly half again as normal. We played from 1:00 to 5:30 p.m. and I need to add, our defense proved inadequate for the job. We lost 34-27.

I'm momentarily lost in the mechanics of time keeping, gears, changing time, basketball versus football.

Another interesting game in the sequence, which was, at that time, a record breaker as far as scoring and offense was concerned, was our game with Ottawa University of Kansas.

"Coach, hold on a second. You're saying the clock had two different ways of counting down time?"

He chuckles as if remembering something humorous. "You can't let anything go, can you?"

I grimace and shrug. Maybe this is a poor use of our short time together. I start to stop him, but he seems already firmly committed.

"Football and basketball used the same clock. We saved money taking it back and forth from the football field to Darby."

I remember Darby Gymnasium, built during World War II using wood instead of precious steel. Fascinating architecture, and no air conditioning.

"Basketball has two halves of 20 minutes. Football has four quarters of 15 minutes each. I guess I should say the time of the game was approximately 25% longer."

"I'm still not sure how the clock worked. Time is time, right?"

"Time is time. I believe you are correct." He smiles. "But you'll have to ask someone smarter than I how the clock worked. I just know it didn't work so well for us that particular day, which made a situation much worse, at least for us, not for our opponents. But," he pauses as if to center himself in another time and place, "Concerning the Ottawa University of Kansas game—

This time we double checked the clock. The score was 48-46, Ottawa, one of the truly amazing games which I have ever been a part of. Some of the greatest offensive long runs ever produced on Iowa football turf were run that day. One was run by Nick Ryan, one of our Captains, one of the finest football players ever to play at Grinnell.

The point is that this team did play well and played particularly well offensively. They played well enough to be in every game, to have a chance to win against nearly everyone. That might be why their frustration was clearly apparent to me a week after the season when a contingent of the players led by Nick Ryan appeared in my office with this request: they wanted the team to be allowed to divide themselves up into two teams, freshmen and seniors vs. sophomores and juniors, and to play a game on Ward Field under the lights on Thursday, to win one.

I had not even thought of such a thing. I was trying to get ready for the basketball season, which also was my responsibility. I was also a little surprised, but pleased that they had enough desire and energy to want to play such a game.

So it was that we played the game. It was a cold night and not too agreeable conditions, but the game was a hard hitting affair played with a good deal of emotion, resulting in as you could guess, a legitimate 13-13 tie, a perfect sequel to a completely defeated season.

At this point in time my analysis of the situation was that we played such close games in at least four cases that had we had a little more energy, I'll call it that for lack of knowing what else to call it, we could have won any of those contests or possibly two or three. Of course, had the opponents had a little less energy the result might haves been a combination of the two situations. We also would have won two or three games.

"Or four or five."

"Yes."

I imagined what it would have been like had that happened, for the boys and for me, for my good wife, who had to put up with all of my frustrations. Desperately I tried to find an answer which could swing the balance. I came up with what I will call the 'Bucket Theory.' I vowed to put it into affect for the next season and went on my way to the basketball court.

The bucket theory, over simplified, went something like this. I decided there must be a total amount of energy which was the accumulated energies of the individuals on the team to spend throughout the eight game season and that if you proportioned from the tank of energy eight buckets holding equal amounts of energy to expend on each game that that was all there was to use. You might spill some of the energy from the buckets in the course of the week, injuries, poor practice, etc. There seemed to be a ceiling on the amount of total energy the team could spend on one game if each game was given equal emphasis or consideration!

If this were true—

"Coach, you realize a premise is pretty important. If it isn't true, what you are about to say isn't worth a lot." He smiles, nods, and continues.

—it would also be true that, if you took the tank of energy and poured out in different size buckets the amount of energy from the tank you thought necessary to win the first game and then proportioned the remainder of the contents of the tank according to the amount of energy you estimated was necessary, you would have varying size buckets of energy, each carefully calculated for the job on that day. But you could not have more than the total accumulation in the tank.

I look at him with more puzzlement than doubt. On some level, it made sense.

My reasoning was that if we could have more energy in bucket number 3 than our opponents had on the day we played, we could win. Or, looking backwards, we could have won those three games I alluded to, if we had arranged the buckets right.

My reasoning further was that this bucket of energy could take the form of dynamic psychological energy and that all I had to do was figure out how to get the team to visualize itself along a formula such as I had dreamed up.

"Dynamic psychological energy?"

"Yes." He doesn't skip a beat.

I set about to think about this during the winter and did come up with a plan which I had courage enough to try in the next season. The results from this experiment became the original model for many similar experiments in the years following. The success of this experiment was the greatest of all, so the hypothesis I have stated is clearly the result of this experience reinforced by several others since then.

First, I conferred with my two captains, Dave Norris and Nick Ryan, and developed my general feelings and conclusions and proposal. I decided I needed to have the approval and support of the captains, and, if possible, the team.

Ownership. I recognize what I call ownership, but I'm not sure what the scientific term would be or if anyone has ever tried to define it for research purposes. I wonder if Coach's "dynamic psychological energy" is the same as athletes' level of belief or trust in something, like Bucket Theory, and the depth of their commitment to it.

Ryan and Norris were not surprised at my concern but quite surprised at my proposed play to solve the problem. After talking it over, they decided it was worth a shot, but only if the squad was in on it and at least the majority agreed. They thought that it would take a good sales pitch to explain and overcome the question of why they should put different effort—conscious at least—into some games.

All athletes in the USA perhaps are mentally patterned to think it a disgrace if you played a game without trying to win and in my explanations of my proposal for super effort in the games which we concurred that we had the best chance of winning and not preparing as much for the ones we had less chance of winning implied, giving up on the latter games. I tended to agree with that but was very interested to see the results. For I surmised in the games we took the pressure off might turn out to be better played due to less tension than the ones we consciously prepped for.

"Okay. So if you were losing the tough games because you were overly anxious or stressed about them, in effect, you were 'spilling energy' and wasting what you could use on winnable games. If you—" I hesitate, then continue with resolve to stay with Coach's line of thinking and terminology. "If you took 'dynamic psychological energy' away from those tough games, you might win them because you were more relaxed, you had nothing to lose, which would leave more energy, more positively focused energy, for the ones you need more energy for, that is, if that's why you lost them in the first place."

"Yes. I think you have a firm understanding. The lack of energy coming from too many losses, low morale, eventually producing poor attitude for 100% performance when games were winnable.

At any rate we spent the greater part of two early practices discussing this revolutionary procedure and the squad slowly, reluctantly at first, came around to agreeing to the experiment.

I wonder how close "coming around to agreeing to the experiment" is to belief in Bucket Theory, or trust in Bucket Theory, or trust in a coach or teammates, or even ambivalence. They could be complying or cooperating. I keep my reservations to myself, while my thoughts continue flowing chaotically amidst countless variables and alternative hypotheses. I wonder if Grinnell College will replicate the TCU scenario: (1) buy into mental prep, (2) win big, (3) decide mental prep isn't needed, (4) lose big. Belief and trust: tough variables to measure and control, possibly the core of Coach's "dynamic psychological energy" and Bucket Theory. Again, his terminology resonates with me. Could dynamic psychological energy be the "magic" behind mental training? So many times we can't explain positive results. We're reluctant to use and measure terms like belief and trust, scientifically difficult terms. Could success simply correlate to the amount of belief and/ or trust we have in our preparation? On some level we know these variables are tantamount to confidence, discipline, and dedication,

201

other difficult concepts to manipulate and measure. Bucket Theory is a hornet's nest of variables.

Then I advanced the specifics of how we would in fact accomplish what we had agreed to do in theory.

First, I asked the team, led by the captains, to study this impending schedule which was nearly the duplicate of the last season 0-8 schedule with one non conference game change.

Second, I asked the team to rate the opponents, select the predictably weakest, and combine that information with our traditional rivalries to select four teams which we should prepare ourselves for 100% mentally. The other four games were to be played with zero mental preparation other than what mental preparation comes from the physical aspects of practice.

"So zero or 100% mental preparation. All or none."

"Yes."

Third, I asked them to try to implant the priority and the importance of winning the four selected from that point on as well as taking a point of view that we will play the other four teams for practice, as if they had called up and asked for a scrimmage for mutual benefit.

"Genius, Coach, that is, if this Bucket Theory holds any water." I giggle.

"There's more."

He must have heard that one before.

Fourth, I pointed out that we would treat the 100% games as we had traditionally greeted all games, i.e., movies, scout report, game plan procedure on Monday, arrange practices to correlate with game plan and scout report, review on Thursday, simulate opponents with scout team during scrimmage, have a final motivational chalk talk 24 hours before game time, etc. For the other four games we would eliminate all of those aspects during the week preceding the game and work to perfect our own offensive and defensive aspects of the game with reference to no opponent.

"So, you hadn't started using 72 Hour Rule yet."

"No. Correct."

"That might be good in some ways—one less confounding variable."

"Right."

I lean forward, anxious to hear results of his experiment and quickly admonish myself for thinking of it as an experiment. But wow! This could have been the experiment of a lifetime for a sport psychologist: defining and manipulating a huge variable, "dynamic psychological energy." I admonish myself again for using a term undefined by science. It's easy to understand how Tom McCullen and so many others followed this man's lead.

The season played itself out basically under those circumstances. In all fairness, I must say that we did not completely recognize the 'backwash' influence of outcomes.

Backwash? Oh no. Another term muddying the waters.

And this, of course, turned out to be a very interesting point, which I will discuss.

I audibly exhale.

But first, to all of our amazement and happiness, the season ended with our winning four games, yes four, tying two others, and only losing two. A quick summary showed that three of the games we prepped for were won, one ended in a tie. We lost two of four games against the strongest teams we did not prep for, but won one and tied another. In addition, the record enabled us to tie for second place in the conference and I was selected as coach of the year by one errant newspaper. Needless to say, the reversal of a completely defeated previous year, last place in the conference to second place, was too big a step for us to make in that time frame as the sequel to this story will show. But, the euphoria for the team was tremendous, to say the least, and one of the more memorable to me of my career.

Also, it was the beginning of me getting smart, for in this area of group dynamics I had learned something big, which saved many teams from disaster, frustration, etc., in the future, to say nothing about myself.

In other words, I learned there was much to the bucket theory, even if amounts of energy in symbolized buckets was not necessarily an accurate explanation. Perhaps it was an amateur example of brainwashing, or a concentration technique projected over a long time span, or a visualization technique in group dynamics, one which involves a self-fulfilling outcome, one without considering the opponent's psyche at the same moment.

Right! There are so many possible explanations. "Coach, regardless, I think you were onto something with Bucket Theory. Those are amazing, well, at least interesting results." He's helping me dial my excitement down a notch.

I did not think I was psychic or that there was some super power intermediating there. But rather I believe the outcome exemplified the organizing and harnessing the power of the combined mental concentration abilities of a group willing to try to use mental energy toward the same goal, and that effort, in fact, enabled us to play games much closer to 100% than when we consciously tried to put all energy into all games.

I open my mouth—

Before we go into any more analysis of what happened in this experiment, let me tell you the story of the sequel, the story of the 1954 season, for the comparison of it and the two preceding seasons does shed additional light on the conclusion.

When we started to organize for the 1954 season, I personally was convinced that our change in preparation had been the reason for the vast improvement in results. I felt we should continue similarly. However, I admit our basic mental set in 1954 was not the same in 1953.

In 1954 we were on a high, in 1953 on a low, to put it crudely. In 1953 we had nothing to lose and in 1954 we had much to lose. So, when I met with our captains, one of which was the same as in 1953, I was not clear in my own mind what I thought we should do. When I proposed to the captains a similar procedure, I got immediate resistance, much stronger than the year before, with good argument, at least sounding good to me. Albeit I believe they were talking to my ego, not my good rational self.

"You thought since you won games in '53, you were a better team in '54 and therefore needed to have higher expectations—put more in the buckets for stronger opponents."

"Correct."

"What did you do?"

I suggested we do the same thing only modify our preparation to include some 25% preparation and try to prep for some stronger teams rather than just the weaker. For we now thought of ourselves as close to number 1, if not number 1, I discovered.

"Hmm. You thought you could possibly win them all, be number 1."

"Yes."

Also I discovered that the team, when reminded of the procedural change, tended to shuck it off as if it had not been too important and that the reality of the thing was their skill improvement. In other words, we are just better than those guys and we can win all our games. Why play around with all this psychology stuff? Why not go out and play them one at a time?

I laugh. The hobgoblin of research minds: not seeing the obvious when it isn't compatible with expectation, or ego. Practitioner minds deal with the same hobgoblin. Maybe all minds deal with the same hobgoblin: pride. Maybe it's too difficult to believe in the power of an abstract notion like dynamic psychological energy or Bucket Theory, at least when other plausible and ego-stroking alternative explanations are available: skill, intelligence, ability, cunning, work ethic. "Who needs mental practice and prep when you're so skilled and tough? This story is beginning to sound like the TCU story, and a bit like a lot of other mental training stories."

"Yes." Coach sets his jaw.

Of course my ego was as big as theirs and I wanted to believe we in fact were that good. The crowning blow to my proposal to do the same thing in 1954 as in 1953 came when we looked at the schedule. It was the same number of games and opponents but the order of the games had been changed. Our first opponent was St. Olaf. St. Olaf was the conference champion in 1953 as well as two successive years previous. St. Olaf was a perennial power in the conference.

The idea of not preparing 100% for the first game in the season because we were saving ourselves for other lesser opponents was impossible to swallow.

The thought of prepping 100% for St. Olaf and the big upset and to prove ourselves the best was much more to our liking. But Coe, another power in the conference, had been moved to the second game. We were to play vs. Coe following our home opener with St. Olaf. I succumbed to the players desires and agreed to go back to the old idea of 'playing them one at a time' and prepping the same for all games. So we entered the 1954 season 'high' and on top of the world with upset on our mind. I did not mention that St. Olaf had defeated us at Northfield in 1953, 60-13, in a no contest sort of game, and of course St. Olaf had been undefeated in conference play and conference champions.

"Oh boy."

"Yes.

Now, with decks cleared, we commenced. We were up for the first game.

The weather was hot, temperature in the 90s. St. Olaf came down from the north and wore wool uniforms. The players were slow and methodical, but confident. We played high keyed, and frenzied. We scored first and were flushed with possible victory. They scored a tying touchdown before half time, 7-7. They scored again in the third quarter, but then, either from overconfidence or fatigue or both, faded. We scored the tying touchdown in the fourth quarter and finished the game with a 13-13 tie. The tie was a terrific moral win for Grinnell. The headlines in the Des Moines Sunday Register carried the story. It was sensational from our point of view. But being a worrier, and particularly after my 1953

206

experience, I could not help but think, how and when were we going to get off the high and how can we prep 100% for Coe?

"You thought you might be overconfident for Coe?"

"Exactly."

"Less than your best effort or focus."

"Yes.

My concern was our 100% Coe prep will mostly be euphoria from St. Olaf or backwash. If that is the case, our 100% prep effort will result in 50% performance, which will not be nearly enough.

"Coach, this term 'backwash'—I assume you mean over-confidence and low effort due to previous success."

"Yes. Well, that and other possibilities."

My mind spins into high gear with the potential for complex, interacting, and confounding variables: overconfidence, complacency, last minute anxiety. "Backwash opens another Pandora's Box of variables, the kind of thing that drives researchers crazy."

"Yes, well, coaches, too.

My premonition turned out to be true. We went to Cedar Rapids, confident on the surface, almost cocky.

We played a night game, which was new to us, against a team which was ready and dedicating a new stadium. We soon found out we were not ready. We knew very early we were in one of those games I had learned to dread so much, a flat performance. Score: 52-0, Coe.

"Oooh. Flat doesn't really capture it." I squint as if I could squeeze a more complete explanation from my brain, something more illuminating than simply "flat" or "over confident." What does "flat" mean in this case? What variables does it encompass? How do they all fit into Bucket Theory?

Crestfallen, frustrated, down hearted, any negative descriptive phrase could not reach the depths my team and I were driven to that evening. To put icing on the cake, the game was televised. Those were early stages of TV, for small college football at least. We were flattered to be on TV before the game.

After, I watched the game replayed for regional viewing on Sunday and Monday nights. I had much opportunity to review the procedures and decisions and facts leading up to the decisions on procedures in a very painful sitting. To say the least, 'our balloon had burst,' and in fact, the season was nearly ruined. I say nearly because psychologically or emotionally the fellows and staff felt the season was already a failure in comparison to the 1953 season.

We did have the power to regroup, reconsider and play out the rest of the games. The results of which were two wins, one more tie, and three more losses. I tried to inject varying emphasis on the remaining games, but I found the damage had been done. It was really impossible to rearrange the team's mental set to get more energy into the buckets than our opponents did on the days we were supposed to perform, or to engender enough mass positive reinforcement for superior performance on a given day. Perhaps it was a good way for me to learn the lesson. I would have preferred to have learned or relearned a different way, but there it is, the sequel to the story, and with it much drama, emotional gamut, and learning.

"I'm sorry, Coach."

He looks away. "Maybe it was the best thing, not at the time, but eventually."

"Because you thought more about Bucket Theory, success in the '53 season compared to the '52 and '54 seasons?"

"Yes. Although, it's a stretch to believe Bucket Theory completely explains it all. If the boys had prepared more appropriately for each contest, without the inflation of ego we all experienced, and the subsequent deflation of ego after the Coe game—"

"Backwash."

"Yes. If we'd internalized our game plan and stuck to it, I can only suggest the outcomes would have been more in our favor, and in my favor."

208

I look for his smile, but it isn't there. He takes a deep breath, and I feel the depth of his commitment to his world of sport, his athletes and their potential for 100% performance.

I hope to tell young coaches about procedures and concepts which should benefit them. Obviously every team is in a group dynamic situation unique to itself. If there are any values here, they must be somehow applicable to situations other than those of our teams of 1952, 1953, and 1954. Our situation was different in each of the three years. In retrospect, I believe the psychological procedures used in 1952 and 1954 were not good for either of those teams, yet they were essentially the same as ones I have seen used for literally hundreds of teams, and I believe they are traditionally used by most sport teams.

"Coach, you sound more and more like a scientist."

He grunts.

"Do you believe when we approach a season without a realistic view of our odds for winning, about our potential for victory, we—Well, in one case we artificially deflate our expectations. In other cases we artificially inflate our expectations. Both cause problems."

"Yes. Many."

"I think we're onto another situation where acceptance—"

He nods, but his eyes show fatigue. I stop speaking. Somehow I know it's not necessary.

After the season of 1954, I quit coaching football and concentrated on basketball. I did try to apply the Bucket Theory to basketball. However, I was not sure enough of its validity and particularly the application of it to basketball, mostly because of the greater numbers of games and the close proximity of the games, even back to back games. So, until late in my career, I did not use the exact principle used in the 1953 football season.

Sometime after 1953, I had the opportunity to attend a coaching school in which the late Bear Bryant was lecturing. I was quite impressed by most of what he preached and enjoyed his

209

humor and knowledge. But on one lecture, he particularly gained my intellect with a discussion of schedule-making and playing.

He explained that it was wise to schedule some very strong teams and also some weak or at least weaker teams. This, as I understood it, was good for Alabama, a team interested in a national ranking and bowl games. National ranking came about easiest with long winning streaks, winning them all; winning them all was easier if you had some 'soft spots' in the schedule.

Following that suggestion was a humorous description of how that was done and I remember having difficulty telling when the Bear was being fictitious or totally honest. I did get the idea, however, that he gave much credence to this idea and that he attempted to control the schedule with regards to quality of opposition and sequential order of opposition as much as possible.

He intimated that mental preparation for the long run was inherent in having teams of varying quality and spaced judiciously throughout the length of the season.

After that exposure I took great interest in studying Alabama schedules. I must say that moving into the modern era, there seemed to be fewer and fewer soft spots in Bear's schedules. However I feel sure he prepared his teams accordingly. I'm sorry I never had the chance to engage him in discussion on the subject, for I am sure I would have been enlightened as to the validity or non validity of my own ideas.

I have developed a theoretical model to explain the application of the Bucket Theory for a team, whose goal is to win every game and whose potential level is considered capable of that, at least when you pair it up theoretically with each opponent on the schedule one on one.

"A no. 1 team."

"Yes."

"And all teams on the schedule are evaluated by coaches."

"Yes.

For the purposes of this model, the teams on the schedule, when rated by your coaching staff on three basic levels—A, B, C, are as follows:

Team	Ranking
1	A
2	B
3	A+
4	B+
5	C
6	C
7	A+
8	B
9	C-
10	B

Most high schools and small college coaches do not have the privilege of making their own schedules and must play schedules given to them by the authorities or the conference to which they belong. These people already alluded to possible explanations of results from the procedures I used applying the Bucket Theory. I claim no real psychological expertise. I think that the maneuvering of the environment as I have described will produce results which are better than other procedures we have seen applied.

I am personally interested in knowing what actually happens or the why's of the results, but I do not think the coach is to know the exact truth.

I stare at the columns and ponder Bucket Theory variables. "Exact truth" might escape us all.

Coaching is a precarious business and techniques which will work are worth much to any coach or any team. The Bucket Theory if applied well to any team will work and work better than the traditional methods of prepping a team.

If there was opportunity to change the order of games, an order more favorable to our chances would be:

Team	Ranking
2	B
5	C
1	A
8	B
6	C
3	A+
4	B+
9	C-
7	A+
10	B

The general pattern looks like B-C-A-B-C-A.

The playing of the varying qualities of the opposition in this manner, middle strength, weaker, stronger, lends itself to less backwash if you are upset.

"You're planning on a loss?"

"No. Preparing for, not planning on. In the unfortunate situation of a loss to a B team, low morale could be the result. Even with low morale, 50% performance might be sufficient to win against a C team, the next opponent. In the unfortunate situation of being upset by a C team, morale might be at a very low point and a loss to an A team, the next opponent, might be predictable and acceptable. But, the squad might be in the 'nothing to lose' state of mind going into it, more relaxed and possibly—this would be predicted and handled skillfully by leadership—the team might produce closer to 100%, that is, if the coach's explanations came into play."

"Explanations?"

"If the team believed the loss to a C Team was due to being 'fat in the head,' they would know they can turn it around. It's a case of visualizing and hard practice. If leadership let's the players believe they are not as good as they thought they were, you might have a problem on your hands."

"You're using Attribution Theory now."

"As you know, I don't believe it matters what you call it—the name of it. You don't have to name something for it to be true. It is what I believe has happened often, and to my dismay. I have become aware of the mechanisms causing the various outcomes: less than 100% performance due to athletes' lack of concentration and internalization of their visualization; less than 100% performance due to being fat in the head. Whatever the reason, if there is not a high effort on their part to visualize, thereby internalizing the outcome they want to see, there will be a drop in the quality of performance."

"So however you do it, or they do it, they need to be motivated to visualize the goal until it's internalized. If possible, mix up the quality of opponents to obtain the pattern of B-C-A to minimize backwash. That's the ideal to strive for, if you have control over your schedule?"

"Yes.

The variation decreases the pressure felt by the team throughout the season. The principle advantage of this technique is to achieve a total conscious picture of the entire season by the squad which, when internalized, causes the squad to play with less conscious buildup, that is, more relaxed, but efficient. After the schedule is set, we could make the plan for % emphasis for the total season.

It can be seen that we will need three levels of mental preparation. We can call them ABC to match the opponents rating. The level of preparation matching the opponents rating needs necessarily to be high enough to insure better performance than that anticipated by the opposition. Now all we need to do is to arrange three types of mental preparation schedules and apply them correspondingly.

I suggest following these principles. For the A games, orient your mental preparations specifically toward the opposition. For the C games orient your mental preparations on improvement of aspects of your own game, defense, offense—whatever needs improvement or emphasis based on your experience in this

213

particular season. For the B games you are in between. Use your judgment as to whether the game deserves more opponent orientation or your own team orientation. A B+ team perhaps needs more orientation toward the opponent.

This system therefore enables you to have flexibility after the season begins to unfold. Say a C rated team begins to roll and its rating might improve by the time you play. You change your mental prep plan.

I said change the plan not upgrade it to B or A. It is important to understand that plan C mental preparation is just as valid and important to the whole scheme of things as A. And the real important point of this whole concept is that the team thoroughly knows the entire schedule at the onset of the season and understands how the procedure will function, including changing mental preparation plans in the middle of the stream.

Give them something to believe in.

If this initial visualization is accomplished well and given time for what I will call internalization, that is, thoroughly digested mentally and placed into the subconscious, I believe the team will perform as a group or produce at the approximate expected level.

The power of belief. Some benefits from physical training can be obtained with or without belief in the methods. I believe the same is true about mental training. BUT, what happens when you add belief in the methods used? What if you add *strong* belief in the methods used? Why would belief in the methods make a difference if the athletes showed discipline anyway?

I can see many questions you will ask, one of which is 'Why?' to my last statement.

If you only knew, or, maybe you know. I'm confused as to what I need to say out loud.

We played quite well on days when we had zero mental preparation. We won one and tied one and played pretty well in the two losses. One factor is the backwash, that is, after we had won one of two, the positive reinforcement carried over into the week of no conscious preparation and so necessarily had an effect on motivation.

"So 'backwash' can have a positive effect, too?" I ask.

"Yes.

The other factor seemed to be the positive effect of zero mental preparation to cause greater relaxation and less tension during the week of practice as well as in the games themselves, thereby resulting in performance which was judged by many as superior to some of the performances we had with 100% preparation.

I shake my head in amazement. "There's a tremendous loss of potential when coaches and sport psychologists don't work together, don't you think?" He isn't listening. I sigh. "And so many variables."

There are many things occurring in these situations, none the least is the 40-50 different people combining to make a team.

Maybe he was listening.

To assume a coach can control their environment and their thinking with respect to emphasis placed on a game may be farfetched. Since I have had the opportunity to try these techniques and observe others doing similarly, I do believe the coach can organize and control to a great extent the productivity of a group of athletes. I think the factors which we have talked about which are most important are:

(1) The onset examination and evaluation of the schedule, game by game, by the coaching staff and by the team led by the coaching staff.

I need to add that by onset I mean preseason. It will not work after the season has begun. And secondly, the onset examination and evaluation should be thorough. I know this from experience and I believe it refers to the principle of Firstness. For any given season, athletes are already primed from the past and are looking forward to a climax, the season, and, like learning anything, the things learned first are learned best. Thus, this work internalizes the schedule analysis, the strengths, weaknesses, goals, and imagined necessities, if this procedure is followed before the season begins.

Also in this internalization is the concept of the length of season, 'Rose Bowls,' conference playoffs, NCAA playoffs, state championships, district championships or otherwise. If those goals are distinctly internalized they will be much more likely to actually materialize than if the end is left open and you play using the traditional one-at-a-time basis.

"I agree. You can tell when a team made a plan to compete in the post season versus not. It's like, 'Now what?' They almost look lost. They might ride out a high they were on after making it that far, like momentum—positive backwash—but if the playoffs are not immediately played, their mindset needs to be reestablished— the power of Firstness lost—and Bucket Theory."

"Correct. Without a plan, no internalizing of goals and outcomes, preparation would be minimal, 50% at best.

(2) The second point refers to thoroughness. Thoroughness means getting all the possibilities out on the table, the possibility of changing ratings, possibility of injuries, possibilities of bad weather, and possibilities of bad luck, in other words, negative possibilities as well as positive, and the development of a rational possible season game plan with goals which all concerned know and have time to internalize.

I love it that Coach includes coping techniques, well supported mental training for enhanced resilience, not to mention acceptance.

Coach smiles before continuing.

Following the ONSET mental preparation, the coaching staff can, with or without the squad's assistance, set up the weekly mental prep plan and carry it out through the season. Weekly plans in fact positively reinforce the original seasonal game plan which essentially maximizes group positive reinforcement on a rational possible basis. In other words, the team should feel the plan is rational, sincere, and possible, the last being the most important.

They really must believe in it, or at least trust it, which promotes discipline and dedication to the plan. Trust is fundamentally important.

If they do feel that way, they will play with reckless abandon, yet controlled, and with considerably less fear of failure syndrome, which in my opinion is the cause of most choked or flat games played by any team.

"And there's that." Such a huge statement. It places Coach's Bucket Theory firmly in the wide array of variables predicting 100% performance. "Interesting stuff, Coach. Bucket Theory definitely utilizes the power of trust. But researchers have a hard time—" My voice trails off as I notice his jaw is set, his countenance firm. He's on a roll with his goal in sight. "Sorry."

Another question which bothered me regarding this total problem is why does the traditional 'game by game' procedure produce such varying results? I have heard coaches advise their players specifically as if individual players' mental set must be consciously arranged by the individual and if enough players do in fact succeed in achieving proper attitude then the results will be good. There will not be flat performances, but always near 100% performance.

I speak, but I hear Dr. Rotella's voice: "Train versus Trust. We achieve much by adopting a training or practice mindset: questioning, criticizing, analyzing, until game time. Performance depends much more on our ability to trust. By the time it's time to trust, we're experts on training, seeking out and analyzing error, a process which erodes trust when we need it most."

A "consciously arranged" mindset sounds like a training mindset, purposeful, analytical, calculated, sometimes overly so. Whereas 100% performance depends on "reckless abandon, yet controlled, less fear of failure": trust.

I feel light and giddy, sensations arriving the moment I realize I'm standing on the shoulders of giants. I'm enlightened by two very experienced professionals, mentors, both teachers and coaches, both respected in their own right, in their own eras and in their own circles of influence, in one case, the sport elite, in the other, underdogs of small college athletics, both saying the same thing, using different language, but with the same meaning, suggesting there's a mindset for practice and a mindset for performance. The trick, we all know, is mastering both, and transitioning from one to the other.

"I'm glad you are seeing it."

I jump in surprise.

"You didn't think I could hear your thoughts?"

My eyes widen as he smiles with a hint of pain curling his lips at the edges.

He asks, "Do you mind if I continue on to a slightly different business?"

"No. Of course not." I revel in the joy of discovery and synthesis; Coach stops for nothing.

Also I have seen and heard coaches admonish their teams or individuals to not get 'fat in the head' after victories or strings of victories as if a conscious knowledge that too much success follows a period of realization in concentration and that that period often lasts long enough to include the next game and the so called fat in the head syndrome from the last game or series of games causes failure, less than required % of effort to win or even play well.

"So you're suggesting too much success—winning—can create a loss of concerted effort, as if their success says they don't have to go back to the training mindset. They can proceed in practice with 'reckless abandon' and no 'fear of failure,' which actually makes them underprepared for the next game?"

"Yes."

"So, you could say too little fear is not good. Too much fear is not good." Now that I know he's reading my thoughts, I think, "Some fear is juuust right, like porridge." I chuckle to myself.

"You're smarter than you look, Goldilocks."

"Thank you, Coach." I'm all grins. This is fun, and a bit disconcerting!

He adds, "It's really negative thoughts and distraction due to negative thoughts that cause a loss of confidence and concentration."

So true.

His eyes glaze over. "Some of anything might not be all bad." I think he's speaking of fear.

"More water, Coach?" His lips look dry and cracked. His face more ashen. I stand up to fill his glass.

He says, "Most people believe fear of failure— Because this business of fear is the most important in sport, at least for the athletes I've had the honor of coaching, it is the most important. It isn't— They don't— It isn't so much fear of failure as it is, possibly fear of getting hurt or— It's a small— It's a lighter person running into a larger, heavier person. Fear is something young men are not likely to reveal to you. It's— There are many different reasons for— Different kinds of fear. I like this idea of your advisor's— Trust. That's why it was extremely important for us to stick to the game plan, at least close to 100% of the time. Trust the game plan, show we were confident in our mission."

Yes! Inspire and maintain trust in the process.

"And if we could encourage visual imagery using the 72 Hour Rule and Firstness and otherwise focus our attention and energy in the correct amount, mostly to move these kids from fearful to not so fearful category. Just knowing, being exposed to the way things are, and, of course, the way we want things to be in visualization, there's a calming effect without taking away desire."

Coach leans back and pulls up the blanket. I keep standing, listening, thinking he is about to call it a day, enthralled by his insights. His theories are coming together. Even if they aren't based in science, solid science, I can see how Bucket Theory fits into sport psychology theory, how 72 Hour Rule, Firstness, Discipline, and Visual Imagery work together toward producing trust and 100% performance, catalyzed by the Umbrella's overarching presence, even if the connections form an ethereal web of—

And then of course we are all familiar with Grantland Rice's immortal line, 'It's not whether you win or lose, it's how you play the game,' and the analysis of games according to this precept. Rice's 'how you play the game' is the 100% effort, for coaches who like that phrase, for excellence.

I sit back down with a phluff, as if his spirit nudged me back into the soft embrace of the sofa.

Emily comes in to refill his water glass.

We hear in the sports pages following professional or college games in pregame shows, post game shows the analysis and explanation of the cause and affect of all possible factors explaining the losses especially and you hear constantly the admission by coaches that their team just did not play well or that so and so and so and so had a bad day. Those are the flat days I speak of. Those are the days when the player, the coach and anyone really close to the team knows that the team is not 'up to par,' not excellent as Grantland Rice said, and often as not it may be when the team won the game, so the enigma goes on. I suppose in a way it is best that it does for it adds that imponderable question about each contest making it a mystery and so interesting for the fans and the players, as they say, we just have to wait to see how it comes out.

The ethereal web and its allure.

From the coach's stand point I can testify that I would have given anything to be sure that when all games my teams were playing were over we could in reality say we really did play the game up to our potential. I went through many a game with many a team in which I knew better than anyone else that was not the case, that had been a driving motivation in my life since I decided to devote my life to coaching young men to achieve.

The depth of his commitment to his athletes leaves me in awe and reverence and openness. I want more than ever to reveal the genius of his ideas, no matter how ethereal. Our minds fuse and flutter with the fundamental notions of fear, acceptance, trust, dedication, motivation, and the list goes on. Despite the infinite possibilities within the web, I know the concepts of acceptance and trust are fundamental to Bucket Theory and 100% performance. They wind throughout the unique patterns of human individuality, hold the web together, and make it possible for athletes to persevere through adversity. They make 100% performance possible.

I recently watched the AFL playoff game between the Dolphins and the San Diego Chargers. Two fine teams playing each other in the Orange Bowl.

I find it easy to come back to his words, his story, our minds now harmonizing, not bumping and thumping.

The game was not much of a game from the spectators' point of view because Miami won easily. It was a game that was not close or that did not include the visual closing of the difference in the score in the last quarter, for it was a game from my point of view as a coach that one team was terribly flat at the very time when I'm sure they wanted the opposite to be true, it was a game for the cynics about professional football to point their suspicious fingers at and wonder if it was not fixed.

It was a game in which although a neutral fan and one with considerable experience could only be empathetic with both Coach Coryell and his players from San Diego because unless it was fixed, which I do not believe, it had to be the epitome of frustration for a fine group of athletes who had earned the position in the playoffs with excellent play game after game. I wondered and still wonder what were the factors that caused them to be flat on that Sunday.

Me, too. Infinite explanations. Mysteries entangled in mysteries, ones we may never solve. Suddenly I'm tired, very tired. But I sense energy remaining in his voice, a home stretch, fourth quarter, final seconds kind of intensity, and I grab onto it. Together, we will bring our conversation to a close.

Chapter VIII
Coach's *Conclusion*

A summary of the core of this discussion includes the psychological concepts which apply both to individual learning and efficiency and group learning and efficiency. In my quest for wisdom particularly in the psychological area of team sports, the concepts enumerated and discussed here were the ones which gradually became known and believed to be true through experience in coaching over 100 different teams, mostly in small college competition, but including one stint of coaching a European Club, which was semiprofessional.

A summary of the information here includes six different concepts and resulting advice for aspiring coaches.

"—and sport psychologists."

He winks.

They are:

(1) the Umbrella or development of a continuing environmental climate of positivity which specifically implies good motivational goals, an organized pecking order based on seniority, representative leadership from captains, definite system of advancement, participation, and reward, plus the use of the challenge as the motivational goal.

"The importance of positive reinforcement and giving athletes opportunities for mastery and control is and will probably remain steadfast in education, psychology, motor learning, and sport psychology. Your advice to 'reinforce lesser players' and criticize 'technique not personality' might be less studied per se, but is noteworthy, particularly in relation to another concept I observed under your Umbrella, an old concept, one that disappeared from research literature years ago, but didn't disappear from your coaching approach. You know what I'm about to say. The concept is "acceptance," or having basic respect for athletes regardless of their strengths and weaknesses, successes or failures. Acceptance is

222

caring about your athletes 'win or lose.' Whether you realized it or not, I believe acceptance was a key variable in coaching the difference between 100% and flat. And, call me picky or politically correct, but I love your use of the word 'challenge.'" I smile.

"No old dog?"

"Ha! No. Although, you do remind me of my chocolate Lab, Mocha."

"I thought I reminded you of Rotella, the wise one. Now I'm an old dog?"

"Can't explain my brain, Coach. But, when Mocha grew older, she still ran as fast as she could after squirrels and rabbits. She'd come back, breathing hard. It was like she couldn't help herself."

Coach is breathing hard, too. But he's moved closer to the edge of his seat. "So you forgive me for comparing you to a horse?"

I laugh. "Of course," of course. I wonder if he remembers Mr. Ed.

He laughs before he continues. He remembers Mr. Ed.

"The acceptance business is good—not something I studied or wrote about." He hesitates. "If you write about it so people can understand, you may have— It may amount to something, so coaches don't look at it as psycho bologna." Coach leans forward. "The Xs and Os will always be what they talk about most." He seems to ponder a moment before adding, "I might experiment with it more."

I think he spotted a squirrel.

(2) Firstness or the recognition that initial quality exposure is an absolute necessity for each season for the development of good techniques, habits and the best possible execution of tactical patterns. The obvious follow up is organizing the early portion of the season to conform to this concept.

"Clearly there is research to support the rule and the exceptions we talked about, but I don't know if we'll ever see it tested in the field like you did. Too difficult. Regardless, I like Firstness."

"Yes. I do, too."

Coach clears his throat.

(3) Visual imagery or recognition that other than Firstness Concept, the concept that athletes learn best from is visual imagery as compared to verbal and therefore it is imperative that seasonal planning include methodology which emphasizes the visual techniques as much as possible. This concept is universal as far as timing is concerned as compared to the Firstness Concept.

"Fascinating, Coach. You were such a pioneer!"

The outer edges of his mouth rise ever so slightly.

"There are many lines of research crossing here. I'm partial to the ones suggesting athletes are best left to imagine the details of their own paths to success. Choose individual and group goals and make a plan to capture them, including contingency plans for potential setbacks, mistakes, and obstacles. Then practice restraint."

"Yes."

"Fight the urge to continually verbalize how to do it with more and more detail, especially after the opportunity for Firstness is past." I smile at Coach. "You shined the light on the issue of visual v. verbal. When it comes to verbal instruction, especially in the later stages of a season, less is more."

I notice Coach staring, steadily and thoughtfully. He might be reminiscing the many hours he spent guiding athletes through visualization. He blinks twice and looks my way as I continue.

"Verbal instruction has the potential to interrupt flow, interfere with automatic motor tasks, and increase tension, sabotaging a good effort and 100% performance. Athletes who visualize their own way to obtaining their goals feel great joy in 100% performance. The outcome will be the best you can obtain."

"Couldn't have said it better myself," he says with a smile.

We share another moment of connection, beyond science and reason. I sense his pleasure.

Coach smiles, clears his throat and says, "72 Hour game plan."

I look down at my notes. "Coach, did you skip Discipline?"

"Discipline. Oh yes. Discipline." He looks at his manuscript.

"(4) Discipline." He hesitates.

"Not your fondest memories?"

"Hm. Well— Maybe—"

"Freudian?" I smile.

"Well, yes, I suppose, of all the— It happens to be— It's a very important concept, not one to forget." He clears his throat again. "It is— Simply stated— Discipline is a combination of a willingness to repeat skills, strategies, preparation, whatever is necessary to further a team or individual toward success or to the point of conditioning the mind and body for success, and secondly, the amount of control a coach has over such willingness."

"Coach, sounds like you've memorized your definition."

He straightens and says, "Yes. Well— But— That would be— Discipline."

"Ahh." I laugh.

"It's important— Such that— I believe no skill, strategy or game plan is as important. I have been on both sides. On both sides, I wish— If only discipline could be gained with a simple verbal order."

We sit in silence for a moment. I realize he's experienced discipline from a wide range of perspectives: a child and a parent, a student and a teacher, an athlete and a coach, a soldier and an officer.

He shuffles the pages of his manuscript and continues to speak as if lecturing. "In all cases, the athlete must possess what we call a 'good attitude,' which means a strong positive commitment to do whatever is necessary, for as long as necessary, to accomplish whatever goals he has visualized. Firstness, Imagery, 72 Hour Rule, and Bucket Theory are not effective without discipline. And discipline is not possible without respect."

"Or fear. Earlier, didn't you say respect or fear?"

He looks up. "Respect or fear. Yes." He seems distant and speaks slower than usual. "Or both. I don't believe— We— It's possible to have a mixture of both to sufficiently overcome a person's natural desire to avoid the difficult mental and physical work necessary for success."

"To persevere and hold firm to the plan."

"Yes."

I fight the urge to reiterate the connections between respect and acceptance, his Umbrella, high morale, and the importance of these variables to 100% performance.

"Yes," he says. "The foundation for good team morale is respect, mutual respect, which is the key to good discipline and therefore, highest proficiency, 100% performance."

"So discipline can be motivated by fear and/or respect; either way, a team will experience some degree of success."

"Yes. Discipline leads to success, albeit limited if the motive is fear: fear of failure, injury, punishment."

"And if high team morale is a goal—" I ponder theoretical lines of causation: a respectful environment leading to greater discipline, discipline leading to success and high team morale. Or does respectful environment lead to high morale, which leads to discipline and success? The variables tumble together in my mind. I wonder how fear changes the process and outcome. Coach says discipline based on fear limits success. But even with an infinite number of ways to measure success, I'm not sure how we measure 100% performance. Coach's Umbrella, his years of experience, tip the scales toward fostering respect, not fear. An accepting environment lessens fear of failure. I want to believe mutual respect brings out the best athletes and coaches have to give. But fear can be a powerful motivator. Might a coach use the power of fear like an officer on the battlefield—to motivate soldiers to their maximum effort? Fight for honor. Fight for life. I look at Coach and remember he has been on the battlefield, figuratively and literally. He's experienced the difference in process and outcome and believes in the superior efficacy of respect over fear, at least when it comes to team and individual discipline and his scholar-athletes' potential for 100% performance.

I feel the familiar exhilaration of an investigator on the trail of insight leading to powerful research questions. Answers depend upon research.

Or are they in front of me? Am I discounting years of experience, rejecting the facts of Coach's "real world?"

I consider drawing a new diagram with all the variables, returning to the library to cast my net more broadly. I'm so tired. Maybe all I need to do is think this through again, examine the causal connections again.

I've been staring at Coach, but now he comes into focus. He drops and narrows his gaze at me, instantly reminding me that real life variables seldom fall neatly into place to answer questions and explain outcomes. Life is complex and mysterious. Certainty is elusive at best. However the connections line up in future research, I can't deny high morale, discipline, and respect sound and feel like a recipe for 100% performance, the best athletes can give. This awareness might be the best I can do today.

I take a deep breath and say, "The concept of discipline is complex. So many interrelated variables. Even *definitions* vary."

"That's a problem for you, Professor Waite."

For an entire research community, I think. I draw a star in the margin next to my notes on discipline, a reminder to explore these questions with a clearer head.

(5) 72 hour game plan or a group dynamic concept which indicates that a team of athletes applying deep mental concentration on a visual or verbally presented plan approximately three days before game time will in fact enable the team to produce considerably closer to 100% efficiency on game day than the team using other traditional methods, the other methods principally varying in the timing of the concentration.

"This is an idea requiring trust on your part as coach, don't you think? Trust and respect for your athletes."

"So many times I've broken that rule."

"Yet, you're sticking by it?"

"It's a good one. Timing might vary from sport to sport or be impossible in some sports due to tight schedules and more games being played, but that's where more experimentation is necessary."

"More research."

"That, too."

I smile.

"If they play smart, follow the plan. They don't always play smart— When Cornell— I believe it was 1964—"

"Coach. I can see the finish line. Bucket Theory."

"Yes." His voice cracks. He swallows hard and clears his throat. "Bucket Theory."

The adrenaline surge from approaching the finish line must be wearing off. He's tired, maybe exhausted. As he takes a drink of water with shaky hands, he looks up at me. The twinkle reappears. I believe once again he's embracing, even enjoying the moment of challenge. He's striving to stay in flow, reaching for his 100%. He clears his throat again and again before continuing.

(6) Bucket Theory, or the seasonal planning concentration or total season mental planning is a concept bearing the cliche 2+2=5, and it states that a group of athletes prep a prescribed way for a common season if they are directed to or challenged to evaluate the opponents, classify them by estimating strength. It desires coming up with a seasonal game plan which in fact predicts the relative energy expenditure of their team for each effort. This mental concentration work will in fact set psychological goals for the team which will be fulfilled better than the more traditional technique generally identified by the cliche 'play them one at a time.' The point of this system, if done with enthusiasm, the positive reinforcement from the efforts will result in performance better than usual or 2+2=5.

Coach pauses. He's not moving. I panic. Is he ill? Is he breathing? Certainly he won't— *I* won't stoop so low. Coach can't expire while speaking his final words like some Hollywood drama.

"Coach!" He jumps. I jump. I calm my voice before saying, "Coach, this one, I don't think has a chance either. I don't think Bucket Theory can be tested scientifically."

He moves. His hands tremble. He slowly reaches for the water glass at his side, the glass he just put down. I lean forward and help him raise it to his lips.

"So many variables, tough variables to measure and control."

Together we place the glass back onto the table.

He leans toward me and looks into my eyes. "Admit it." His words rumble over the gravel in his throat as his tone reaches a new level of low. "You like it."

I smile and breathe easier. "I do. But, I bet I like it for different reasons than you." I'm tweaking him, prodding him at his most vulnerable.

He squeezes his eyes into two tight lines. His body sways as he straightens.

I like Bucket Theory. I like all of his ideas, because they are compatible with acceptance.

His eyes widen. "It's not only a problem of acceptance."

"I suppose not," I say. "But it's my biggest hammer."

I feel his subconscious push. It's not gentle. It turns into a solid shaking. And, he's the tired one! He's looking at me, metaphysically challenging me. I take off my glasses and rub my eyes. When I put my glasses back on, I look directly at him and begin thinking out loud.

"I like Bucket Theory—maybe more than the others—because it *requires* acceptance. It wouldn't work without acceptance. As you painfully know, in my mind, all things relate to acceptance or a lack there of. But, acceptance is particularly relevant to Bucket Theory because when coaches and athletes are more accepting, they have a greater capacity to bring reality into their minds unaltered by things like ego, judgment, or emotion. They see more clearly—a loss or a mistake—because their worth isn't riding in the balance. They're not so stressed or scared when faced with challenges. Naturally they see challenges more clearly, more realistically."

I raise my forefinger on my right hand. "Team A is a tough opponent. For Bucket Theory to work, you have to accept this and all that it means." I raise my forefinger on my left hand. "Team C is not a tough opponent. You have to accept this, too. You can't allow 'baggage' from previous encounters to cloud judgment or change game plans, lower morale after losing or 'fatten heads' after winning."

"Backwash."

"Yes!"

I open my palms toward him. "If you use Bucket Theory, you lay it all out there, talk about it, hold nothing back. It's about acceptance and appropriate responses to knowledge obtained from the process of acceptance. Team morale and confidence stay higher despite losses, because, in a way, losses or stumbles along the way, are part of the plan, a plan admitting no team or individual is perfect. 100% performance relies on acceptance. Oh my gosh. Here's a new concept: *team acceptance*, basic respect for fellow members of a team no matter what the score—so to speak—literally and figuratively. Why not?"

His expression doesn't change, which, I quickly decide is a good thing.

"I'm not saying players have to be best friends or *embrace* mistakes. It's a commitment to reality without judgment, which promotes a basic level of respect, acceptance of who they are and what they're about despite weaknesses and mistakes. There's less conflict and tension. Players work on appropriate skills and choose appropriate starters and leaders, raising overall confidence and trust in what they are doing—all so important to Bucket Theory. The team would more readily be on board with 'positively reinforcing lesser players' and 'criticizing techniques not personalities.' They'll make better captains. You were so ahead of this one, Coach! Team acceptance, a basic level of respect for one another 'win or lose,' could be a team goal right along with buying into Bucket Theory. 100% performance is possible with Bucket Theory—probably the least scientifically supported of all! If you win more than you predict, icing on the cake. 2+2=5! And of course you accept the true reasons for success or failure, not what your ego tells you in an effort to protect itself or build itself up. Success—or should I say 110% performance—"

Coach laughs.

"2+2=110!" I laugh, too. "Admit it. You know it's true. 100% performance depends on Bucket Theory and Bucket Theory depends on acceptance."

He's still chuckling.

"I just wish you'd been able to test Bucket Theory more." I inhale sharply. Agh! What did I just say? It sounds suspiciously like respect for his methods, the use of experiments cluttered with confounding variables and alternative hypotheses. Coach looks pleased. He's shaking his head up and down, smiling, now laughing. My eyes roll back.

He startles me when he slaps both legs and exclaims, "*Team acceptance*. I like it. An improvement made to Bucket Theory by taking focus off outcomes. It might reduce this business of anxiety."

"Yes! Let's find out! We could use a pre/post design. Measure competitive state and trait anxiety, achievement motivation, self-efficacy, and self-acceptance. We'll design a new instrument to measure team acceptance. If the team buys into Bucket Theory— Measuring belief will be challenging. The power of belief on its own might explain success with Bucket Theory. But if the team does buy into Bucket Theory, they'll do their best, a pre calculated and visualized 'best' in all situations. Or another way to put it: 100% performance! Oh jeez. So many alternative hypotheses: size of team, home team or away, new coach or veteran, experimenter effect. So many variables. Everyone, or at least key players must trust and take ownership. That's where senior leadership—"

Coach is laughing loudly now. "You have a much bigger—"

"Hammer!" I exclaim.

His eyes light up. "I was going to say research study!"

We laugh like children, eventually smiling, breathing slower, and shaking our heads in wonder. Coach appears enthused with energy from our revelations and I'm suddenly overwhelmed with respect for his legacy, not only his theories and ideas, but the seed and spark of creativity, leadership, achievement motivation, a basic respect and fondness for others, confidence, perseverance, and so much more, living on through his family and the athletes he coached.

He looks at me and I at him. I lean forward and reach out with my hands. He places his in mine. They feel cool and rough. I wrap my fingers around them and squeeze. He squeezes back. We're holding on to our moment together, knowing it's time to conclude, like recovery at the end of an exhausting workout. It's time to call it a day, a very long, phenomenal day.

In the moment before it becomes awkward—just as I think it might become awkward sitting so close and holding hands—Coach doesn't seem bothered. He straightens and says, "I need to make final comments." I straighten, too. He inhales noisily and releases my hands to arrange the papers in his lap as if restarting his lecture. When they're squared away, he says,

The general message is that these concepts applied well should produce a team of well trained athletes regardless of the sport involved with a minimum number of less than potential performances, and in fact a maximum of near 100% efforts.

Interspersed throughout this discussion are anecdotes. They are there to provide evidence for the concepts being discussed. They are all true stories of my teams. The facts are taken essentially from memory and sparse small college official sports records. The names of persons, teams, and schools are as accurate as memory allows. I would like to include all the names of the players involved in all games. The ones I used were the principle characters as I remembered them particularly in regard to the points being made.

I feel the need to state similar remarks and jot down a note to do so.

He lifts his hand.

One last point. I feel a great personal debt to all the young men who I have had the privilege of coaching. Like having hundreds of sons—I feel enriched. The concepts reported here are but a small part of what I have learned from them and from their reactions to the various situations which I was able to observe them in.

Silence fills the room.

"Coach, you're known for your never-ending stories. This can't be the end."

"Well— Yes, it can." His face, grim with seriousness, has lost all color now. "I found my way. There are new ways, more intelligent ways to tell the story of it and it probably needs to be continually rewritten for the current mentality. I probably would write it again today in much the same way. That's why it's up to you to take this business and make something new of it."

"Coach, when you— When a person connects with, and is touched by, and touches so many people in such profound ways—" Tears fill my eyes and my throat tightens. I swallow hard and take a slow, deep breath. "As long as there's respect for one another, the learning never ends, does it? Life as you know and love it continues."

"It does. We do. We learn and relearn as best we can. At this moment I'm convinced of the basic truths in the premises of this book. Tomorrow will bring new revelations."

"No matter what happens to the ideas in this book, you connected with the young people you coached. Each one was a gift to you, but you gave each one a gift, too, something special."

"You don't want to do the same?"

"I do. But I'm searching for answers beyond one group or one individual. I think research will lead to the general rule rather than the exception. I think it can reach more people. Now I'm convinced both approaches are necessary to prove the existence of each rule, the truths that touch us." I look Coach in the eyes. "It takes courage to learn by real life experimentation and to write about it without research support."

He seems to mentally drift before saying, "The Scholar-athletes at Grinnell College were a different bunch."

"They needed someone like you to respect them, accept them, and learn from them, learn how to coach them. You did that. When it comes to an individual or a group, the concepts developed through scientific research are just part of the picture. It's like saying, 'Visualize for 15 minutes every day because research says so.' Some scholar-athletes will never visualize at all because 15 minutes seems overwhelming. Some will visualize for 30 minutes because if 15 is good, 30 must be better. Each individual and each team is so different, how can a coach know what to say or do? In one era the rousing fight talk works. The next era it's laughed at. Research can't be ahead of the best coach, a coach in tune with changes as they happen, with individuals and unique athletes changing by the minute."

"But, research— You— Science has a place. In my early years, I didn't know shit from Shinola. Faux pas after faux pax I made due to my ignorance and ego. I read what I could. Even if I had known exactly what to read, I probably wouldn't have understood it. That's your job, to gather and communicate information so others can understand it. *The Inner Game* filled me with ideas and helped me in positive ways because I understood it and it made sense to me." He paused. "Write your version of truth. You have research to guide you, data. They tell a magnificent story, too. Make it interesting and helpful and understandable."

"Here we are, the practitioner and the researcher, expressing respect for each other."

"I'm not certain I'd go that far." His eyes glitter like a sparkler as he suppresses a grin.

I laugh out loud and purse my lips before saying, "We need each other, don't we? We validate each other, enrich each other. It's too bad it doesn't happen more often."

"Practitioners talking with researchers?"

"Yes. Or professors *being* practitioners or practitioners *being* professors."

He pulls at his chin. "I think you're describing physical education and athletics at Grinnell College."

"I'm concerned it won't be long before coaches will only coach and teachers will only teach, even at Grinnell College. What is it about academia and athletics? What makes them such adversaries?"

"Winning, I suppose. So many academicians see coaches as all about winning contests, not about intellectual development." He pauses before saying, "Sometimes we are wrapped up in the winning."

"The best ones get it."

"Yes. The best ones— The best ones on both sides get it."

He arranges his blanket with trembling hands and looks at me. The twinkle catches my eye as he smiles. He asks, "Do you have what you need?"

I frown and shake my head not so much to say "no" as to say "never." I grit my teeth and feel fear creeping back in.

This time he extends his hands. Mine are cold and clammy. He takes them, squeezes them. I squeeze back. He says, "We can't rid ourselves— We don't want to completely cure ourselves of fear. We can't. We're human. We learn to deal with it, use it, accept it." He winks. "Maybe accept it first."

I smile at Coach as his quiet and calm become mine.

Post Game Commentary

Coach Pfitsch tackled big, tough questions like he learned to tackle big, tough football players, with 100% performance, no matter what the outcome. He tackled the kind of questions scholars have in their hearts and minds when they enter graduate school, the kind of difficult questions often left on the drawing board, questions abandoned due to "unmeasurable concepts" and "uncontrollable variables," questions that may never be answered using scientific methods.

You won't find Coach Pfitsch's theories in a textbook. His ideas were raw, constantly evolving, and "out there." In many ways, research wasn't there to guide him and others like him: true pioneers. I realize that's the definition of a pioneer, someone who courageously goes forth without prior knowledge or certainty.

Being a pioneer agreed with John Pfitsch. He spent 50 years challenging himself and others, gaining comfort from learning and knowing what he knew in the moment. Yet, when I came along, he accepted data with interest and eagerness. If science had disproved his theories, I think he would have shrugged his shoulders and changed his practice to test new theory. If revised practices proved unsuccessful, he would have changed them again.

He put acceptance into practice, the kind of acceptance that came from his core, a core influenced by parents and coaches who modeled acceptance and ultimately placed respect and love above winning. Maybe it came from experiencing the worst a world can throw at a person, a world at war, feeling a need to move on, to live the remainder of life to the fullest. Fact is, science will always have a difficult time keeping up with the likes of Coach John Pfitsch.

Besides the personal gratification from the pursuit of answers, I believe John Pfitsch took satisfaction from knowing he modeled a scholarly attitude for the young people he cared so much about, his scholar-athletes. If you spent any time with him at all, you saw the wonder in his eyes—the twinkle—the desire to constantly strive and learn, like my Alaskan Malamute in a frenzy of digging. You could almost hear her say between pants and pawfuls, "It's here somewhere. I know it is. I know it is." Sorry, Coach, for one more animal metaphor. It truly doesn't do justice to the excitement you must have felt striving with and watching scholar-athletes, colleagues, and beloved family members experience their own 100% performance.

Coach's son, Bill, said, "His preeminent quality was his love of people." And yes, with children at home, time and energy for them was sacrificed or kept in precarious balance. No doubt, his love for others was his biggest hammer. Caring about people, win or lose, his love for Emily, his children, their children, and their love for others might be his greatest legacy.

Coach might not have had our names on the tip of his tongue as we entered the room, but he reacted with joy upon seeing us. He remembered details of our lives. He often remembered what was on my mind the last time we talked. He listened as well as he told a story, maybe not as often or as long, but as well. He listened more as the years went by. He listened more to me after he was gone, in my imagination. My sweet revenge made us both smile.

Coach spent the last years of his life fighting a number of serious health concerns, conditions that would have undoubtedly brought down others long before they brought down his tough-minded spirit. After seeing him battle back from life-threatening infection and multiple surgeries, his body must have given him a "last call."

He stopped attending Grinnell College events. He had good days and bad days. I began to panic. How would I write the book —his book—after he was gone? I comfort myself with our metaphysical conversation and remind myself, "some fear is good, or at the very least, a reminder of our shared humanity."

Regardless of his physical well-being, Coach continued to greet others as if they were the greatest gift. He engaged with them, gave them a chiding in a way they recognized from past visits. The love flowed so strongly, it didn't matter if he remembered a name or past times spent together. In that moment, you were his long lost friend.

One long lost friend after another came to visit Coach in his final days. One of his closest long time friends was George Drake, former President of Grinnell College and current Professor Emeritus. He described the phenomenon surrounding Coach's relationships in this way: "John would reel in those he was with, make them a part of his world, a world that included as many people as John could grab, and once grabbed, that person was always a part of John Pfitsch's narrative."

The last time I saw Coach, he was in a wheelchair at Mayflower Health Center in Grinnell. He'd recently had a number of small strokes. His major organs had shown sharp decline; his body was finally shutting down for good. We were told he had less than two weeks to live. I'm not sure what they told him, but we and hundreds of his friends, family, and students, came flooding in to say final goodbyes. He was chipper as always. He told Deanna Shorb, Chaplain of Grinnell College, "If I'd known it was going to be this good, I'd have done this a long time ago."

While a few of us were sitting with him for the last time, his face took on an unusual expression. Serious. Focused inward. He broke through the trance and looked out at all of us and said, "I don't want you to be scared. I've been having what they call little seizures. They come and go. I feel one coming now." I panicked. I wanted to call the nurse. I looked for Emily. The others seemed calmer or stunned, I'm not sure which. Within a few moments, he seemed to return to us, this time with less of a twinkle in his eyes. He wasn't able to speak. I think that bothered him. His time with friends cut short.

I thought my pearl diving had come to an end that day. Selfish me. I still wanted Coach to look at me with that mischievous grin and twinkle in his eyes and say, "Who the hell are you? Sit down. Tell me what you're doing." Then he'd start a story. And I would listen.

As I write these final words, my pearl diving days *are* coming to an end. I hear the gravelly voice I've come to know so well say, "Get on with the business of your life, whatever the hell it is." The voice doesn't burst out of nowhere any more. I have to work a little harder to hear it, even harder to see his stubbly beard and questioning expression.

"Coach, before you go this time, I have something to say."

"There's a— I don't think anyone— I'm not surprised. What revelation is burning a hole in your brain today?"

I see him clearly now. He's quiet. Waiting. He's a man who spent his professional life studying scholar-athlete behavior, pondering and hypothesizing it. Why would he want to listen to me? But, he does. And I'm comforted, empowered. I feel myself grow as a person because Coach cares. As usual, I sense Emily's presence nearby.

"I want to thank you for giving me your manuscript, telling me I could do what I wish with it. I'm sorry I couldn't fill in all the asterisks and dashes. I'm sorry for all the mistakes. I know you wouldn't want to leave someone out or slight anyone."

"Well that's—"

"Wait. There's more. I want to thank you for writing it. I don't think many people realize how courageous, not just intellectual, even brilliant, but how courageous you were to write it."

Coach's chin trembles.

"Writing is difficult. But writing without leaning on research, writing as a pioneer, as a physical educator and coach— You fought stereotypes, too."

He shakes his head in agreement and shrugs and says, "When I began using my manuscript as our text, I heard someone say, 'I didn't know he could spell.'"

The comment hits a nerve with me. I'm offended.

"Laugh! Laugh, Professor Waite! Laugh at yourself." He quietly adds, "It's a great laugh. Laughter will take you further."

I swallow hard. "And keep my knees bent."

"Yes." He grins. "Bend, roll, and spring."

239

"Start with acceptance."

"Yes."

We're singing the same tune again, in harmony.

"They were and are pearls, you know: your ideas. You gave me beautiful pearls. I might have scrubbed off a few barnacles here and there because they've been buried for a long time, but they are pearls. I hope you are pleased with the outcome."

"Well—uh hum— It wasn't— It might— What matters— Was it 100% performance?"

I'm grinning through tears running down my cheeks.

He smiles. His mind seems to wander and his focus dims, but only for a moment. He reappears as clear as ever and opens his mouth. I settle back into the softness of the sofa.

"100% performance is possible, you know. It was a different time, the 60s— Bob Musser, George Grey, John Sundell, Gar Smith, and Danny, Danny— In 1962— The Conference Championship was at stake. After much preparation of the kind we have been discussing, we met our long time rival…

About the Authors

John Alfred Pfitsch, October 28, 1919-June 15, 2012, was born in Miraj, India to medical missionary parents. He moved back to the United States at the age of five where his life plan was influenced by years of youth sport and high school and college athletics. He played all major and many minor sports from season to season at Pflugerville High School, Texas Lutheran Junior College, and University of Texas at Austin where he graduated in 1940. His graduate education at The University of Kansas was interrupted by World War II when he served in the 35th Division of the Army, landing on Utah Beach on Day 3 of D-Day. He returned to Kansas in the Fall of 1945 to graduate with a masters in physical education and serve as Phog Allen's first assistant coach in the 1945-46 basketball season. He met Emily Hollis at University of Kansas. They were married on August 3, 1946 and moved to Fremont, NE, where he coached all sports and taught physical education at Midland College. In 1948 he was hired to coach basketball, tennis, and football at Grinnell College. He became athletic director in 1953. During his 50 year career at Grinnell, he initiated women's intercollegiate sport programs and eventually coached almost every men's sport. John Pfitsch is also co-author of *Pfitsch Tales: 50 Years of Grinnell College Athletics* with Suzanne Kelsey.

Barbara Teetor Waite grew up in Fort Wayne, Indiana playing all the major sports from season to season in her back yard and neighborhood. She was fortunate to live in a city offering a youth baseball league initially organized to feed the All-American Girls Professional Baseball League, which gave her the opportunity to play competitive baseball. Summer camp broadened her sport knowledge and skills. United States Tennis Association tournaments challenged her to compete locally and regionally in tennis. She pursued athletics, competitive flying, and a degree in general studies at The University of Arizona. She attended graduate school at The University of Virginia where she earned a masters and doctorate in sport psychology. As a visiting assistant professor, she directed the Sport Psychology Program at The University of Iowa from 1990-93. During her years at Grinnell College, she coached tennis and softball, taught physical education, and directed the staff/faculty wellness program. Barbara pursues a variety of passions, the most enduring of which are writing, music, and the great outdoors via the "silent" sports of hiking, biking, paddling, and sailing. She credits her family for instilling her life-long love of learning. Her writing can be found on line, in bookstores, and at frendshippublications.com.

www.ingramcontent.com/pod-product-compliance
Lightning Source LLC
LaVergne TN
LVHW051501080426
835509LV00017B/1851